Teaching English

Reflective Teaching and Learning: A guide to professional issues for beginning secondary teachers

Edited by Sue Dymoke and Jennifer Harrison

Reflective practice is at the heart of effective teaching. This core text is an introduction for beginning secondary teachers on developing the art of critical reflective teaching throughout their professional work. Designed as a flexible resource, the book combines theoretical background with practical reflective activities.

Developing as a Reflective Secondary Teacher Series
These subject-specific core texts are for beginning secondary teachers following PGCE, GTP or undergraduate routes into teaching. Each book provides a comprehensive guide to beginning subject teachers, offering practical guidance to support students through their training and beyond. Most importantly, the books are designed to help students develop a more reflective and critical approach to their own practice. Key features of the series are:

- observed lessons, providing both worked examples of good practice and commentaries by the teachers themselves and other observers
- an introduction to national subject frameworks including a critical examination of the role and status of each subject
- support for beginning teachers on all aspects of subject teaching, including planning, assessment, classroom management, differentiation and teaching strategies
- a trainee-focused approach to critical and analytical reflection on practice
- a research-based section demonstrating M-level work
- a comprehensive companion website linking all subjects, featuring video clips of sample lessons, a range of support material and weblinks.

Teaching Mathematics
Paul Chambers

Teaching History
Ian Phillips

Forthcoming:
Teaching Science
Tony Liversidge, Matt Cochrane, Bernie Kerfoot and Judith Thomas

Teaching ICT
Carl Simmons and Claire Hawkins

Teaching English
Carol Evans, Alyson Midgley, Phil Rigby, Lynne Warham and Peter Woolnough

Teaching English

Developing as a Reflective Secondary Teacher

Carol Evans, Alyson Midgley,
Phil Rigby, Lynne Warham and
Peter Woolnough

Los Angeles | London | New Delhi
Singapore | Washington DC

SAGE Publications Ltd
1 Oliver's Yard
55 City Road
London EC1Y 1SP

SAGE Publications Inc.
2455 Teller Road
Thousand Oaks, California 91320

SAGE Publications India Pvt Ltd
B 1/I 1 Mohan Cooperative Industrial Area
Mathura Road, Post Bag 7
New Delhi 110 044

SAGE Publications Asia-Pacific Pte Ltd
33 Pekin Street #02-01
Far East Square
Singapore 048763

Library of Congress Control Number: 2008933667

British Library Cataloguing in Publication data

A catalogue record for this book is available from
The British Library

ISBN 978-1-4129-4817-3
ISBN 978-1-4129-4818-0 (pbk)

Typeset by C&M Digitals (P) Ltd, Chennai, India
Printed in Great Britain by TJ International, Padstow, Cornwall
Printed on paper from sustainable resources

Mixed Sources
Product group from well-managed
forests and other controlled sources
www.fsc.org Cert no. TT-COC-2082
© 1996 Forest Stewardship Council
FSC

10/0/09

CONTENTS

ACKNOWLEDGEMENTS

Chapter 2:
Sarah Cody, Laura Shipsides, Jemma Sugden, Kate Thornton, Jonathan Thorpe and Matthew Whittle: PGCE Secondary English trainee teachers at Edge Hill, 2006-7.

Chapter 3:
Sutton High Sports College, St Helens, Monika Maloszyc (Acting Head of English, SHSC), Ian Jackson (ITT Trainee), Isobel Browett

Chapter 4:
Emily Parr and Katie Unsworth: PGCE Secondary English trainee teachers at Edge Hill University, 2007-8.
Stephanie Davies: PGCE Secondary English trainee teacher at Edge Hill, 2006-7.
Joe Felce: Ex-Deputy Head of Birkdale High School, Southport.

Chapter 7:
QCA, Jo Wallace, WJEC, AQA

Chapter 8:
Jean Raybould: PSHE Co-ordinator and English teacher, and other members of the English department, Range High School, Formby.
Dr Bethan Evans: lecturer in Human Geography, Manchester Institute of Social and Spatial Transformations, Manchester Metropolitan University, and colleagues at Loughborough University.
Sarah Cody: PGCE Secondary English trainee teacher at Edge Hill, 2006-7.
The Head Teacher, Professional Mentor, English department teachers, Learning Support Assistant and year 7 pupils of Rivington and Blackrod High School, Horwich.
Angela Mayer: Assistant Head of Lower School, Year 7 PSHE Co-ordinator and Food technology teacher, Parklands Specialist Language College, Chorley.
Anthony Rider: PE/PSHE teacher, Holy Cross Catholic High School, Sports and Science College, Chorley.
PGCE Secondary English trainee teachers at Edge Hill University, 2002-2004, who took part in PSHE research.

Chapter 9:
Rachel Swann, Lisa Charnock, Sylvia Williamson and Paul Duvall: Former Edge Hill staff instrumental in devising and designing ICT activities for the VLE.
Chris Warren: Teachit and NATE.

HOW TO USE THIS BOOK

This book is designed to help you to make a success of your training course. It shows you how to plan lessons, how to make good use of resources and how to assess pupils' progress effectively. However, its main aim is to help you learn how to improve your classroom performance. In order to improve, you need to have skills of analysis and self-evaluation, and you need to know what you are trying to achieve and why. You also need examples of how experienced teachers deliver successful lessons, and how even the best teachers continually strive to become even better.

As practising teachers, we wanted this book to have a practical focus and to be user- friendly. We want not only to demystify English teaching but also to demonstrate how special this subject is. This book will help you to feel more comfortable about what is expected from you in teaching practice, through demonstrating good practice in English teaching, but also through putting that good practice into a whole-school and a national context. You will, for example, find suggestions about how English teachers can contribute to the national *Every Child Matters* agenda.

When we started to write this book, we were very conscious of two key issues: first, there were five different teachers writing the book and you, as a reader, would note the difference in voices and, perhaps, emphasis. We see the different voices as an added strength to the book, because you will experience different perspectives and be able to make your own judgements. Secondly, English as a subject does not have designated boundaries, and information intentionally overlaps from one chapter to another. We feel that the overlap reflects the fluidity of English as a subject, which in turn will enable you to see how the subject's multiple elements link together.

A key feature of this book is the accompanying website. The icon shown in the margin will appear throughout the text where additional material is available on the website www.sage pub.co.uk/secondary. The website contains links to all of the websites featured in the various chapters, together with additional links to sites that provide useful support to trainee teachers of English. The book makes extensive reference to filmed English lessons and video files of these lessons appears on the companion website. As you read the book, you will be able to view how a trainee teacher puts into practice key aspects of planning, teaching and assessment. The video clips are available in Windows media video file format (.wmv), and give the best quality visuals if viewed with Windows Media Player. (Players that support this file type are: Windows Media Player 7, Windows Media Player for Windows XP, Windows Media Player 9 Series, Windows Media Player 10 and Windows Media Player 11.) The clips are also available as Flash files (.flv), which may play more quickly on your computer. You will need Flash Player to view these, and this programme can be downloaded for free from www.adobe.com/products/flash.player/ The clips also link to transcriptions of trainee teachers' views.

This book also provides a key link to the Professional Standards for Qualified Teacher Status (September 2007). Table H.1 gives a summary of how this book and the accompanying website cover these professional standards.

Table H.1 Professional Standards for Qualified Teacher Status
Professional attributes. Those recommended for the award of QTS should:

Standard		Opportunities to learn more
Relationships with children and young people		
Q1	Have high expectations of children and young people including a commitment to ensuring that they can achieve their full educational potential and to establishing fair, respectful, trusting, supportive and constructive relationships with them	Explicit throughout the book. Each chapter emphasizes the importance of enabling pupils to fulfil their potential through lesson plans, lesson resources and lesson transcripts
Q2	Demonstrate the positive values, attitudes and behaviour they expect from children and young people	*Chapter One*
Frameworks		
Q3a	Be aware of the professional duties of teachers and the statutory framework within which they work	*Chapter 1* *Chapter 1*
Q3b	Be aware of the policies and practices of the workplace and share in collective responsibility for their implementation	Explicit throughout the book. Each chapter emphasises the importance of enabling pupils to fulfil their potential through lesson plans, lesson resources and lesson transcripts.
Communicating and working with others		
Q4	Communicate effectively with children, young people, colleagues, parents and carers	*Chapter 2* *Chapter 4*
Q5	Recognize and respect the contribution that colleagues, parents and carers can make to the development and well-being of children and young people and to raising their levels of attainment	Explicit throughout the book. Each chapter emphasises the importance of enabling pupils to fulfil their potential through lesson plans, lesson resources and lesson transcripts.
Q6	Have a commitment to collaboration and co-operative working	Explicit throughout the book. Each chapter emphasises the importance of enabling pupils to fulfil their potential through lesson plans, lesson resources and lesson transcripts.
Personal professional development		
Q7a	Reflect on and improve their practice, and take responsibility for identifying and meeting their developing professional needs	Explicit throughout the book – each chapter contains Points for Reflection. These sections are designed to reflect on information, consider and consolidate and add to the professional skills.

Table H.1   (Continued)

Standard		Opportunities to learn more
Q7b	Identify priorities for their early professional development in the context of induction	Explicit throughout the book – each chapter contains Points for Reflection. These sections are designed to reflect on information, consider and consolidate and add to the professional skills.
Q8	Have a creative and constructively critical approach towards innovation, being prepared to adapt their practice where benefits and improvements are identified	*Chapter 2* *Chapter 4* *Chapter 5* *Chapter 6* *Chapter 8* *Chapter 9* *Chapter 10*
Q9	Act upon advice and feedback and be open to coaching and mentoring	Explicit throughout the book – each chapter contains Points for Reflection. These sections are designed to reflect on information, consider and consolidate and add to the professional skills.
Professional knowledge and understanding. Those recommended for the award of QTS should:		
Teaching and learning		
Q10	Have a knowledge and understanding of a range of teaching, learning and behaviour management strategies and know how to use and adapt them, including how to personalize learning and provide opportunities for all learners to achieve their potential	*Chapter 1* *Chapter 2* *Chapter 3* *Chapter 4* *Chapter 6* *Chapter 7* *Chapter 8* *Chapter 9*
Assessment and monitoring		
Q11	Know the assessment requirements and arrangements for the subjects/curriculum areas in the age ranges they are trained to teach, including those relating to public examinations and qualifications	*Chapter 5* *Chapter 7*
Q12	Know a range of approaches to assessment, including the importance of formative assessment	*Chapter 5* *Chapter 7*
Q13	Know how to use local and national statistical information to evaluate the effectiveness of their teaching, to monitor the progress of those they teach and to raise levels of attainment	*Chapter 5* *Chapter 7*

(Continued)

Table H.1 (Continued)

Standard		Opportunities to learn more
Subjects and curriculum		
Q14	Have a secure knowledge and understanding of their subjects/curriculum areas and related pedagogy to enable them to teach effectively across the age and ability range for which they are trained	*Chapter 2* *Chapter 4* *Chapter 7*
Q15	Know and understand the relevant statutory and non-statutory curricula, frameworks, including those provided through the National Strategies, for their subjects/curriculum areas, and other relevant initiatives applicable to the age and ability range for which they are trained	*Chapter 2* *Chapter 4* *Chapter 7*
Literacy, numeracy and ICT		
Q16	Have passed the professional skills tests in numeracy, literacy and information and communication technology (ICT)	Not addressed
Q17	Know how to use skills in literacy, numeracy and ICT to support their teaching and wider professional activities	*Chapter 1* *Chapter 2* *Chapter 3* *Chapter 4* *Chapter 6* *Chapter 7* *Chapter 8* *Chapter 9*
Achievement and diversity		
Q18	Understand how children and young people develop and that the progress and well-being of learners are affected by a range of developmental, social, religious, ethnic, cultural and linguistic influences	Explicit throughout the book. Each chapter emphasizes the importance of enabling pupils to fulfil their potential through lesson plans, lesson resources and lesson transcripts.
Q19	Know how to make effective personalized provision for those they teach, including those for whom English is an additional language or who have special educational needs or disabilities, and how to take practical account of diversity and promote equality and inclusion in their teaching	*Chapter 2* *Chapter 6* *Chapter 9*
Q20	Know and understand the roles of colleagues with specific responsibilities, including those with responsibility for learners with special educational needs and disabilities and other individual learning needs	*Chapter 7*

(Continued)

Table H.1   (Continued)

Standard		Opportunities to learn more
Health and well-being		
Q21a	Be aware of current legal requirements, national policies and guidance on the safeguarding and promotion of the well-being of children and young people	*Chapter 2* *Chapter 4*
Q21b	Know how to identify and support children and young people whose progress, development or well-being is affected by changes or difficulties in their personal circumstances, and when to refer them to colleagues for specialist support	Explicit throughout the book. Each chapter emphasises the importance of enabling pupils to fulfil their potential through lesson plans, lesson resources and lesson transcripts.
Professional skills. **Those recommended for the award of QTS should:**		
Planning		
Q22	Plan for progression across the age and ability range for which they are trained, designing effective learning sequences within lessons and across series of lessons and demonstrating secure subject/curriculum knowledge	Explicit throughout the book. Each chapter emphasises the importance of enabling pupils to fulfil their potential through lesson plans, lesson resources and lesson transcripts. *Chapter 2* *Chapter 6* *Chapter 7*
Q23	Design opportunities for learners to develop their literacy, numeracy and ICT skills	*Chapter 2* *Chapter 6* *Chapter 7* *Chapter 9*
Q24	Plan homework or other out-of-class work to sustain learners' progress and to extend and consolidate their learning	*Chapter 2*
Teaching		
Teach lessons and sequences of lessons across the age and ability range for which they are trained in which they:		
Q25a	Use a range of teaching strategies and resources, including e-learning, taking practical account of diversity and promoting equality and inclusion	*Chapter 2* *Chapter 6* *Chapter 7* *Chapter 9*
Q25b	Build on prior knowledge, develop concepts and processes, enable learners to apply new	*Chapter 2* *Chapter 5*

Table H.1   (Continued)

Standard		Opportunities to learn more
	knowledge, understanding and skills and meet learning objectives	*Chapter 6* *Chapter 7* *Chapter 9*
Q25c	Adapt their language to suit the learners they teach, introducing new ideas and concepts clearly, and using explanations, questions, discussions and plenaries effectively	*Chapter 2* *Chapter 5* *Chapter 6* *Chapter 7* *Chapter 9*
Q25d	Manage the learning of individuals, groups and whole classes, modifying their teaching to suit the stage of the lesson	*Chapter 2* *Chapter 4* *Chapter 5* *Chapter 6* *Chapter 7* *Chapter 9*
Assessing, monitoring and giving feedback		
Q26a	Make effective use of a range of assessment, monitoring and recording strategies	*Chapter 2* *Chapter 5* *Chapter 7*
Q26b	Assess the learning needs of those they teach in order to set challenging learning objectives	*Chapter 2* *Chapter 5* *Chapter 7*
Q27	Provide timely, accurate and constructive feedback on learners' attainment, progress and areas for development	*Chapter 2* *Chapter 5* *Chapter 7*
Q28	Support and guide learners to reflect on their learning, identify the progress they have made and identify their emerging learning needs	*Chapter 2* *Chapter 5* *Chapter 7*
Reviewing teaching and learning		
Q29	Evaluate the impact of their teaching on the progress of all learners, and modify their planning and classroom practice where necessary	*Chapter 1* *Chapter 10*
Learning environment		
Q30	Establish a purposeful and safe learning environment conducive to learning and identify opportunities for learners to learn in out-of-school contexts	*Chapter 4*

(Continued)

Table H.1   (Continued)

Standard		Opportunities to learn more
Q31	Establish a clear framework for classroom discipline to manage learners' behaviour constructively and promote their self-control and independence	*Chapter 4*
Team-working and collaboration		
Q32	Work as a team member and identify opportunities for working with colleagues, sharing the development of effective practice with them	*Chapter 1* *Chapter 2* *Chapter 6*
Q33	Ensure that colleagues working with them are appropriately involved in supporting learning and understand the roles they are expected to fulfil	*Chapter 1* *Chapter 2* *Chapter 6*

AUTHORS' NOTE

This book had gone to print when the decision was made to abolish Key Stage 3 SATs. The authors hope the information contained in the book about these tests may be of use to readers as a point of comparison, when the government announces detail about any new KS3 assessment regime.

1 ENGLISH TEACHERS AND ENGLISH TEACHING

Phil Rigby

This chapter considers:

- the nature of the English curriculum and the way it is viewed, both by society at large and by English teachers themselves
- external pressures on the English curriculum
- internal conflicts about the nature of English as a subject
- the development of the National Curriculum, its style, content and structure
- the Framework for secondary English
- the teaching of grammar and the standards debate
- Shakespeare and the literary canon
- frequently encountered texts within English lessons.

Finally, in focusing upon a discussion between four experienced teachers around the topic of planning to deliver an aspect of a GCSE set text, the chapter reflects upon different ways of presenting material, according to the particular needs of the pupils in a class.

INTRODUCTION

English is vital for communicating with others in school and in the wider world, and is fundamental to learning in all curriculum subjects. (QCA, 2007: 1)

Literature in English is rich and influential. (QCA, 2007: 1)

This is it: your opportunity to train as an English teacher; your chance to play your own unique role in the development and evolution of the English curriculum! This opening chapter deliberately begins with two key quotations from the English National Curriculum programme of study (2007), each emphasizing the importance and centrality of the subject to all pupils. The very nature of English is 'vital' because it is in a constant state of change: it moves and breathes in the same way as the English language itself. It is 'influential' because of the way that it impacts not only on every subject area, but also on pupils' lives beyond school. Equally, English is 'rich' because of its unlimited diversity. In essence, these two quotations encapsulate the significance and the enjoyment of English teaching.

As a successful practitioner you will need to develop the skills to discuss, explore and evaluate the learning and teaching within your classroom in an informed manner. Equally, you will need to develop the reflective, evaluative and critical thinking skills which are a crucial part of developing Master's-level professional practice. This opening chapter is deliberately designed to be thought-provoking, raising issues and asking the kinds of questions that you will encounter not only during the course of your English training, but also throughout your teaching career.

THE NATURE OF THE ENGLISH CURRICULUM

In order to begin to explore the centrality of English as a subject, it is first important to understand its position within the school curriculum as a whole. Just as, within the early years of primary education, reading impacts disproportionately upon every other area of the curriculum with the result that the good reader is at an advantage over other children in a whole range of subjects, so in the secondary age-phase English has a unique relationship with every other subject area. As an English teacher, that places you in a rather special position, a member of a key department in the school, one that links with every other subject and whose influence is felt across the whole school. However, like many of life's benefits, such privilege also has its drawbacks. For instance, your colleagues will think nothing of berating you for their pupils' poor spelling in their lessons; worse still, as native speakers of English, many will consider themselves experts on the subject, and consider it their duty to explain to you what and how they feel you should be teaching, in ways that you would never even consider doing with them.

Similarly, on a wider and more public stage, the more vocal elements among the press will relish every opportunity to comment on what they perceive to be poor levels of spoken and, particularly, written English among school leavers (it makes no difference when you point to pupils' consistently rising examination performance; to them this is merely another manifestation of falling standards and further serves to fuel their argument). They salivate over spelling errors on public signs, incorrect word choice and – the worst sin of all – misplaced apostrophes! Such lapses in public standards are again clearly the fault of – you have guessed it – English teachers. The English teacher is singled out by society at large in ways that simply do not happen to, for example, the geography teacher, the biology teacher or the information and communications technology (ICT) teacher.

The two viewpoints mentioned above are linked to the 'anyone can teach English' discourse that has been in existence almost as long as the subject itself. Everyone has been to school, so the logic goes, everyone can speak English; therefore everyone must be an expert on English teaching. However, if you are anything like me, that is at least part of the attraction of wanting to be an English teacher: to be involved in teaching such a crucial subject, one that has such a profound and lasting impact on pupils, affecting them and staying with them in ways that other subjects do not. When you chance to meet former pupils, sometimes many years after they have left your class, they will often tell you how English was not only the subject that they enjoyed most at the time but that its relevance has become increasingly apparent with the passage of the years.

Point for reflection

The Spanish teacher tells you in the classroom that the pupils in his class do not understand what a verb is; how do you react? The geography teacher tells you that her pupils cannot spell the simplest of geographical terms; what do you say? The science teacher tells you that she never corrects grammatical errors in her pupils' work because, as far as she is concerned, it is science that she is teaching, not English; does she have a point? On passing the notice board outside the head's office you notice an absolutely howling error (surely you can't be the only one to have noticed it); what do you do?

As you begin to explore others' views, both of English as a subject and of English teaching itself, it is important that you consider what English really means to you. How do you view the subject? What kind of English teacher will you be? Perhaps these are questions you have never considered up to this point; however, they are valid questions that you ought to be aware of and consider at this early stage in your career. It is important that you reflect upon and develop an opinion about English teaching and what it means to you, otherwise you will find yourself buffeted by the vagaries of public opinion or by circumstances as they change.

EXTERNAL PRESSURES

Because English is such a crucial subject, so central to pupils' educational, cultural and social development, it can become subject to significant external pressures, often of an overtly political nature. In a sense, this is simply a manifestation of its importance: people have strong and diverse opinions about it and want to influence the way it is taught precisely because it matters so much. Such pressures on the content and structure of the English curriculum derive, broadly, from two sources: first, from other groups and individuals within education and, second, from society in general, often in the form of comment in the press or statements by politicians.

> English, after all, is the subject at the heart of our definition of national cultural identity. Since English teachers are the chief custodians of that identity we should not be surprised to find that revolutionaries intent on using the subject to transform society have gained a powerful foothold, attempting to redefine the very meaning of reading itself. (Phillips, 1997: 69)

As a member of the English teaching community, it is important both that you engage in the debate and that you are prepared to be flexible, but it is also important that you remain resilient in order to stand up to the pressures, the questions and, at times, the criticism that you will face as a member of the profession.

I have already hinted at some of the types of comments that you will face from your colleagues in school. This may seem an obvious point, but experience shows that it is worth making: it is important that your colleagues do not see English simply as a service subject, as a content-free, skills-based curriculum shell whose only justification for existence is to benefit other subject areas. That is not to say, of course, that there can be no carry-over from English into other subjects: the best learning is one that is deeply contextualized; one that actively seeks to create links between different facets of the curriculum; where subjects (and here I mean subjects, not just teachers) do actually talk to each other and benefit from such dialogue. Because of its position in the curriculum, English is almost uniquely placed to involve itself in cross-curricular initiatives; to develop skills and understanding; to explore through literature the human aspects of social or historical situations in ways that will certainly benefit other subject areas. Yet it certainly does not exist simply to service the particular demands and needs of other curriculum areas; indeed, if you were to follow such a route through to its natural conclusion, you would find yourself in a situation where other curriculum subjects totally dominated and controlled the shape and structure of the English curriculum, and where English as a subject was left without a core, intellectually, emotionally or morally.

In recent years, attitudes such as these from among the teaching profession have become less widespread, as the National Strategies have become embedded, with their clear emphasis on the development of cross-curricular literacy and of the particular literacies of each different subject area. It has now become more widely recognized and accepted that pupils' progress in individual subject areas is inextricably tied up with the development of the particular literacy of that subject. So the Spanish teacher wanting his pupils to understand verb formation will be expected to find ways to teach it so that pupils can see its importance in context; similarly, the geography teacher wanting her pupils to develop sound strategies for knowing how to spell key geographical terms cannot simply pass the responsibility for the pupils' prowess at spelling to their English teacher.

Over 30 years ago a seminal report on English teaching entitled *A Language for Life* (DES, 1975), more commonly known as the Bullock Report after its author Lord Bullock, advocated the development of language across the curriculum and put forward the view that every teacher is a teacher of language. However, in the years between the report's publication and the launch of the National Literacy Strategy in 1998, language across the curriculum became seen almost as the Holy Grail in language development, an almost unattainable target. Responding to the Bullock Report's recommendations, individual schools and local authorities had adopted a number of creative schemes in an attempt to develop a cross-curricular approach to language teaching; however, by and large, such small-scale and individual approaches had failed to achieve a breakthrough at a national level, until the advent of the National Literacy Strategy with its focus on every teacher's responsibility to develop the literacy of their own subject.

If the pressure upon the English curriculum from within schools could be identified as being driven by debate over standards and the accuracy of spoken and written expression, the pressure from outside the educational community tends to come from the same direction. There are a number of contentious issues within the field of English that could attract such comment: the importance of the literary canon, the role of new media in textual study, the teaching of Shakespeare, to name but three. All these do attract comment from politicians and the press from time to time, usually as a part of the 'dumbing down' discourse. However, as in schools, the main area for comment is in terms of standards and accuracy. In terms of vitriol and vehemence, the days leading up to the introduction of the first National Curriculum document in 1988 probably saw the most outspoken comments on what was wrong with English teaching.

Typical of the criticism were the remarks of Norman Tebbit, then Chairman of the Conservative Party, who pointed out the causal link between the decline in the teaching of grammar and the rise in street crime:

> If you allow standards to slip to the stage where good English is no better than bad English, where people turn up filthy at school ... all these things tend to cause people to have no standards at all, and once you lose standards then there's no imperative to stay out of crime.(Cameron, 1995: 94)

In similar vein, Prince Charles raged about standards of English teaching:

> We've got to produce people who can write proper English. It's a fundamental problem. All the people I have in my office, they can't speak English properly; they can't write English properly. All the letters sent from my office I have to correct myself, and that is because English is taught so bloody badly ... The whole way schools are operating is not

right. I do not believe that English is being taught properly. You cannot teach people properly unless you do it on a basic framework and drilling system. (28 June 1989, cited in Cater, R., 1997, p.7)

This is not the place to start to unpick and explore the underlying message of such remarks. However, hopefully they serve as useful examples of the type of comment and criticism that English teaching attracts. Recent years have seen a decrease in both the vehemence and the frequency of such views, yet from time to time they do still emerge, placing English teachers at the heart of the debate about standards, not just in classrooms but in society as a whole.

INTERNAL CONFLICTS

In looking at the external pressures on the English curriculum, you begin to understand some of the key influences in shaping the current state of English teaching and how English teachers feel about their subject. However, there are similar internal conflicts among the English teaching fraternity about what English is and what it should be. Depending on their own particular personal beliefs, social background, life experience and area of interest within the subject, teachers will adopt a particular standpoint and view English in a particular way. This describes a healthy situation – the fact that there is such a wide range of views is not a reason for criticism – it is reflective of the breadth, the depth and, indeed, the strength of the subject. People have such wide-ranging views on English teaching, expressing and defending them so vehemently, because it actually matters to them.

In discussing the first English National Curriculum in 1991, Professor Brian Cox identified a number of different views of English teaching:

- A 'personal growth' view focuses on the child; it emphasizes the relationship between language and learning in the individual child, and the role of literature in developing children's imaginative and aesthetic lives.
- A 'cross-curricular' view focuses on the school: it emphasizes that all teachers (of English and other subjects) have a responsibility to help children with the language demands of different subjects on the school curriculum, otherwise areas of the curriculum may be closed to them.
- An 'adult needs' view focuses on communication outside the school: it emphasizes the responsibility of English teachers to prepare children for the language demands of adult life, including the work place, in a fast-changing world. Children need to learn to deal with the day-to-day demands of spoken language and of print; they also need to be able to write clearly, appropriately and effectively.
- A 'cultural heritage' view emphasizes the responsibility of schools to lead children to an appreciation of those works of literature that have been widely regarded as among the finest in the language.
- A 'cultural analysis' view emphasizes the role of English in helping children towards a critical understanding of the world and cultural environment in which they live. Children should know about the processes by which meanings are conveyed, and about the ways in which print and other media carry values.

Here, we begin to see some of the philosophical standpoints underlying particular epistemologies of English teaching. Often, teachers will have adopted such viewpoints instinctively, without entering into an inner debate on the relative merits of particular cases. Positions taken will be intimately tied up with individual teachers' personalities and areas of interest; indeed, some teachers may be unaware of their own natural inclination, never having questioned the rationale behind their own particular approach.

The teacher taking a 'personal growth' view considers the transforming power of literature, of pupils seeing their world in new and different ways as a result of explorations inside the English classroom. The teacher who adopts a 'cross-curricular' view might consider the overlap between English and literacy, asking where one ends and the other begins and seeking to identify links between the literacies of individual subjects across the curriculum, perhaps looking for opportunities to design and implement integrated arts projects across a number of subjects. The teacher with an 'adult needs' view sees English very much as a transactional subject, one that prepares pupils for the particular demands of the work place and of adult life in general, keeping an eye on changing technologies and seeking opportunities to utilize these within the English classroom, with life skills such as letter and report writing being paramount. In the 'cultural heritage' view, literature is at the heart of the curriculum, with classic poetry, prose and drama being studied in order to gain an understanding of our nationhood and as an exemplification of our national heritage. For the teacher with a 'cultural analysis' view, new media – television, film, the press, the Internet, text messaging and blogging – are explored, both as texts for study and as vehicles for writing, alongside newer literary texts, often from non-English settings.

Of course, such distinctions are artificial; there is scope for overlap. They are certainly not mutually exclusive, nor is there an implied hierarchy, with one particular viewpoint seen as the 'norm' or the most preferred. However, they are useful in summarizing the different standpoints within English teaching, and the majority of teachers will probably find themselves instinctively drawn towards a particular standpoint. In a sense, these artificial divisions are less evident in teachers' everyday practice now than they were at the time of writing, certainly since the establishment of, the National Curriculum and the embedding of the Framework for secondary English. Today, English teaching is far less polarized. However, pre-National Curriculum, such distinctions were crucial, as teachers had the freedom to follow their own areas of interest almost to the exclusion of other areas.

In a recent straw poll survey with the Postgraduate Certificate of Education (PGCE) English trainees at Edge Hill University, by far the largest contingent (over 65 per cent) identified themselves most strongly with the 'personal growth' viewpoint. Of the remainder, the trainee group was split almost evenly between 'cross-curricular' and 'cultural analysis' viewpoints, with 'cultural analysis' just shading second place. Significantly, not one of the trainees felt particularly attracted to either the 'adult needs' or 'cultural heritage' viewpoints. Interesting though these figures are, it must be stressed that this was a relatively small sample (57 trainees) in a room together on one particular afternoon, and as such should not be seen as particularly representative of a wider group.

Point for reflection

Relate these views to your own memories of learning English at school. To what extent they might apply today. Where do your own educational priorities lie?

THE NATIONAL CURRICULUM

After a debate over the future of education that had started with Prime Minister James Callaghan's speech at Ruskin College, Oxford, in 1976 and had lasted for over a decade, the National Curriculum was eventually introduced in 1990. It seems almost unthinkable now that, prior to this point, apart from the examination syllabuses for 16- and 18-year-old pupils, there was no real agreement as to what the English curriculum should comprise. At individual local authority, school and department levels teachers did discuss and debate the curriculum, but by and large this was principally a matter for individual choice. Within the bounds of reason, teachers were free to teach not only how they wanted but also what they wanted. With such a lack of structure, either agreed or imposed, it was little wonder that many teachers simply followed their own interests: poetry, media, spoken English, drama – each could easily fill a teacher's curriculum planning if left unchecked. This was not out of a lack of professionalism or ambition for their pupils: it was simply that teachers were operating in a virtual void. At this time it was taken for granted that particular teachers had particular interests, and heads of department frequently took the view that pupils who experienced a mix of teachers from across the department would receive a relatively broad and balanced curriculum spread over a period of five years.

Since its introduction in 1990, the National Curriculum for English has been through four different iterations. The original document, presented like all the other subjects in a hefty A4 ring-binder, introduced the three attainment targets of Speaking and Listening (EN1), Reading (EN2) and Writing (EN3); it provided detailed assessment criteria on levels of attainment within each; it introduced the notion of 'expected' levels of achievement, and it provided both statutory and non-statutory guidance on curriculum planning – perhaps the most useful yet least used aspect of the document. Other notable features of the 1990 version were the status given to speaking and listening alongside reading and writing and the inclusion of media texts within the reading section.

Its 1995 revision, more commonly known as the Dearing National Curriculum (DfE, 1995), saw few really major structural or philosophical changes, yet there were some real differences from the earlier document, mostly political in nature and not always for the better. It was a significantly slimmed down document; this time the non-statutory guidance had been removed; at the forefront were the level descriptors for each of the attainment targets, which resulted in several years of largely assessment-driven curriculum planning within English departments. Instead of starting from the programme of study and planning to ensure coverage of the breadth of the curriculum, teachers found themselves starting from the attainment targets and working backwards to try and reach a suitable starting point. The result was a well-intentioned but ultimately unproductive period in which teachers, in trying to adapt to the new curriculum, were attempting to fit their teaching to the attainment targets rather than vice versa. Perhaps the two most controversial features of the revision were the relegation of the role of media within the English curriculum and the strengthened emphasis on the English literary heritage and on works 'of high quality by contemporary writers'.

The third version, introduced as part of the 'Curriculum 2000' revisions, though similar in size to the 1995 version was very different in tone and presentation (DfEE, 1999). The major changes were at primary level, where the programme of study was revised to ensure alignment with the National Literacy Strategy. Reflecting the mood and values of the early years of the New Labour government, this document included 12 pages on inclusion, which will be explored in fuller detail in Chapter 6. Interestingly, though, the document retained its compulsory lists of classic authors and poets, included for the first time guidance on non-fiction writing, and reinstated media as a key element of the curriculum.

This section is certainly not intended as a detailed historical trawl through the intricacies of the National Curriculum. If, however, you do want to read more, there are numerous texts dealing in depth with the introduction and development of the National Curriculum. The further reading section at the end of this chapter provides details of some of these. However, before going on to consider the structure and demands of the most recent iteration of the National Curriculum for English, there are two key points that do need to be made. First, the National Curriculum is statutory in nature: it is a legal document, set up by Act of Parliament and can be amended only by Act of Parliament. What this means in simple terms and in practice is that the National Curriculum is compulsory if you are teaching within the maintained sector in England and Wales. Second, although it comes with the full weight of statute behind it, remember, too, that this is an entitlement document. It exists to establish a common curriculum that all pupils must follow in English over the course of their 11 years of compulsory education. However, it is not the entire English curriculum; it does not build a fence around English teaching and say to teachers, 'You must not pass beyond this point'. This means that teachers are still free to enrich the English curriculum using their own interests and professional judgements, providing that they first ensure that the National Curriculum is being fully covered.

Any introduction of the revised National Curriculum for English (2007 www.qca.org.uk) needs to begin in 2005, when the QCA initiated a national discussion, 'English 21', with the aim of exploring future directions for English over the next 10 years. The project focused on four principal areas:

- how changes in society, work and knowledge would change the skills pupils need
- choice and flexibility in 14–19 qualifications
- the impact of new technologies on the nature of texts and on assessment
- how assessment should develop.

Over 5000 individuals and organizations participated in the exercise, which was eventually summarized in *Taking English Forward*, the QCA's response to the consultation (QCA, 2005). This document, together with the comments of those who had contributed to the discussion, informed the revision to the programme of study for Key Stages 3 and 4, which was eventually published in 2007.

The revised National Curriculum for English (2007) signals a move towards greater professional independence for English teachers and constitutes an explicit acknowledgement of the importance of creativity, personalized learning, functional skills, cultural awareness and criticality. Links to the new programme of study can be found on the companion website www.sagepub.co.uk/secondary. The actual documents are structured and expressed with genuine clarity (see Figure 1.1).

The fact that all subjects in the new National Curriculum are presented in the same format is particularly helpful for teachers. This means that cross-curricular and interdisciplinary links are made explicit, and the role that each subject has to play in the holistic development of pupils is emphasized. Looking at the National Curriculum for English (2007), it is evident that this version has tried to provide teachers with the opportunity to personalize learning according to the particular needs of the individuals they teach. Hence we find less prescription in the range of texts for reading (QCA, 2007: 70–1) and teachers being explicitly encouraged to select reading matter that will engage their pupils.

Main sections of the National Curriculum for English

Statement of the Curriculum Aims

Statement of the Importance of English

1. Key Concepts:
competence
creativity
cultural understanding
critical understanding

2. Key Processes:
the essential skills and processes that pupils need to learn to make progress in terms of speaking and listening, reading and writing are detailed

3. Range & Content:
outlining the breadth of the skills and processes that teachers should address, in terms of speaking and listening, reading and writing

4. Curriculum Opportunities:
detailing the contexts and kinds of activities pupils should explore to develop their skills in speaking and listening, reading and writing.

Figure 1.1   Structure of the National Curriculum for English

The 2007 National Curriculum for English has been built around the development of the 'four Cs': key concepts of competence, creativity, critical understanding and cultural awareness (Figure 1.2), which first appeared during the 'English 21' consultations. Perhaps unsurprisingly, there remain here distinct traces of the viewpoints that Professor Brian Cox noted within the first National Curriculum for English in 1991, although now labelled differently.

The 2007 National Curriculum has also been written to take account of the five requirements of the *Every Child Matters* agenda (DfES, 2004). Within the curriculum, all children should:

- be healthy
- stay safe
- enjoy and achieve
- make a positive contribution
- achieve economic well-being.

English, like every other National Curriculum subject area, is expected to provide contextualized opportunities to ensure that these five key requirements are addressed.

In summary, the revision of the National Curriculum for English (2007) offers opportunities for schools to:

- personalize the curriculum
- provide focused support and challenge
- ensure coherent learning experiences
- embrace more creative teaching/learning
- choose how learning is organized
- effectively utilize Assessment for Learning (AfL).

Competence:	Creativity:
• The ability to communicate effectively and adapt to different situations • Being clear, coherent and accurate in spoken and written communication • Reading and understanding a range of texts, and responding appropriately • Demonstrating a secure understanding of the conventions of written language including grammar, spelling and punctuation • Being adaptable in a widening range of familiar and unfamiliar contexts within the classroom and beyond • Making informed choices about effective ways to communicate formally and informally	• Drawing on a rich experience of language and literature to make fresh connections between ideas, experiences, texts and words • Using inventive approaches to making meaning, taking risks, playing with language and using it to make new effects • Using imagination to convey themes, ideas and arguments, and create settings, moods and characters • Cultural understanding: the appreciation of the best achievements of our literature and language, and new ways that culture develops • Critical skills: being able to evaluate all forms of media and communication
Cultural awareness:	Critical understanding:
• Gaining a sense of the English literary heritage and engaging with important texts in it • Exploring how ideas, experiences and values are portrayed differently in texts from a range of cultures and traditions • Understanding how English varies locally and globally, and how these variations relate to identity and cultural diversity	• Engaging with ideas and texts, understanding and responding to the main issues and developing their own views • Analysing and evaluating spoken and written language to appreciate how meaning is shaped

Figure 1.2   The four Cs

Point for reflection

Now take a few minutes to consider your immediate reactions to the four Cs and the *Every Child Matters* agenda. Is anything missing that you now think should be in the National Curriculum? Given that you have a statutory responsibility to 'deliver' the National Curriculum, how might you make it accommodate all these requirements and what purpose do you think a secondary English curriculum should serve?

THE FRAMEWORK FOR SECONDARY ENGLISH

In 1996 the government's taskforce on literacy produced the blueprint for the National Literacy Project, seen as fundamental in continuing the drive on standards and improvement that had categorized discussions over the shape of the English curriculum since the launch of the National Curriculum (NC) almost 10 years earlier. Its major product was the *National Literacy Strategy Framework*, introduced in all primary schools in September 1998. The Framework had clear content, clearly prescribed ways of operating and a rigid structure, designed to maximize the time teachers spent directly teaching their class. Its intention was to shift the balance of teaching away from individualized work, especially in the teaching of reading, and towards more whole-class and group teaching.

The National Literacy Strategy was designed to operate principally through the Literacy Hour, which would run each day in primary schools. The structure of the hour was clearly set out: the lesson would begin with 15 minutes of shared text work led by the teacher, a balance of reading and writing. This would then lead to a further 15 minutes of focused word or sentence work, again led by the teacher, covering spelling and vocabulary, together with the teaching of grammar and punctuation from the sentence-level objectives. From here, pupils would go into 20 minutes of guided group work; all pupils grouped according to ability, the teacher working closely with one group and circulating through the course of the week to ensure full coverage. The hour would conclude with a 10-minute plenary, often remarked upon as potentially the most effective yet in practice the least likely to be covered properly, in which the teacher and pupils would reflect together on key aspects of the learning, with particular points emphasized and reinforced.

Three years later in 2001, the National Literacy Strategy was introduced into secondary schools, this time in the form of the *Framework for Teaching English: Years 7, 8 and 9* (DfEE, 2001), which took many of the more recognizable features of the primary strategy and reworked them for a secondary setting. For those interested in such things, the nomenclature was deliberate. Whereas, in the primary phase this was the National Literacy Strategy, at Key Stage 3 it was quite pointedly the Framework for Teaching English. This illustrates a key distinction: the question of where literacy starts and finishes and how much overlap there is with English. Clearly there is much common ground between the two, but they are not synonymous. Literacy points to a set of skills, concerned with accuracy, appropriateness, clarity of expression. English, as we have already seen, is significantly broader than this.

When the Framework for Teaching English was introduced, observers noted that a number of key features of the literacy hour had vanished (not every secondary school operated a 60-minute lesson timetable; it was impractical to expect English to be taught each day), yet a number of the established ways of working were retained. There were also key changes in focus: there was an emphasis on Speaking and Listening that was missing from the primary Framework; equally, there was a clear expectation that it would be supported by cross-curricular work across all other subject areas. Starter activities and plenaries, the focus on shared text work, teachers working to support ability groupings of pupils, a phonic approach to the teaching of spelling, transferability of skills and a fast pace of learning were all to be seen in the Key Stage 3 Framework. However, just as the headline feature of the National Literacy Strategy within the primary phase was the Literacy Hour, so in secondary schools the major innovation was the way that it objectivized the National Curriculum, in order to provide an outline curriculum planning framework covering the three Key Stage 3 years.

In 2008, a secondary National Strategy for school improvement was launched, with the key strategic aim of raising 'standards of achievement for young people in all phases and settings'. The secondary National Strategy for school improvement forms the spine of the government's reform programme for transforming secondary education in order to enable children and young people to attend and enjoy school, achieve personal and social development and raise educational standards in line with the *Every Child Matters* agenda.

Alongside mathematics, science and ICT, central to the secondary National Strategy was a revised and updated Framework for secondary English, based on the programme of study for the new secondary curriculum and designed to build upon the success of the previous Framework document. A key change here was the inclusion of Key Stage 4 in the Framework.

The Framework identifies yearly learning objectives that encourage ambition and provide challenge for all pupils, showing progression in the subject. The objectives have been designed to ensure coverage of the programme of study at both Key Stages 3 and 4 and to establish a minimum expectation for the progression of most pupils. The new objectives for English build on the previous Framework and are now:

- expressed as objectives for pupils' learning
- based on the new programme of study
- extended to Key Stage 4 (and include a number of higher-level extension objectives related to more complex and challenging learning)
- organized by the three language modes of Speaking and Listening, Reading and Writing plus a fourth section, Language.

Speaking and listening

The objectives for speaking and listening are arranged under similar headings to those in the original Framework (listening and responding, speaking and presenting, group discussion and interaction, and drama, role-play and performance). The new speaking and listening section begins with listening and responding (Figure 1.3) in order to give more emphasis to this strand.

Speaking and Listening	
Pupils will explore, develop and respond to a range of skills and strategies, in a variety of contexts, adapting language according to task, audience and purpose.	
Strands	**Substrands**
1 Listening and responding	1.1 Developing active listening skills and strategies
	1.2 Understanding and responding to what speakers say in formal and informal contexts
2 Speaking and presenting	2.1 Developing and adapting speaking skills and strategies in formal and informal contexts
	2.2 Using and adapting the conventions and forms of spoken texts
3 Group discussion and interaction	3.1 Developing and adapting discussion skills and strategies in formal and informal contexts
	3.2 Taking roles in group discussion
4 Drama, role play and performance	4.1 Using different dramatic approaches to explore ideas, texts and issues
	4.2 Developing, adapting and responding to dramatic techniques, conventions and styles

Figure 1.3 Speaking and listening

Reading	
Pupils will engage with, and respond to, a rich variety of print, electronic and multi-modal texts, developing analysis and awareness of the forms and purposes of writing, and the contexts and cultures within which they were written.	
Strands	**Substrands**
5 Reading for meaning: understanding and responding to print, electronic and multi-modal texts	5.1 Developing and adapting active reading skills and strategies
	5.2 Understanding and responding to ideas, viewpoints, themes and purposes in texts
	5.3 Reading and engaging with a wide and varied range of texts
6 Understanding the author's craft	6.1 Relating texts to the social, historical and cultural contexts in which they were written
	6.2 Analysing how writers' use of linguistic and literary features shapes and influences meaning
	6.3 Analysing writers' use of organization, structure, layout and presentation

Figure 1.4   Reading

Reading

The reading objectives reflect the format used by the new programme of study, with just two main headings: 'Reading for meaning' and 'Understanding the author's craft' (Figure 1.4). However, a notable change is the introduction of a separate sub-strand concerned with Reading and engaging with a wide variety of texts, which links to the need for a wide repertoire of opportunities, including the need to develop wide independent reading, as suggested by the range and content and curriculum opportunities sections of the programme of study.

Writing

The renewed Framework describes writing in three strands (Figure 1.5).

- Composition: generating ideas, planning and drafting
- Composition: shaping and constructing language for expression and effect
- Conventions: drawing on conventions and structures.

Language

The exploration of language change and variation, and the development of a meta-language (the terminology we use to comment on and analyse language) are included in this area (Figure 1.6).

Writing	
Pupils will write a wide range of texts on paper and on screen for different purposes and audiences, adapting features and techniques to create a range of effects and impact.	
Strands	**Substrands**
7 Composition: generating ideas, planning and drafting	7.1 Generating ideas, planning and drafting
	7.2 Using and adapting the conventions and forms of texts on paper and on screen
8 Composition: shaping and constructing language for expression and effect	8.1 Developing viewpoint, voice and ideas
	8.2 Varying sentences and punctuation for clarity and effect
	8.3 Improving vocabulary for precision and impact
	8.4 Developing varied linguistic and literary techniques
	8.5 Structuring, organizing and presenting texts in a variety of forms on paper and on screen
	8.6 Developing and using editing and proofreading skills on paper and on screen
9 Conventions: drawing on conventions and structures	9.1 Using the conventions of standard English
	9.2 Using grammar accurately and appropriately
	9.3 Reviewing spelling and increasing knowledge of word derivations, patterns and families

Figure 1.5   Writing

Language	
Pupils will explore the significance of English and the variations in its use and development, and comment on how language is used across a variety of contexts and situations.	
Strands	**Substrands**
10 Exploring and analysing language	10.1 Exploring language variation and development according to time, place, culture, society and technology
	10.2 Commenting on language use

Figure 1.6   Language

Before moving on, a key point does need to be made about the Framework for secondary English (2008) www.standards.dfes.gov.uk/secondary/framework/english. Unlike the National Curriculum, the Framework is not statutory in nature; its status is 'Recommended'. However, so closely does it align with the National Curriculum that English teachers find it invaluable as a curriculum planning tool, allowing an overview over half a term, a year, even a key stage, and thus ensuring a balanced coverage of the National Curriculum.

Point for reflection

Look closely at the Framework for secondary English (2008), at its content and implied structure. A link can be found on the companion website. To what extent do you think it allows for a flexible and open-minded English classroom to be developed?

GRAMMAR AND STANDARD ENGLISH

One of the most acrimonious battles in the debate over English teaching has been that over the role of Standard English in the curriculum. Closely aligned with concerns over standards, both professional and among the wider public, it has raged both outside the profession and among English teachers themselves. Some have said it is symptomatic of cultural colonialism, others that it is the only form of English that should be studied as it is that which is 'correct'; some have said that it is one of a number of forms of English worthy of sustained study; others that it is the only fair way to present pupils with the skills to equip them to perform well in later life. In one sense such different approaches bring to life the different epistemologies of English teaching explored earlier in the chapter under 'Internal conflicts' and it could be said that there is at least some reason in all of them.

Part of the problem with Standard English, of course, is its cultural dominance – a feature that English teachers have tried to counter in other areas. The National Curriculum has stated that: 'the phrase Standard English refers to the grammatically correct language used in formal communication throughout the world. To become competent users of Standard English, pupils need to be taught to recognise its characteristics and the rules which govern its usage' (DES, 1989: 51).

The Standard English debate perhaps reached its height in the battle over the Language in the National Curriculum (LINC) project. Set up in the early 1990s in response to the Kingman Report into the teaching of English language (DES, 1988), the LINC project had actively promoted an investigative, descriptive approach to language study, rather than the more formalized, prescriptive approach favoured by ministers and members of the government. It had encouraged pupils to enjoy language study, to see it as relevant and to base it upon their own experience of language use. However, its lack of prescription, together with its refusal to endorse Standard English as the desired model, ultimately resulted in the government's withdrawal of all the materials developed and circulated, and retaining Crown Copyright over them in an attempt to block their further dissemination and use. In a sense, though, this was a futile gesture and many English department stockrooms still contain copies of the materials developed, with teachers continuing to use them today in order to explore and develop children's understanding of language in use.

Point for reflection

Is there a 'Standard' English and, if so, (how) should it be taught?

The debate over Standard English is not a new one, as the following comments show. Do you feel that any of these have a particular resonance or relevance for English teachers today?

A poor intelligent boy who is compelled to come to school has a clear right to have his language cleansed and purified, and we must accept the burden of the effort. (Sampson, 1921: 27)

One of the disadvantages of the prescriptive approach to language teaching is its negative aspect ... This kind of teaching has often inhibited a child's utterance without strengthening the fabric of his language. (DES, 1975: 170)

The great divide is not between those who can read and write and those who have not learned how to. It is between those who have discovered what kinds of literacy society values and how to demonstrate their competencies in ways that earn recognition. (Meek, 1992 : 9)

Standard English demands great sensitivity from the teacher. It is dangerous to tell a five-year-old boy or girl that his or her mother uses language incorrectly. Adolescents are going to be embarrassed and ashamed if a teacher suggests that their dialect, which is a part of their identity must be radically changed. How to teach spoken Standard English needs continual discussion among teachers. (DES, 1989: 58)

We should aim to correct what is wrong because it is ugly, unclear or not conforming to accepted standards. The terminology of grammar should be subservient to our need to help pupils with their expression, and not an end in itself. Be flexible on common usage, warning pupils of the possible consequences of errors like 'it's me', while accepting that it is a commonly spoken form. (1980, Unpublished secondary school English department policy document)

The desired uniformity could be achieved by adopting the forms used by the underprivileged, but it never is — they are the ones who must demote their own language and learn a new one, replacing the threads that join their minds and feelings to reality — like the operation of reconnecting the flesh and nerves of a severed limb. (Bolinger, 1980: 52)

competence in language is not seen as very much to do with an ability to write correct Standard English. Bullock does not accept the concept of correctness in English, but prefers to talk about 'appropriateness'. Prescriptive approaches to grammar, spelling and punctuation are dismissed by the report, not so much with contempt as with amusement. (Marenbon, 1987: 8)

Ultimately, we should continue to focus our energies on teaching children to learn language accurately and appropriately, in ways that are responsive both to — rather than prescriptive about — the realities of how language is used, and how young people learn to use it ... To be literate in the twenty-first century will involve interacting with Information and Communications Technology in ways that we are now only beginning to think about ... this technology will relieve us of many of our worries about correctness (for example, spell and grammar checks) and will also increasingly offer us predetermined forms of appropriateness. Our freedom as communicators in general and as writers in particular, will be both more extensive and less autonomous. We need to start thinking about how we want to use these possibilities and about how we want to teach young people to use them, right now. (Davison and Moss, 2000: 117)

Point for reflection

- Compose three statements about whether/why you think Standard English does or does not have a place in the secondary English curriculum.
- Devise three 'shoulds' and 'should nots' that you think English teachers should bear in mind when approaching spoken language.
- What place do you think dialects other than Standard English should have in the English classroom?

Point for reflection

SHAKESPEARE AND THE LITERARY CANON

One of the more controversial elements of the National Curriculum since 1995 has been the inclusion of a canonical list of 'approved' authors for compulsory study. Situated firmly within the 'cultural heritage' camp, the list has been praised by traditionalists as a sign of standards being upheld and the great tradition of English literature being passed on to future generations. Simultaneously, it has been vilified by modernizers within the profession, who see it as backward-facing, designed almost as an aversion therapy to deter young people from engaging with literature.

Point for reflection

What is the literary 'canon'? Who chose it and why is it taught?

Point for reflection

Within the National Curriculum for English (2007), at Key Stage 3 the range of literature identified for study includes:

- stories, poetry and drama drawn from different historical times, including contemporary writers
- texts that enable pupils to understand the appeal and importance over time of texts from the English literary heritage, including works by the following pre-twentieth-century writers: Jane Austen, Elizabeth Barrett Browning, William Blake, Charlotte Brontë, Robert Burns, Geoffrey Chaucer, Kate Chopin, John Clare, Samuel Taylor Coleridge, Charles Dickens, Arthur Conan Doyle, George Eliot, Thomas Gray, Thomas Hardy, John Keats, John Masefield, Alexander Pope, Christina Rossetti, William Shakespeare (*Sonnets*), Mary Shelley, Robert Louis Stevenson, Jonathan Swift, Alfred Lord Tennyson, H.G. Wells, Oscar Wilde, Dorothy Wordsworth and William Wordsworth
- texts that enable pupils to appreciate the qualities and distinctiveness of texts from different cultures and traditions

- at least one play by Shakespeare
- forms such as journalism, travel writing, essays, reportage, literary non-fiction and multimodal texts, including film.

Point for reflection

'A dead white men's curriculum': how relevant is the National Curriculum's list of prescribed authors for a twenty-first century, multicultural, British population?

A similar list exists at Key Stage 4, with a revised and expanded list of pre-twentieth-century authors.

In practice, however, the effect of this list has not been to swamp the English curriculum with classic works of literature, but to make English teachers selective and judicious in their choice of texts. Narrative poems and the Sherlock Holmes stories have grown in popularity, as have works of fiction by authors such as Robert Louis Stevenson and H.G. Wells. The importance of studying whole texts rather than extracts has led to a rise in the popularity of the short story as a way of maintaining pupils' interest in and engagement with the text.

At Key Stage 3, the compulsory study of at least one play by Shakespeare has usually tended to result in pupils studying a Shakespeare play during the second half of Year 9, in readiness for their Key Stage 3 standard assessment tests (SATs) (a number, of course, will have been introduced to Shakespeare in earlier years). Since the inception of the Key Stage 3 SATs in the mid-1990s, the following texts have been selected for study on a rolling programme, with teachers able to choose from among the three plays offered each year: *As You Like It, Henry V, Julius Caesar, Macbeth, The Merchant of Venice, A Midsummer Night's Dream, Much Ado About Nothing, Romeo and Juliet, The Tempest, Twelfth Night* and *Richard III*. As a representative list of the plays by Shakespeare that any English teacher involved in teaching up to GCSE level might be expected to know, this is fairly comprehensive. Remember, though, that you will not be expected to know all of them immediately; once selected for SAT study, each play will remain on the list for at least three years. Alongside your Key Stage 3 Shakespeare play, you will then need to select another for study at GCSE level. In that way, as a teacher you can build up your knowledge of the plays over a number of years. Remember, too, that one of the principal influences on what you will be studying with your classes is what is available in departmental stockrooms!

Point for reflection

Read the following comments on the literary canon. Written some years ago, to what extent do you consider that they still apply to the current National Curriculum?

The so-called 'literary canon', the unquestioned 'great tradition' of the 'national literature', has to be recognised as a *construct*, fashioned by particular people for particular reasons at a certain time. There is no such thing as a literary work or tradition which is valuable in itself, regardless of what anyone might have said or come to say about it. (Eagleton, 1983: 11)

The 1995 NC was criticised as elitist, 'elevating writing produced by and about a particular Anglo-Saxon class and gender, so that the 'universal meanings' it embodies are only universal for those who define the world from that perspective. Other people are not only under-represented as authors in the canon, but have to read about themselves and their experience as constructed by authoritative others. Raymond Williams (1973) ... argued that a truly popular culture representing the voices and interests of the working class should be supported and valued. Critics have complained that people from cultures outside Britain are presented in the Leavisite canonical texts (if at all) as alien and inferior, women are represented as the objects of male desire and defined in their relation to men, and the working classes are depicted as pitiful or quaint. The existence of this canon as a whole may be experienced as a form of oppression, and a denial of everyday personal experience'. (J. Maybin, Davison and Moss, 2000: 186-7)

STANDARD TEXTS

So what are the standard texts that you might expect to find within departmental stock cupboards? Some will say that class sets of novels are less ubiquitous than was the case, maybe, 10 or more years ago. The introduction and establishment of the Framework for secondary English might be cited as a part of the reason behind this – indeed a criticism that is sometimes made of the Strategy is that, in seeking to ensure adequate coverage of a range of genres, pupils only ever get to read extracts, that they no longer study complete texts and that this is just another manifestation of children and young people becoming unable to sustain their attention over a period of time, preferring instead to focus on extracts and sound bites.

However, many would argue that the shared class text remains as central and vital a part of the English curriculum as it ever did. Certainly, an exploratory visit to departmental stock cupboards around the country would corroborate such a statement. The following is a necessarily brief sample of some of the novels for children currently in use in secondary schools. You should, from the outset, become familiar with as many children's authors as possible.

A brief introductory list, aimed at Key Stage 3 classes, might include the following texts:

Vivienne Alcock	*The Trial of Anna Cotman*
David Almond	*Skellig*
Nina Bawden	*Carrie's War*
Malorie Blackman	*Noughts and Crosses*
Frank Gardner Boyce	*Millions*
Roald Dahl	*Boy*
Anne Fine	*Goggle Eyes*
Nicholas Fisk	*Grinny*
Janni Howker	*The Nature of the Beast*
Elizabeth Laird	*Red Sky in the Morning*
Michelle Magorian	*Goodnight, Mr Tom*
Michael Morpurgo	*Kensuke's Kingdom*
Michael Morpurgo	*Private Peaceful*
Michael Morpugo	*War Horse*
William Nicholson	*The Wind Singer*

Philip Pullmann	*Northern Lights*
Philip Reeve	*Mortal Engines*
Louis Sachar	*Holes*
Robert Swindells	*Abomination*
Rosemary Sutcliff	*Eagle of the Ninth*
Jean Ure	*Tea-leaf on the Roof*
Robert Westall	*The Kingdom By The Sea*
Robert Westall	*The Machine Gunners*
Benjamin Zephaniah	*Refugee Boy*

This is a very small selection from a vast number. A few, such as *Carrie's War*, *The Machine Gunners* or *Goodnight, Mr Tom* have already attained 'classic' status; other, more recently published works, such as *Kensuke's Kingdom*, *Private Peaceful* or *Holes* look certain to follow suit. Many of the authors mentioned above are prolific writers, and you should try to read other books by them. You should read as widely as possible in the field of children's literature, and especially those books used most frequently as shared class texts – look out for what is in use when out on teaching placements.

Point for reflection

Select a shortlist of authors or works that you consider should be included in a twenty-first century National Curriculum for English.

At Key Stage 4, the stock cupboard is ordered according to the demands of the examination syllabus, with examiners tending to be rather conservative in their tastes. Next summer, my younger son sits his GCSE English Literature examination. The text chosen for detailed study is *To Kill a Mockingbird* – the same novel I studied for O level English Literature, over 30 years ago. *Of Mice and Men*, *Lord of the Flies* and *A Kestrel for a Knave* are similarly widespread. In the Drama stakes, Shakespeare still dominates, with Arthur Miller in second place in what is virtually a two-horse race. In spite of such cultural conservatism, there are newer texts that have been introduced over recent years: for instance, poems by Simon Armitage and Carol Ann Duffy; poetry from other cultures and traditions and an engaging study of current non-fiction and media texts.

Point for reflection

What are the particular challenges that you as a teacher might face in teaching some of the books on the list above? Might any classroom situations prevent you from studying a particular text?

PLANNING TO DELIVER A GCSE ENGLISH LITERATURE TEXT

Finally, let us consider some of the different possible approaches to planning to teach a GCSE English Literature text. The examination texts available for study will depend upon the particular examination board that your department has chosen to follow. There are currently five examination boards offering GCSEs: Assessment and Qualifications Alliance (AQA), Oxford, Cambridge and RSA (OCR), Edexcel, the Welsh Joint Education Committee (WJEC) and the Council for the Curriculum, Examinations and Assessment (CCEA). Regardless of which examination board is selected, all pupils must demonstrate evidence of assessment in the following six categories of literature:

- prose published before 1914
- prose published after 1914
- poetry published before 1914
- poetry published after 1914
- drama published before 1914
- drama published after 1914.

Each board differs slightly in terms of the texts selected for study and the categories of literature selected for assessment by coursework or examination.

For instance, in AQA English Literature Specification A, all candidates compile a coursework folder worth 30 per cent of the total available marks and comprising three pieces: pre-1914 drama, pre-1914 prose and post-1914 drama. In addition, there is one examination paper worth 70 per cent of the total available marks; this is divided into two sections: Section A (post-1914 prose) and Section B (pre-1914 poetry and post-1914 poetry). In 2009, the following texts have been selected for the post-1914 prose section of the examination:

- *Green Days by the River* by Michael Anthony
- *Heroes* by Robert Cormier
- *Lord of the Flies* by William Golding
- *I'm the King of the Castle* by Susan Hill
- *A Kestrel for a Knave* by Barry Hines
- *To Kill a Mockingbird* by Harper Lee
- *The Catcher in the Rye* by J.D. Salinger
- *Of Mice and Men* by John Steinbeck
- Short stories included in the *AQA Anthology*.

Four teachers, Steve, Jan, Angela and Ann have agreed to meet to discuss possible ways in which they might approach the teaching of the novel *To Kill a Mockingbird* to a GCSE class. The outcome of the conversation will hopefully illustrate the range of different approaches to one text: in planning an approach to a text, you are not looking for the 'right answer'; instead, you need to consider the approach that you feel will engage your pupils and elicit the best response from them.

JAN   I always set the novel as a reading task over the summer holidays between Year 10 and Year 11. That way, hopefully most of the class will have a fair idea of what the novel is about before we actually come to study it in detail.

ANN   Yes, I'll always try to get them to read it before we come to study it in detail in class. For me, the key is to get the pupils to understand the characters and the setting right from the outset. It's such a wonderful book; I don't want them to miss any of the details, so I'll get them to focus on small details throughout Part One. For instance, towards the end of Part One I'll get them to draw a map of the street where Jem and Scout live, not because they especially need to know where all the different houses are but because by doing that it makes them go back to the text and read it closely — you can actually do it quite accurately.

STEVE   That's interesting because, for me, I just want the class to enjoy Part One and to get a sense of the characters, but to get through it quickly. For me, Part One is like a collection of short stories about the characters in Maycomb, but in a sense, it's just there to create a sense of background detail about the place where the main action is going to take place in Part Two.

ANN   I know what you mean but I just prefer to take some time over the details of Part One; for instance without being aware of some of the more peripheral characters like young Walter Cunningham and Burris Ewell, I think that the pupils might not make the link properly when other members of their families come to the fore during Part Two. I think that you also need an understanding of Boo Radley and the Radley family too, so that you're not left in the lurch at the end of the novel — it needs to be a surprise without being completely unexpected.

JAN   Yes — I agree totally about the importance of Part One. Get the pupils to find the briefest of quotations from the text to describe each of the characters: Dill was 'a pocket Merlin', Miss Stephanie Crawford was 'a neighbourhood scold', Boo Radley was 'a malevolent phantom', Mrs Dubose was 'pure hell'. That way, the pupils have at least some details to hang their hats on.

ANGELA   And don't forget the mockingbird motif. You need to draw the pupils' attention to the mentions of mockingbirds throughout Part One, even if you don't actually do anything substantial with them until towards the end of the novel, when Scout begins to understand what it's about for herself.

ANN   That's the thing — for me time spent on the first part of the novel building up the pupils' knowledge of the characters and the small town setting is time well invested. Really, I want to take my time over this part of the novel, so that in Part Two we can pick the pace up. You're right about Part One being like a collection of short stories — for that reason, I think that Part Two merits a faster paced reading, which I think you can do once you've got that knowledge of the characters and the setting.

STEVE   And alongside the mockingbirds, there is also scope for work on courage too, when you think of Atticus' words after Mrs Dubose dies, particularly after the children have not long before seen him shoot the mad dog. That then means that further on, towards the end, you can discuss the different ways that courage is shown in the novel, and look back to incidents such as Scout's fighting at the start of the book and the lynch mob before the start of the court case.

JAN   Do you do anything with the part on the first page about Jem breaking his arm? I'm always in two minds about that: part of me wants to say 'Just remember that line — it'll all make sense at the end of the book' and part of me thinks that that will spoil it for the pupils.

ANGELA   I know what you mean. I never point that out myself, but then at the very end I will go back to the very beginning to point out the link. It's surprising though, how many pupils have remembered the opening and made the connection.

JAN   What you said earlier about the small town setting, that's really important to me, that sense of everybody knowing everybody else's business, so that the characters know how the people round them will act and react, and the whole small-mindedness that goes with it.

STEVE   But how do you first start teaching the book — what do you do during the first lesson?

ANN   Start with basic work on the characters and the setting. Read Chapter One, then look at Jem, Scout, Dill, Atticus, Calpurnia, Boo Radley and what we find out about each of them. Discuss what we've worked out so far about where the novel is set and why.

JAN   Discuss the title and the book cover, get the pupils to speculate about what they think the book might be about.

ANGELA   A lot of the pupils who are doing History GCSE are studying the Depression, so that gives a useful background too. If you talk nicely to the History Department, they usually have some useful resources to lend you. I think it's always worthwhile showing the pupils something to give a sense of time and place, otherwise they think it was set just around the corner.

STEVE   Do you make much use of the film?

JAN   It's a great film, but it's not a patch on the book. It's confusing too, the way it mixes up the characters. It's useful once you've got to the end of the novel and the pupils are really comfortable and confident with it. Then you can use it as a way of reinforcing some of the bigger themes and plot lines.

ANN   Is it a book that you feel you could teach to any groups of pupils?

ANGELA   I've usually taught it with middle and upper sets. It's not that it's too complicated or difficult for lower ability classes; I just think there are other set texts that are more appropriate.

STEVE   I know what you mean. It's a great book, and the plot line is relatively straightforward, but it's fairly long and quite detailed. With middle to lower groups, I prefer to work on *Of Mice and Men*.

Point for reflection

Discuss with your mentor potential approaches to this or another of the set texts for GCSE English Literature examination study. Select another of the books from list of set texts: how might you approach the teaching of this with a class?

Point for reflection

WHAT THE RESEARCH SUGGESTS

In approaching the research underpinning current developments within the English curriculum, a practical starting point is Roger Beard's *National Literacy Strategy: Review of*

Research and other Related Evidence. Published to coincide with the National Literacy Strategy's (NLS's) launch in primary schools in 1998, the review explores the extent to which the rationale and pedagogy principally associated with the Strategy were underpinned by findings from then current research into literacy development from Britain, Australia and the USA. Although situated squarely within the primary years, this review provides a thorough introduction to key research studies pertaining to school improvement; to teaching quality; to the NLS model itself and to each of the individual generic teaching areas associated with the literacy strategy. The review was useful in demonstrating how the key approaches associated with the introduction of the National Literacy Strategy were grounded in and guided by both current and ongoing research.

In terms of a useful summary of research based on the development of the Framework for secondary English, the most thorough and comprehensive review is probably Colin Harrison's *Key Stage 3 Strategy: Roots & Research* (2002). This time specifically focused upon the secondary age-phase, the document synthesizes research findings from Britain and the USA in order to explore the development of literacy skills among pupils aged 11–14. Adopting a scholarly but readable approach and providing individual chapters on reading, writing and spelling, Speaking and Listening, together with critical summaries of what research shows about the teaching sequence, about supporting pupils who have fallen behind and about the challenge of staff development, this is an excellent introductory review.

Also worthy of note and in keeping with current developments designed to encourage teachers to become more critically reflective is the recently established What Works Well website, on which teachers are able to share case studies which have improved learning and teaching. Although lower key in nature by design, these are the kinds of practitioner-based research that all teachers can become involved in, and which will prove invaluable when moving towards Master's-level study.

The intention in this opening chapter has been to raise some of the broader, more wide-reaching issues in order to give a general overview of the subject and of English teaching, in order to answer the question, 'What is it that actually makes this subject and the teaching of English so different from others?'

In subsequent chapters, you will move on to consider particular aspects of English teaching in greater depth and finer detail. However, it is important that, throughout, you remember and bear in mind the broader questions in this first chapter, as they raise issues, both philosophical and practical, that have implications for every aspect of English teaching.

Key points from this chapter

This chapter has asked you to consider:

- what English means as a subject
- the key issues facing English teachers
- what it actually means to be an English teacher.

Further reading

Any of the texts mentioned in this chapter will help develop your understanding of the issues involved in teaching pupils with individual abilities, aptitudes, interests and needs. You might find the texts below particularly helpful, in terms of further reading.

Clarke, S., Dickinson, P. and Westbrook, J. (2004) *The Complete Guide to Becoming an English Teacher*. London: Sage.
Links educational theory, historical perspectives and current practice in a way that encourages the reader to engage with the issues and critique approaches. Chapters 1 and 2, on the National Curriculum and the Framework for teaching English, are both comprehensive and encourage a reflective approach.

Davison, J. and Dowson, J. (2003) *Learning to Teach English in the Secondary School: A Companion to School Experience*. 2nd edn. London: Routledge.
Provides a range of advice, planning ideas and templates for schemes of work and lessons. Chapters 1–4 explore the background, philosophies and influences upon English teaching, together with the battles that have raged around the subject, before going on to examine the National Curriculum and the Framework for teaching English in some depth.

Fleming, J. and Stevens, D. (2004) *English Teaching in the Secondary School: Linking Theory and Practice*. 2nd edn. London: David Fulton.
Adopts a topic-based approach to English teaching, with chapters on, for example, speaking and listening, reading, writing, teaching poetry, drama, ICT. The approach is scholarly but practical; Chapters 1 and 2, on the National Curriculum and the Key Stage 3 Strategy, are detailed and thought-provoking.

Marshall, B. (2000) *English Teachers: The Unofficial Guide: Researching the Philosophies of English Teachers*. London: Routledge.
Traces the competing traditions of English teaching and considers their relevance to the current debate through an analysis of English teachers' views about themselves and their subject.

Pike, M. (2004) *Teaching Secondary English*. London: Paul Chapman.
Takes a thematic approach to English teaching. Chapter 1, 'The Art of Teaching English' explores the philosophical background to English as a curriculum subject.

Williamson, J. (2001) *Meeting the Standards in Secondary English: A Guide to the ITT NC*. London: Taylor & Francis.
Provides detailed subject and pedagogical knowledge needed to teach English in secondary schools, together with support activities for work in schools.

Wright, T. (2005) *How to be a Brilliant English Teacher*. Oxford: Routledge.
A lively and realistic approach, which suggests practical strategies for implementing the statutory curriculum and is as entertaining as it is stimulating. Chapter 7, entitled 'The Framework', offers a practical, realistic introduction to the demands of working with the Framework for teaching English.

Useful websites

Live links to these websites can be found on the companion website www.sagepub.co.uk/
secondary.

www.curriculumonline.gov.uk
www.literacytrust.org.uk/index.html
www.qca.org.uk/qca_5600.aspx
http://whatworkswell.standards.dcsf.gov.uk/

PLANNING FOR LEARNING

Carol Evans

> **This chapter considers:**
>
> - what purposes curriculum planning serves
> - the three levels of curriculum planning: long, medium and short term
> - how good curriculum planning can address the key aim of any teacher: to enable all learners to learn to their potential
> - how to go about planning in a systematic and secure way.
>
> This chapter relates closely to Chapter 3, which offers you two detailed analyses of how plans emerge and are put into practice.

WHAT PURPOSE DOES PLANNING SERVE?

Whenever I hear the word, 'plan', it brings to mind the mantra of the disarmingly optimistic Baldrick, Mr Blackadder's servant and stooge, 'I have a plan – a cunning plan!' Maybe this is the way to start thinking about planning in teaching: Baldrick's plans were inevitably formulated as a means of escape from potentially catastrophic situations; and many trainee teachers have probably felt in equally vulnerable positions if facing a class of disaffected Year 9s – or even a co-operative but astute group of mature, adult students – without having prepared a very clear plan for the lesson ahead. But that's where I hope the similarity will end, for Baldrick's plans frequently backfired, and that is not what I hope will be the case when you go into the classroom.

The most obvious purpose of planning is to ensure that pupils make progress as they move through the education system – to avoid a situation in which learners are asked to learn something that they have already learned. Clarke et al. see this purpose as clearly linked to any commitment to raise standards, whether at central government or individual teacher levels: 'Teachers … need both a "bottom up" pedagogical approach and a "top down" centralised government approach to progression. The two are not mutually exclusive … Progression is firmly linked to the raising of standards as manifested in school league tables' (2004: 60).

Before the publication of *The Statutory Order: English in the National Curriculum* (DES and Welsh Office, 1990; later updated as *The National Curriculum for England*, DfEE, 2000, and again revised, 2007), referred to in this chapter as the National Curriculum, there was no requisite, formal co-ordination between teachers, across year groups and certainly among schools regarding what was to be taught and learned at any stage in English, or anywhere else in a child's schooling. Those who moved from one area to another, one local authority

(LA) to another and even one school to another within the same LA were vulnerable to finding themselves either repeating work that they had done before, or missing out aspects of learning altogether. Similarly, planning is essential to ensure smooth progression in pupils' learning as they pass from primary to secondary schools. Clarke et al. cite 'much evidence of a "learning loss" or dip in achievement in the Key Stage 2/3 transition' (2004: 59). In short, until the advent of a *national* curriculum, before the age of 14, after which examination boards dictated curriculum content, there was no overview of the curriculum and no one was accountable for what pupils learned and when.

The various versions of the secondary National Curriculum have aimed to address these issues, laying down a body of knowledge, skills and understanding which learners in the 11–16 age phase should be taught, and on which they should be assessed. Subsequent curriculum guides, particularly the Key Stage 3 Strategy's non-statutory *Framework for Teaching English: Years 7, 8 and 9* (DfEE, 2001) revised as the *Framework for Secondary English* (2008), referred to in this chapter as the Framework (see Chapter 1 for further information), have gone further in specifying the skills which teachers should address with each year group, so that the situation in the early twenty-first century is a very different, and more centrally controlled one than it used to be. The 2008 Framework aims to:

- support schools in raising standards and closing attainment gaps through guidance on planning and teaching to ensure effective progression
- promote continuity and progression from Key Stage 2 through to the end of Key Stage 4 in line with the new programmes of study
- provide a basis for target setting and promote high and consistent expectations for the achievement of all pupils
- give a sharper focus to tracking pupils' progress by integrating existing guidance on assessment
- emphasise the place of personalised learning, thinking skills and functional skills in the English curriculum
- provide a flexible electronic format to support planning for progression
- build on existing National Strategies resources and further develop guidance, especially on the new areas of the curriculum (www.standards.gov.uk, accessed 8 May 2008) (details of the Framework can be accessed via the companion website www.sagepub.co.uk/secondary).

While many teachers feel that their professional judgement and freedom are challenged by what is seen by some as over-centralized curriculum and pedagodic control, adopting the perspective of a pupil who may be subject to the difficulties mentioned earlier suggests that some measure of organization in curriculum content must be prudent, if pupils' knowledge, skills and understanding are to be built on secure foundations and to be progressive.

LEVELS OF PLANNING

Long-term planning

A long-term curriculum plan sets out what will be covered over a key stage, and within that key stage, by each year group. This plan will normally be drawn up by/under the guidance of the head of department, perhaps in consultation with other departmental staff, and it will address the requirements of the National Curriculum, National Strategy documents such as the Framework and examination syllabi, as relevant to the age phase and ability levels of the pupils, thus targeting particular attainment levels and learning objectives. The long-term plan is probably one which you, as a trainee or new teacher, will have least involvement with, hence its brief mention here. You will, though, be wise to ask your head of department to show you the long-term plan, so that you can contextualize your own medium- and short-term planning within the bigger picture.

Medium-term planning

Medium-term plans are often referred to as 'schemes of work', and generally cover a period of a term, half a term or a few weeks. In a recent teacher training session at Edge Hill University, the trainee group identified five key purposes for schemes of work:

1. To ensure that the statutory learning requirements are covered. These 'flesh out' the long-term plan, with regard to the National Curriculum – reading, writing, speaking and listening, media and drama – and any relevant examination syllabus. This purpose has a clear implication for teacher accountability: is the teacher delivering the required specifications for each age group?

2. To ensure, as in the long-term plan, that pupils are not frustrated by 'learning' the same things (knowledge, skills and understanding) at the same level as they have done before. This purpose aims to ensure progression, and is addressed by building the scheme of work around clear, specific, progressive learning objectives. At Key Stage 3 (Years 7, 8 and 9) and Key Stage 4 (Years 10 and 11) these will follow the Framework's learning objectives, organized into four main areas of English study – speaking and listening, reading, writing and language; at Key Stage 4 (Years 10 and 11) they will additionally relate to GCSE examination criteria and assessment objectives. Progression also requires teachers to plan what material (for example, within a text) will be covered and what the focus and outcome (work produced) will be, in each lesson in the scheme.

3. To ensure that that progression is incremental. This means that learning expectations are based on realistic and carefully staged steps, similar to building blocks. In turn, this means that each child could well be working at a slightly different level than her/his peers – even within a streamed or setted class – though it is likely that several children in each class will be working to common goals. Lev Vygotsky (1986) referred to children's 'zones of proximal development', meaning the carefully graduated levels of further, potential learning which each child has. If learning expectations are carefully planned to move children to the next stage in their development potential – the next 'zone' – their learning will be secure. Thus, plans need to 'personalize' learning objectives to each individual. The Framework guidance on planning states that:

> The key to successful planning for particular classes and groups and for personalising learning is the process of constructing the learning objectives into a coherent scheme of work – by grouping objectives, from across as well as within years, and aligning them to appropriate contexts, activities and resources. The renewed Framework supports this process by enabling teachers to combine objectives, which are arranged progressively in a limited number of strands and substrands. (www.standards.dcsf.gov.uk – access via the companion website www.sagepub.co.uk/secondary)

4. To ensure that pupils are stimulated and engaged in lessons, that a varied range of activity is planned for and that lessons do not become a 'teacher performance', leaving pupils passive. This purpose serves to address the range of learning opportunities across a series of lessons, ensuring variety.

5. To ensure that teachers and pupils will know what pupils have learned over a given period. This purpose relates to monitoring, assessing and recording individual achievement, so that progress can be measured over a period of time. This also requires teachers to reflect on the ongoing success, or otherwise, of the scheme of work, making changes to it in order to best ensure each child's progress.

There are many possible templates and formats for medium-term planning, and these which follow are offered as examples which have been found helpful and 'fit for purpose', by trainees in the past. The Framework (2008) offers amended formats, which address more closely the 2007 National Curriculum.

Points for reflection

Look at the templates and plans on offer both in this chapter (Figures 2.1–2.6) and on the Standards site. Rewrite the past plans to address the 2008 curriculum requirements, try them out in practice and reflect on their relative effectiveness for you and your pupils.

If you create thorough and thoughtful medium-term plans, you will find that you have already done much of the work needed for your short-term or individual lesson plans, and the advice which follows is equally relevant as you work on both medium-term and short-term (lesson) planning.

Short-term planning: lesson plans

This level of planning relates to individual lessons, and will be the most frequent form of planning which you will do during your training. As a beginning teacher, you need individual lesson plans as a preparatory thinking tool and – in the lesson itself – an aide-memoire, and security blanket! Behind the written plan is significant preparation, thought and research on your part, as you decide on the various ingredients of the lesson.

As you plan, remember to keep *learning* rather than *teaching* as your focus. The crucial questions are:

- What *skills* will pupils learn in this lesson; what are your *learning objectives*? These will usually be based on National Curriculum programmes of study/Framework objectives, but will also address Assessment Foci (AFs) and examination syllabus criteria. In the English lesson plans associated with this chapter, and on the companion website, you will see DfEE (2001) *Framework for Teaching English: Years 7, 8 and 9* objectives listed. These were relevant at the time that these lessons were planned. However, *you* will use the revised, Framework (DCSF, 2008) objectives. (See www.standards. dfes.gov.uk/secondary/framework/english via the companion website.) Learning objectives are often confused with learning outcomes and lesson activities or tasks, and it is important to clarify the differences before you start planning: see below for definitions, examples and advice, and go to the companion website to see how Sarah, Monika and Ian put their learning objectives into practice in their teaching (see for example Sarah's overt use of the learning objectives at 13.55 and 16.17 on the video, phase 2).

- Are you enabling *every child* to learn what you want her/him to learn? This aspect of planning is variously referred to as 'differentiation', 'personalization' and 'individualization'. In effect it is about making your learning accessible and engaging for all the pupils, whatever their ability, preferred learning style, gender, personal, social, ethnic background and so on.

- How will you know whether *all* pupils have all achieved what you set out for them to learn; how will you *monitor and assess* each pupil's learning? The Framework's guidance on planning for assessment makes a clear link with APP (Assessing Pupils' Progress), and states that: 'Making the link between learning objectives and assessment criteria supports periodic assessment, which enables teachers and subject *Framework* to shape planning and related future assessment. In this way curricular targets derived from APP can then inform planning from the Framework and learning in the classroom' (www.standards.dfes.gov.uk).

- Are you setting up a situation in which each child is *actively involved* in learning?

- Are you relating the scheme of work to *progressive skill acquisition* and practice, linked to relevant statutory/non-statutory curricular guidelines? Again, use the National Curriculum and Framework as your first sources.

- Last, but certainly not least, are you including a *range of activities* over time? Trevor Wright includes a lively list of ideas for variety, which he says 'isn't a superficial or trivial issue – it's a central one' (2005: 25), which is important at both the scheme of work and lesson planning stages. Are you keeping in mind, as you plan your scheme, the need to ensure a classroom atmosphere which encourages pupils to think, to contribute, to gain confidence and respect others? This relates to Chapter 1's note about being a creative teacher, which is a key to developing creative learners. As Fleming and Stevens note, 'successful English teaching is as much about creating a culture in the classroom as it is about implementing a programme or structuring a series of lessons' (2004: xvii). They further emphasize the need for balance: 'What we need to do, above all, is to reflect on our own preferences and predilections, compensating when appropriate for any personal shortcomings through a conscious effort to adapt to new ways and areas of English teaching' (2004: 5). Avoid the temptation to plan to your 'default' teaching style – the style which seems easiest on a 'bad day'! Incorporate drama activities, creative tasks and multi-sensory resources, which will stimulate and engage your pupils.

Points for reflection

Before reading on, use the 'crucial questions' as a checklist for any plans that you have already seen. Think back to lessons which you have observed or in which you were a student, yourself. How far was the checklist catered for? Did the learning 'work'? If not, what might have made it more effective?

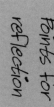

THE PRACTICALITIES

Before planning, find out about basics such as the size, age and ability range of the class, the facilities available, the lesson length, the pupils' prior learning and whether they have covered your proposed topic before. It is crucial to ensuring that you meet every child's needs and address the requirement to personalize learning that you should ask for achievement data (previous National Curriculum levels achieved, standard assessment test (SAT) results from the previous key stage, school reports and test or examination scores, for example: see Chapter 5), and any other information, either recorded in writing or by word of mouth from class teachers or pastoral tutors about particular members of the class who may need special facilities, assistance or support. If learning support staff are working with the class, find out whether they are there for general support or to help one or more individuals, and build into your planning exactly how you would like any additional adults to support the pupil(s). It is your responsibility to work co-operatively with other adults, planning for their deployment and discussing your plans and their role in them.

Points for reflection

If you look at Sarah's lesson on the website, you can reflect on how she uses her learning support assistant (LSA) in each phase of the lesson. Does her plan (Figure 2.1) show that she deliberately planned for her use? To what extent does the LSA use the planned activities to enable her pupils to make progress and achieve the learning objectives?

As stated above, you will usually be advised to start the planning process by deciding on your learning objectives, which indicate what you want your pupils to learn by the end of the lesson. The experience of Mark Pike (2004), in researching his trainee teachers' approach to lesson planning in Leeds University, suggests a common difference of opinion with regard to whether to start with learning objectives or tasks. While one trainee teacher 'started from the tasks and worked backwards so she could fill in the box at the top of her lesson plan labelled "Learning Objectives"', Pike makes it clear that: 'what is not acceptable is to say that your objective is to "get to the end of Act III scene 2 by the end of the lesson". You may well need to get to the end of Act III, scene 2 but need to be clear about what, specifically will be learnt on the way' (2004: 15).

One of the most common causes for muddled lessons is a lack of clarity in learning objectives, on the part of either the teacher or the pupils: unless you are clear about what you want the pupils to learn, you cannot judge how successful they – and you – have been. Keep your learning objectives focused: too many, and your learners will not achieve them. Matt, a trainee teacher on the PGCE course at Edge Hill University, reflected on the planning process and writing. Prior to the course, Matthew had trained chefs in prestigious restaurants and he brought his experience of creating and meeting objectives in that environment to his work on the teacher training course:

Date: Thursday 28 June 2007

Class (including ability range): Year 7, Mixed Ability

Location: L10

Length of Lesson: 50 minutes

Topic: An Introduction to Persuasive Writing

Aims (*What is your overall teaching aim?*)

For pupils to understand language techniques used in persuasive writing.

Learning Objectives (*What do you want pupils to learn in this lesson?*)
By the end of the lesson, pupils will:

LOb1: analyse meaning in the poem ('The Deserted House')
LOb2: extract key pieces of information from a given text
LOb3: identify and use language techniques used in persuasive writing
LOb4: develop peer and self-assessment skills

Learning outcomes (*What will pupils* **produce** *in this lesson?*)
Peer assessment sheet
Written self-assessment comment
Discussions in class and small groups

Differentiation (*How will you cater for differences in your pupils' abilities/learning styles?*)

By questioning – targeted questions to targeted pupils
By groupings – peer support
By stimulus material – addresses VAK learning styles
By support – LSA

Assessment (*How will you evaluate how far your stated learning objectives have been achieved by each pupil?*)

Written assessment – mark and record at end of lesson
Peer assessment
Self-assessment
Homework – mark at the end of the lesson
Oral feedback via questioning and discussion

Resources needed
Peer assessment forms; newspaper reviews; copies of 'The Deserted House'; worksheets; IWB; A4 lined paper; pens

Key NC (2000)/Framework (2001) Objective/Examination Syllabus References
S&L 1b, 3a, 8a, 10a; R 1b, f, 8v; W 1j, 9b – NC
R1, 2, 7, 11; W2, 3, 14; S&L 5, 13 – KS3 Framework

Content, including **introduction,** teaching and learning **methods** and **activities**, **timings** and **review** session:

Figure 2.1   Sarah's PGCE secondary English lesson plan: Year 7

Figure 2.1 (Continued)

Timing	Teacher activity	Learner activity	Notes
10 mins	**Starter** • State teaching and LObs • *Peer and self-assessment* • Pupils assess partners' work • Feedback • Pupils to write 2 stars and a wish at bottom of results (self assessment)	• Pupils listen • Pupils peer assess using worksheet (1) • Pupils respond by offering opinions • Using worksheet (1) pupils assess their own work • Pupils respond by offering opinions	Hand out worksheet 2 while pupils are assessing homework piece
10 mins	**Introduction** • Different types of property programmes • Using PowerPoint slides, go through activity – describing homes. • Ask targeted questions	• Pupils listen • Pupils respond by answering questions and offering opinions	
10 mins	**Development** • Read through worksheet (2) with pupils • Explain task • Circulate – assist LSA where needed • Feedback	• Pupils work on task • Pupils respond by answering questions and offering opinions	
10 mins	**Further development** • Read through poem • General discussion of poem • Ask targeted questions – see *notes* section • Explain task to pupils – estate agent activity • Using PowerPoint slides, explain the focus for each group • Pupils to work in pairs • Hand out envelopes after explaining task • Circulate during activity	• Pupils listen • Pupils respond by answering questions and offering opinions • Pupils listen • Pupils work collaboratively on task – write ideas on A4 paper	*Questions* 1 Find 6 details about the house 2 How do you know the house is deserted? 3 Who might live in the house?
10 mins	**Plenary** • Ask selected pupils to read their suggestions • Ask targeted questions • Collect in written work – explain that we will look at grades for written assessment next lesson	• Pupils respond by answering questions and offering opinions • Pupils hand in resources and homework	*Focus* Persuasive nature of language used: 1. Features of the house 2. Garden area

after using the suggested template and then experimenting around it, I made my own lesson plan template because that's how it works best, easiest, most efficiently for me. I'm planning in a way that helps me to achieve what I want (and I can still prove that I am planning.)

This efficiency helps me to achieve [learning objectives] LObs for THEM – the pupils. LObs are simple and streamlined. Achieve ONE thing, but *nail* it. Don't reach that target, surpass it. Smash it. That LOb should be the most important thing, the fundamental principle of your topic. The driving force. (Matt Whittle, 2007, email to tutor).

Two other trainees, Jemma and Kate, also reflected on the initial challenges of planning:

It does seem tricky at first, getting the aim of the lesson, the objectives, the activities and the assessment all tied together but like many things practice does make it easier (Kate Thornton, 2007, email to tutor).

They also thought about which came first in their planning – the learning objectives or potential activities. Jemma wrote:

I, like Kate, agree that it is difficult at first to tie in the learning objectives, the lesson plan and the *Framework* but rather than thinking about what you *have* to teach I would advise to think about what you *want* to teach. Usually ... and I know this is very simple but I feel something worth pointing out ... you are best thinking of what you want to do (that is, an activity) and then looking at the *Framework* to see what you can get out of it in terms of the curriculum.

I very often think I might like to do something and it might come to me while in the pub or watching TV. I was watching an old Wheel of Fortune on Sky and thought I would like to use the idea for a game/test. When you have thought about the activity it is easier to see which *Framework* objectives fit the task. Then as you get more confident you begin thinking about it the other way round and if you know a class has to cover something in the curriculum, you have learned the easy way how to think up the activity (Jemma Sugden, 2007, email to tutor).

Finally, Jonathan, another trainee, reflected on his experience after a group activity in a planning seminar in university. He found that his approach was out of step with that of others in the group, exemplifying that you, too, will need to find the most productive and accessible method for you:

The preferred method of the group was to get straight on with the first lesson plan, relating it ... to the previous lesson plan, and then fitting LObs to the tasks they had dreamt up. I now think the best approach is to see which LObs I can relate to the Scheme of Work, order them into a progression, and then begin to select texts, tasks, and resources to move through the scheme (Jonathan Thorpe, 2007, PGCE reflective journal).

Another challenge is targeting the appropriate level of challenge for pupils: if your objectives are inappropriate by being either too difficult or too easy for your specific learners, all manner of difficulties can arise – behavioural, motivational and learning. Refer to the Framework, National Curriculum or examination syllabus in order to specify learning objectives and plan how you will make them clear to the pupils, in language that they can understand, and so that they can see a valid reason for doing this work.

Include also in your plans what you want the pupils to produce in the lesson: the learning (or lesson) outcomes. One way of clarifying the difference between learning objectives and learning outcomes is to use the acronyms of imagined characters, WALT (We Are

Learning Today …) and WILF (What I'm Looking For …), which you may see written on many a classroom board. Many trainees find that this method of wording objectives and outcomes helps to focus the whole lesson on learning, as opposed to simply keeping pupils busy with no real gain in learning. To see this method in action, look at the sample lesson plans in this chapter.

Points for reflection

Again, at this point, consider Sarah's plan (Figure 2.1). Does she distinguish between the learning objectives and the learning outcomes? To what extent does this help the pupils to see learning signposted as the lesson progresses? (Look at phase 1 and 2 of Sarah's video, starting at 00.01 and 16.17.) Sarah's learning objectives on the board are specific; in her plan she lists a good many National Curriculum and Framework references for the lesson to target. Check these in the relevant documents and see whether you can prioritize and slim these down to a more specific and focused group.

My advice, in wording learning objectives, is to use *dynamic verbs* rather than verbs which make it very difficult to assess pupils' learning, such as 'understand', 'know about'. J.S. Atherton (2005) is one of many writers (see also advice in the National Strategy, 2004, publication, *Pedagogy and Practice: Teaching and Learning in Secondary Schools. Unit 3: Lesson Design for Lower Attainers*) who uses Bloom's (1956) taxonomy of learning as a source of wording for learning objectives. Thus, dynamic verbs such as define, recall, describe, label, identify, match, explain, translate, illustrate, summarize, extend, apply (to a new context), demonstrate, predict, employ, solve, use, analyse, infer, relate, support, differentiate, explore, design, create, compose, combine, assess, evaluate, defend, give good reason for, are all effective introductory words in specifying the learning that you might want pupils to focus on.

The National Strategy's recommended structure for a lesson is a three- or four-part one: a starter activity (sometimes omitted), introduction, developmental activity(ies) and plenary. Although it may be comforting to adhere to this structure, you may sometimes feel that the learning objectives for that day do not fit easily into it, and you should have the confidence, then, to depart from it. The Office for Standards in Educations (Ofsted's) 2005 publication, *English 2000–05. A Review of Inspection evidence*, reported that, over the five-year period, 'planning has improved, with clearer learning objectives and positive engagement from pupils (para. 19)', and 'teachers are increasingly alert to the different ways in which pupils learn and try to plan lessons that will meet their needs (para. 20)', nevertheless:

some teachers lack the confidence and subject knowledge to respond sufficiently flexibly to what pupils need. They interpret the recommended four-part lesson structure as something to be applied on all occasions. HMCI's Annual Report (2003/04) makes a similar point in relation to secondary trainee teachers, describing 'a tendency towards safe and unimaginative teaching … partly because trainees use the structure and content of the Strategy too rigidly … [and] … many teachers still need to have the courage to be innovative, making greater use, in particular, of group, collaborative and independent approaches and a wider range of teaching strategies to engage and challenge pupils. (para. 20)

The report continues:

> This lack of flexibility also applies to teachers' use of learning objectives. At best, they plan carefully over a sequence of lessons, using realistic objectives that match pupils' needs. For too many primary and secondary teachers, however, the objectives become a tick list to be checked off because they follow the frameworks for teaching too slavishly. As a result, too many objectives are identified and they become impossible to assess in the lesson. (para. 21)

Whether you use the three/four-part structure or not, your lesson should progress clearly through a series of stages, so that you can build pupils' confidence and develop their independence in learning. When working on this aspect of planning with my trainee teachers, I asked them to put themselves in the position of a pupil. Together, we produced the 'pupil voice' guidance (see Figure 2.2), offering advice to teachers on how to help pupils to learn securely.

Adhering to this progressive scaffold will ensure that pupils are at least given a fair chance at becoming confident in their learning. Following research for the Department for Education and Employment into teacher effectiveness, Hay McBer reported that progression is a fundamental premise of effective learning, and has been identified as such by research into teacher effectiveness: 'Our lesson observations revealed that in classes run by effective teachers, pupils are clear about what they are doing and why they are doing it. They can see the links with their earlier learning and have some ideas about how it could be developed further' (McBer, 2000: 59).

Points for reflection

When you go to the website you'll find an extended version (Figure 2.2a) of the 'pupil voice' table in Figure 2.2, including a column in which you can make comments as to whether any of the videoed lessons adhere to this suggested structure. For example, as pupils are completing the peer and self-assessment exercise (09.30–17.00), Sarah leads in to the new learning by asking pupils to make sure they have written down today's learning objectives, and also uses them as a signpost for pupils, so that they know what is coming next in the lesson:

> OK while we're waiting for everyone to get them all done I am just going to go through the objectives very quickly, OK? We have got two objectives today, to be able to extract key pieces of information from a given text which I will explain more in detail later and to understand the language techniques used in persuasive writing. They are your objectives for today (transcript: 5).

When you have watched the footage, ask yourself whether any part of the lesson(s) might have been planned differently, to make the learning more incremental for pupils.

What would a pupil say?	What does this mean to you as you plan?
• Take me through easy stages:	• Provide a 'scaffold' of activities for secure learning:
→ talk to me about it	→ explain what you want them to learn (learning objectives in pupil-friendly language)
→ show me how it works	→ demonstrate/model/deconstruct to the class
→ let me talk about it with my friends	→ sharing ideas to feel safe 'having a go' at analysing the model
→ let me try creating a new one with my friends	→ collaborating/constructing together to build confidence
→ let me try it on my own	→ independence/constructing solo
• We learn to talk before we learn to write, so: → let me talk (with you and with my friends) before asking me to write on my own	→ allow talk time to enable development, according to social constructivist theory of learning (Vygotsky, 1986)
• Keep me motivated and be fair when you assess me!	• Only assess what you have set out to teach:
→ tell me *how* I can get it right	→ tell pupils, *before they start the task*, what you're looking for/assessment criteria
→ tell me *when* I am getting it right	→ use praise/reinforcement
→ give me align a chance in the lesson to realize I'm getting it right	→ refer to learning objectives throughout the lesson and build in mini-plenaries
→ mark my work according to what you said would get me marks	→ use the learning objectives when marking

Figure 2.2   Planning and learning in English: the pupil view

Other things to consider as you plan the structure of the lesson include:

- Optionally devising an appropriate starter activity. How will you open the lesson? Is this a continuation of work begun previously? If so, find an interesting way of beginning with an active recap. For example, pupils tell *you* what went before, rather than you telling *them*, to reinforce learning and build progressively from it. The National Strategy suggests that you open with a specific, interactive, 10-minute activity, such as a game to teach a spelling or grammar rule, for example. These activities can grab the attention of the pupils and act as a 'calmer'. Look for other ways of achieving this result. If this is a new topic, how can you catch their attention, and make them want to know more? Do the lessons on the website do this?
- The organization of pupils needs thought. In what combinations do you want the pupils to work at different times in the lesson: as a whole class, in small groups, in pairs, individually?

Remember that Speaking and Listening requirements include all of these types of situation as requirements. Most effective learning experiences include a variety of class groupings and short, fast-paced activities. Decide what you will do, and at which points in the lesson, for best effect. Avoid planning to 'tell them about' something for longer than five minutes! Get pupils involved and busy: active learning is crucial – even when teaching adults! (Consider your own experiences in the taught sessions of your teacher training course. Do they adhere to this advice? What is the effect on your learning if they do/do not?) Notice the groupings in Sarah's lesson. Would you have organized it differently? Consider, too, whether an off-site activity might be valuable – theatre, museums and similar venues offer a breadth of experience which cannot be offered in a classroom. As a trainee, you will need to shadow an experienced member of staff in organizing a visit as there are legal requirements which mean you cannot do this on your own until you are fully qualified.

- How will you manage the transition from one activity to another, and plan for it? The transition from talking to writing can often be a tricky one, so find ways of making this as smooth as possible. For example, ask the class to have writing materials out of their bags at the start of every lesson, so that there is no disruption while they shuffle about in the middle of the lesson, and forget what they are supposed to be doing. If you want pupils to work in groups, consider putting names on each table and asking pupils to sit in those seats from the start of the lesson: again, this prevents disruption, time-wasting and loss of impetus at a crucial stage later in the lesson. Consider how Sarah plans for such transitions. How well do they work, in practice, when you see the video? Look at the start and end of each phase on the video (phase 1: start 00.01/end 13.00; phase 2: start 16.17/end 30.15; phase 3a: start 30.15/end 37.00; phase 3b: start 37.00/end 44.00; phase 4: start 44.00/end 46.40). For example, notice that all her resources are on the desks ready at the start of the lesson; notice, too, that she introduces the pictures of the house as part of the PowerPoint-linked class discussion (18.00 onwards), then leads fluently into a text-marking exercise, and suggests note-making to follow:

Sarah   OK have you all got a copy of this in front of you? Yep. OK. So these passages have all been taken from estate agents and they've used words very similar to the words that you used to describe the first house but in more detail. Now what I want you to do on your own is underline any words you think have been included to try and persuade people to buy these properties. OK now when I say persuade what do you think I mean?

Pupil   Inaudible response.

Sarah   OK excellent yeah. Just try to … what words have they used to try and make you buy these houses. OK so I'm not going to give you very long just underline any words … If you get to the point where you have done that and are still waiting, have a look at the pictures and maybe make some notes. What has been used in these pictures to make you try and buy, the house? What's appealing about these pictures? OK so you have just under five minutes, off you go (transcript: 7).

Here, Sarah uses her planned availability of resources on the tables to avoid any off-task possibilities or time-wasting.

- How are you going to cater for individual differences in the class? Personalized learning means much more than setting easier worksheets for the less able! At best, it should mean your being aware of the specific needs, personalities and working styles of everyone in the class, and ensuring that your planned lesson allows each person to work at her/his best. There is, of course, value in differentiated tasks, and in assessing to differentiated levels, so that each pupil can be encouraged and can progress to the best of her/his ability. Remember that 'ability' refers to the least able, the most able and those in the middle. The effective use of other adults in your classes can very ably address issues of different pupils' needs. In Sarah's lesson, notice her comment to the class in general and the supported pupil's learning assistant in particular, indicating that pupils 'can brainstorm' as an alternative way of approaching the next activity – a good example of how Sarah is catering for the pupil's best way of learning.

- How long will each phase of the lesson take? It's difficult, at first, to estimate with any accuracy how long pupils will need; but as you get to you know your pupils, you will estimate more realistically. As you watch experienced teachers, make a note of the time they allow for different activities with different classes, and use this information as you create your own plans.

- How will you plan for assessment? (You will find Chapter 7 particularly relevant to this issue, and remember that the web-based Framework allows you to relate learning objectives to APP targets so that you can plan appropriately.) Trainees sometimes think of assessment as coming after the learning experience, or lesson, and this leads to a lack of focus both at the planning stage and as the pupils work. You also have a statutory responsibility to record and report on pupils' achievements and progress, and you can only fulfill this duty if you monitor learning and assess progress regularly and efficiently. The sample plans in this chapter show how assessment can be planned for. It can take many forms, including formative (ongoing) monitoring and summative (end-point) assessment, and includes techniques such as asking questions in class, marking written work to attainment target level descriptions, using examination board assessment criteria, assigning marks for specific objectives in oral work or written work, making notes on particular achievements by individuals in lessons, peer and self-assessment. Sarah uses peer and self-assessment at the start of her lesson (02.00 onwards):

Sarah	Excellent right so now I want you to just quickly at the very bottom — you've all done this before — the two stars and a wish. Someone tell me what I want you to do in this box. Yep Alishia.
Pupil	Replies (inaudible)
Sarah	OK do we all agree with that? Two things you like. One thing that you don't like — everyone agree with that?
Pupil	All pupils say yes in unison.
Sarah	Yep, OK very quickly. You've got about three minutes. Two things you liked about your own review and one thing that you could do to improve it (transcript: 4-5).

 When you watch Sarah's lesson, notice, too, how she links this peer and self-assessment into the learning objectives (12.20–17.00) for the persuasive writing lesson which she goes on to teach today. How do you think this is helping the pupils to progress? How does it relate to their growing independence in learning? The important thing to bear in mind is that you need to be clear about *what* you want to assess in each lesson, and *how best* to assess it, and you must make sure that your pupils know all this, too: all assessment criteria should relate closely to your stated learning objectives, defining how pupils will be able to show they have achieved them. Remember that achievement for each individual may be either a 'small step' or a 'giant leap', but all achievement deserves recognition, praise and recording.

- How to end the lesson. The purpose of a final 'plenary', or drawing together of the learning, is to reinforce what pupils have learned and for you to be able to make a final check on who has learned what. Do the teachers on the website use plenaries, and to what effect for the pupils and themselves?
- Finally, remember that you will use your plan after the lesson, and your reflections on how the lesson actually went in relation to your plan, in order to evaluate how successful you and all individuals in the class have been. This is what makes you into a genuinely reflective practitioner, who will continue to develop as a professional and effective teacher. Although your preoccupation at first will be with your classroom management and control, you must always focus on your pupils' or students' success in achieving the learning objectives stated on your plan. This analysis of what knowledge, skills and understanding have been gained by each pupil will be vital in deciding what worked, what did not, what needs to be changed and how to plan your next lesson … which takes you back to the start of this section …

FINDING RESOURCES

Often, the best resource you can use will be one made by yourself, which has a precise class in mind. Look at Sarah's PowerPoint and peer/self-assessment sheet (all available on the website www.sagepub.co.uk/secondary), which she made herself to suit her class and the learning she wanted them to have access to. How helpful do you think these resources were, both to her and to the pupils?

Published resource packs are plentiful for English language and literature; websites such as www.teachit.co.uk and the Qualifications and Curriculum Authority site (www.qca.org) contain a plethora of pre-planned lessons and resources which will be more or less useful to you, *provided that* you reflect on the appropriacy of each download and personalize it to your particular class of individuals, your learning objectives and your targeted approach. If you are teaching media studies, communications, drama or vocational courses, you will find that many generic resources are equally useful, and there are also tailor-made resources for these courses, both in hard copy and on websites, and a quick search on 'Google' will reveal just how many sites there are!

As English teachers, we are lucky to have newspapers, magazines, adverts, television, radio and a multitude of other, everyday sources on which we can draw. Be on the look out, and collect whatever you can – you will invariably find that it has a use. Do, though, be careful to find out about copyright restrictions, as they apply to educational uses: schools and colleges are required to make these public for all staff to refer to.

Use your ICT skills to make resources look professional, but remember that sometimes the most effective resources can be the most simple. If you need ICT or other equipment – even as basic as felt pens and A3 paper – make sure you arrange well in advance for them to be available to you: the lesson plan template in this chapter includes a space for resources needed to be listed, so that you are sure that you have everything necessary to produce an effective learning experience for the pupils. See Chapter 9 for further help with the use of ICT.

Points for reflection

Review the resources used in the website lessons. How 'fit for purpose' do you judge them to be? As practice, you might try searching for a new resource which you could use if teaching one of these lessons; alternatively, you might redraft one of the resources used, or create a new one with a particular class in mind. Later, reflect on how easy/difficult you found this activity, and how you would approach resourcing in future planning.

In Matthew's written reflection on his own learning, his comments about resourcing his lessons in order to serve his learning objectives are as follows:

> any resources or strategies should be [equally] streamlined. What is the easiest/most efficient way to achieve the LOb? Once you've identified it, USE IT. Once that resource is identified/chosen, make it glam, make it relevant, make it the best it can be. Don't fall into the trap of using the most glam resource and then try to force it to achieve your LOb for you — *you* need to achieve the LOb: tools do not compensate for lack of prep. Equally don't use any resources that will just 'do'. Nothing will ever just 'do' (Matt Whittle, 2007, email to tutor).

EXAMPLES OF PLANNING TEMPLATES

In Figure 2.3 you will see a guided template for planning a medium-term scheme of work. If you go to the companion website, you will find a blank version of the same template which you can download and experiment on. The guided template shows where each of the key elements discussed so far in this chapter can be planned for. As you study it, try to relate it to one of the classes you have observed or even taught already while on placement. Try, too, the various templates offered in the Framework and by your placement institution. Gradually, you will select and adapt to suit your needs and create a working document which you can use well, and which others can understand in tracking your work and that of your classes.

Points for reflection

Now look at Figure 2.4 and see how the template might address the first two lessons in a scheme of work for a Year 7 class, learning about visual and sound devices used in writing. As you read the example, relate this to similar class which you have observed or taught already. Reflect on these questions:

- How far are the opening lessons in the scheme of work likely to challenge the ability range and preferred learning styles of the class?
- Is there a range of learning activities which should engage pupils actively in learning?

Medium-Term Scheme of Work PGCE Secondary English

Title of scheme (for example, Creative writing/persuasive writing/a literary text)
What topic/text/subject within English are you addressing?

Year/class: year group/designation	Dates (from … to …)	Number of lessons: total in scheme

Nature of pupils (for example, specific, individual needs/preferred learning styles/gender balance/additional adults) Give NC levels/pupils' names with specific needs/balance of pupils' preferred learning styles/support available, and so on.

Objectives to be addressed in whole scheme
NC English or cross curricular PSHE and so on/Framework/examination syllabus

When planning this overview, take advice from your HOD/the usual class teacher. Ask which learning objectives (LObs) they want you to cover and particularly what the class has already done in terms of LObs, so that you do not repeat previous work. The same will apply to when you plan the activities and learning outcomes (see below); check with the teachers to avoid hearing, 'We've already done this!' when you start to teach a lesson. Over the whole SOW, you are likely to target a long list of LObs. In this section, use both numerical references and textual description, as in the NC/Framework/syllabus documents.

You should also include cross-curricular objectives, including PSHE/numeracy/citizenship/ICT objectives, as appropriate to this scheme.

Learning outcomes from the scheme
List here the work which pupils will produce. This is likely to be all the work that you will assess, so include oral work as well as written.

Lesson no.	1. Key Nat.Curr./Framework/ examination syllabus references; 2. Learning outcomes	Specific learning objectives (LOb) (use dynamic verb; link to NC English or cross curricular PSHE and so on/Framework/ Examination syllabus)	Brief outline of lesson content and teaching/learning activities	Resources; uses of ICT, if available	Assessment: how will you know whether pupils have met the LObs? (e.g. observation and recording; marking written or oral work …)
1 2 3 … and so on – the easiest bit!	1. Use numerical references from the list you put in the overview section, above. 2. State what pupils will produce by the end of the lesson.	You should list, here, exactly what skills or understanding pupils will be learning. Use dynamic verbs! Number each LOb. (Warning! Do not confuse LObs with a description of activities: this should be in the next column.)	List here what pupils/teacher will do at each stage in the lesson. BRIEFLY indicate content and method	Include a full list of resources you and the pupils will need.	How will you monitor (during the lesson) and assess/record (after the lesson) each pupil's learning success in relation to each LOb?

Figure 2.3 Medium-term scheme of work: guided template

Medium-Term Scheme of Work PGCE Secondary English

Title of scheme (for example, Creative writing/persuasive writing/a literary text)
Using imagery and sound devices in writing

Year/class: Year 7	Dates (from … to …) 3 Sept – 1 October	Number of lessons: 15

Nature of pupils (for example, specific, individual needs/preferred learning styles/gender balance/additional adults) 20 pupils at level 4; 10 at level 3+; 4 at level 3. 20 male/14 female. Adam (dyslexia) helped by TA, Anne; Jane, Jason and Peter (behavioural difficulties/short attention span) helped by TA, Lisa. Mainly visual and kinaesthetic learner styles.

Objectives to be addressed in whole scheme: NC English (2000) or cross-curricular PSHE and so on/Framework (2001)/Examination syllabus

Reading

  2 – use strategies to extract meaning (highlighting/scanning and so on);
  11 – recognize how print, sounds and still or moving images combine to create meaning;
  12 – understand author's craft in creating mood;
  14 – recognize how writers' language choices can enhance meaning (sound effects, repetition, emotive vocab …)

Writing

  8 – experiment with visual and sound effects of language (imagery, alliteration, rhythm, rhyme)

S&L

  12 – exploratory talk;
  13 – work together to solve problems, make deductions, share, test and evaluate ideas;
  14 – justify/modify views;
  16 – work collaboratively.

Learning outcomes

Cloze exercise; descriptive writing; peer assessment forms; text marking sheets; notes in list form

Figure 2.4   Completed example of first two lessons in a scheme of work

Figure 2.4   (Continued)

Lesson no.	1. Key Nat.Curr. (2000)/Frame work (2001)/ examination syllabus references 2. Learning outcomes	Specific learning objectives (LObs) (use dynamic verb; link to NC English or cross-curricular PSHE to /Framework/ examination syllabus)	Brief outline of lesson content and teaching/learning activities	Resources; uses of ICT, if available	Assessment: how will you know whether pupils have met the LObs? (e.g., observation and recording; marking written or oral work …)
1	1. Framework refs: W8 S&L14 R12 2. Outcomes:– cloze exercise; – descriptive writing; peer – assessment forms	LOb1: identify the meaning of 'simile' and 'metaphor' LOb2: construct own similes and metaphors in a short descriptive piece based on picture LOb3: evaluate effectiveness of similes and metaphors	Starter/Intro • Teacher intro • Whole-class discussion • OHT/IWB to show examples • Mini-whiteboards to identify • Buzz session in pairs to discuss effectiveness Development • Cloze procedure: groups of 4. • Feedback from groups – comment on suggestions, evaluate alterna-tives and justify opinions. • Individual or paired composition from picture, using similes and metaphors Plenary • Selected pupils read out; others evaluate using 'two stars and a wish' evaluation frames Homework Write description of room in home, using similes and metaphors.	OHT/IWB; mini-whiteboard and pen per pupil; picture per pupil; evaluation frames	*Starter/Intro:* Teacher observation/target questions (LOb1, (LOb3); use Teaching Assistant to note those unsure and follow up (LOb1) *Development* Monitor when circulating (LOb2); target individuals (LOb3); peer assess-ment (LOb3) *Plenary* Monitor responses; target individuals *Homework* Mark hwk for correct use and effectiveness. (LOb2)

(Continued)

Figure 2.4 (Continued)

| 2 | 1. Framework refs: R2, 11, 14. S&L12
2. Outcomes:
– text marking sheets
– note list for homework | LOb1: review and justify effectiveness of own and peers' writing
LOb2: explain link between written description, sound effects and visual images
LOb3: extract examples of effective sound/visual imagery used in literary extract. | **Starter**
• Pairs discuss hwk. Volunteer effective descriptions.
• Hear samples and class justify why chosen. (Collect hwk)
Introduction
• Listen to music and note five visual responses: what pictures come to mind? Discuss responses in fours.
• Feedback – justify responses.
Development
• Read extract *Wuthering Heights* re moors (display on IWB).
• Model descriptive phrase: pupil comes to front to highlight example in text on IWB. Class decide why effective: annotate on IWB as model.
• Pairs highlight other descriptive phrases re visuals/sounds: feedback. Annotate why effective.
• 4s discuss music to accompany possible film version
Plenary
• In pairs, say 3 techniques used by Brontë to create effective description
Homework
• List three memorable moments from films which use sound effects. Describe the sounds and write why effective. | Extract from soundtrack 'The Piano'; CD player; Printed/IWB extracts *Wuthering Heights* | **Starter:**
Teacher/TA obs in justification session (LOb1)
Intro
Teacher obs in listening and reviewing exercise (LOb1 and LOb2)
Development
Assessment of highlighting exercise after lesson (LOb3)
Homework
Assess ideas in starter next lesson. |

- Do the two lessons allow an initial progression in pupils' skills and understanding in relation to the overall aim of the scheme?
- How far would these activities enable pupils to meet the learning objectives?
- Is an appropriate and effective use of ICT incorporated?
- Are monitoring and assessment strategies likely to be effective and to enable pupils' levels of progress to be recorded?

Now that you have reflected on the effectiveness of the first two lessons in the scheme of work, try this further activity (see Figure 2.5) to practise using the template yourself. If you can work on this with a peer or teaching colleague, even better: remember that working collaboratively makes a useful step in the process of developing independence and confidence alone. The templates are available on/via the associated website. If you prefer, you might use the lesson planning template (Figure 2.6) and produce a full lesson plan instead of the scheme of work summary. Do whichever is more appropriate to your current needs.

When you have tried the activity, reflect again on how easy/difficult you found different aspects of the planning task. You will probably find, in the early attempts at planning, that you take at least as long to plan a lesson as you do to deliver it! Do not despair; practice really does help, and you will become much more efficient as you learn by trial and error – and reflective evaluation – what works and what does not.

Perhaps the best place to end this chapter is to offer you some advice which one of my trainees found particularly helpful. Laura, like the vast majority of trainees, found that planning, in particular, was taking up her every waking minute. I advised her that she should also plan for her own self-preservation, and some time later, she sent me this emailed reflection:

> I don't know if this will be any help [to others], but my biggest bit of advice is something you told me: don't let yourself get too bogged down in work, you need time for yourself. There will always be time for work it may not be perfect but you won't be running yourself down into the process. Back in the beginning just after the Planning assignment, I thought there would be no way I'd be able to cope while on placement doing everything in school. But planning my own time helped.

Imagine that your Head of Department has given you the following brief for the same Year 7 class for whom she has already planned the first lesson:

> I would like Year 7 to spend up to nine lessons investigating how authors use visual, literary and sound techniques to stimulate readers' responses, particularly targeting writing to entertain and the use of imagery/sound devices, such as those commonly used in poetry.

> Your key Framework (2001) objective is Year 7, Writing 8: 'pupils should be taught to experiment with the visual and sound effects of language, including the use of imagery, alliteration, rhythm and rhyme'. You might also choose to incorporate specific speaking and listening skills, drama skills and/or reading skills.

> Please plan the next two lessons, ensuring that the scheme is progressive, pushing pupils' learning towards more sophisticated understandings and developing their own ability to manipulate language and readers' responses to it.

Figure 2.5   Scheme of work/lesson planning practical activity

Class (including ability range): 8M2 (mixed)
Location: Eng 15
Length of Lesson: 1 hour
Topic: Non-fiction texts – Advertising

Aims *(What is your overall teaching aim?)*
   – to enable pupils to see how advertisers manipulate audience response by using music and pictures in adverts

Learning Objectives *(What do you want pupils to learn in this lesson?)*
Pupils will learn how to:
   LOb1 explore what a synonym and antonym are;
   LOb2 deduce and discuss why pictures and sound are used in the advertising industry to affect the appropriate audience;
   LOb3 analyse the effects of music in advertising;
   LOb4 analyse the effects of pictures in advertising;
   LOb5 practise co-operative working skills.

Lesson Outcomes *(What will pupils produce in this lesson?)*
   – individual examples of synonym/antonym
   – discussion and feedback re use of pictures in adverts
   – completion of handout matching songs to products
   – class discussion analysing purposes of adverts/images/sound
   – homework: notes re wider uses of advertising

Personalized learning strategies *(how will you cater for differences in your pupils' abilities/learning styles?)*
   • By questioning. Targeted questions to targeted pupils.[1]
   • By pair groupings. Pairs pre-planned to address individual needs/behaviours.
   • By use of stimulus material. Resources address VAK[2] learning styles.
   • By pace of the lesson and relevant use of starters.
   • By support.[3]
   • By guided modelling

Assessment *(How will you evaluate how far your stated learning objectives have been achieved by each pupil?)*
   LOb1 Oral feedback on ability to give a synonym and antonym at the beginning of the lesson.
   LOb2, LOb3, LOb4 Oral feedback via discussion and questioning in activities.
   LOb2, LOb3, LOb4 Written work: assessment of handouts and ex books at the end of lesson.
   LOb5 Observation during pair work. Written notes will be made on targeted pupils during the oral activity[4]

Resources needed
   Exercise books
   CD/CD player
   Advertisements (photocopies in case class not completed homework)
   Handouts.

Key[5] NC (2000)/Framework (2001) objective/examination syllabus references
   1 R3, R9
   2 Wr 3
   3 S&L 5

Figure 2.6   PGCE secondary English sample lesson plan: year 8

Figure 2.6 (Continued)

[1] You will begin to target pupils' learning as you get to know them via data available and through working with them. You will know who can/will contribute and who has difficulty, so you will be able to cater for individual needs and abilities.

[2] VAK: visual, auditory and kinaesthetic learners. Pupils do not learn in the same ways, so you should include a variety of material to stimulate all learners.

[3] Support in the classroom may only be relevant when you have a TA (teaching assistant). Here, you are addressing QTT Standards Q5: 'recognise the contribution that colleagues ... can make ... ', Q6: 'have a commitment to collaboration and co-operative working'. Q20: 'know and understand the roles of colleagues ... 'Q33: 'ensure that colleagues working with them are appropriately involved in supporting learning ... ' and others.

[4] It is impossible to make notes on every child's progress in a LO of this kind in every lesson. Target a few for written comment in each lesson.

[5] Keep the targeted NC/Framework/examination assessment criteria references to a manageable and realistic number. Only include the KEY ones, based on your learning objectives.

Content, including **introduction,** teaching and learning **methods** and **activities**, **timings** and **review** session:

Timing	Teacher activity	Learner activity	Notes/questions/expected answers/assessment activities
10 mins	**Starter** Class register. Recap yesterday's lesson during registration: explain activity.	When name is called out pupil has to give either synonym or antonym as requested.	Give example: nice → horrible; disappointed → pleased. *Monitor understanding in Starter and all other discussion/feedback activities: ask teaching assistant to note down anyone who is struggling and target for extra support when circulating during group work.*
5 mins	**Introduction** Recap learning so far using question and answer. Target questions to specifically noted pupils.	Pupils answer.	Cover 1. Slogans (*catchword/motto*). 2. Rhetorical questions (*q's which imply the desired answer*). 3. Fact/opinion *(not open to question/open to question).* 4. Adjectives (*word which adds description to a noun or adverb*).
5 mins	**Development** Ask class to hold up adverts brought in. Show examples you have. Brief discussion about *language* used on the ads. Mention the use of pictures. Targeted questions and answers.	Pupils respond.	Cover 1. Why are pictures used in advertising? (*Looking for ...*) 2. What effect might they have on an audience? Remind the class of the definition of audience. (*Looking for ...*) 3. What kind of colours or images might be used to attract an audience? 4. Would the type of picture change according to product or audience? *(Examples)*

(Continued)

Figure 2.6 (Continued)

15 mins	Set task. In pairs, pupils will analyse the use of pictures in an advert of their choice. Show an example: guided modelling of how to look at the advertisement. Ask for any questions. Circulate during task. Work with pairs as needed.	Pupils respond to modelling questions. Pupils work together on task.	Model: 1. Opening statement about the need for pictures in advertising – demonstrate this. 2. What is the advertisement about? 3. How does the picture relate to the advertisement? (Is it the actual product or something else?) 4. How much room does the picture take up? 5. Where is the picture positioned in order to catch the eye? 6. What colours does the advertisement use? Any significance? *Monitor as circulating: select three good examples for feedback later, and alert relevant pairs that you will ask them to lead the discussion.*
5 mins	Ask for feedback. Target three examples. List features on the whiteboard.	Class comments on similarities and differences and any features of the adverts that seem particularly significant (e.g., in persuading audience).	*Ask higher-order questions of more able pupils: 'How does this example ... ? /'Why does the advertiser ... ?'*
15 mins	Move from visuals to sound. Ask class why adverts have music. Play one example. How does the music affect the audience?	Pupils offer ideas. Pupils offer ideas.	e.g., creating a happy feeling/appealing in other ways to our emotions → linking the product with positive feelings. *Target less vocal pupils for answers: paired buzz session for 30 secs to give confidence if necessary.*
	Set task: pupils are working as part of an advertising business. The songs need to be fitted to some adverts. The task is to place the music with the best fit advert.		*As pupils work, circulate, identify examples of achievement and quietly ask each pair to lead the feedback, at the end of the activity, on one specific example.*

Figure 2.6   (Continued)

	Give out handouts. Model one example: write answer on board. Play appropriate music and allow time to complete handouts.	Pupils to work in pairs and complete handout.	
5 mins	**Plenary** Ask pairs for feedback	Pupils justify choices for matching music and adverts. Others support/disagree with choices, **with justification each time**.	
	Finish with open questions. 1. What else do advertisements need in addition to carefully selected words? 2. What is the purpose of adverts?	Pupils offer ideas.	*Monitor: challenge/help any who seem unsure, asking others to build on ideas which suggest learning has not been fully consolidated.*
	Homework Briefly mention what pupils will learn next lesson: other occasions when someone tries to influence us to do something.	To ask friends/relatives for ideas and write down at least three occasions, other than in product adverts, in which people try to 'sell' us something.	Give example of political speeches – selling a political party, an idea or a belief.

I have my school timetable and in my frees I've planned to do something specific – for example, marking, evaluations, sit and relax time (usually Friday afternoon) – and then planned what I want to get done that night, including 'me time' ... Planning is the thing I've found takes the longest and doing it this way – planning when was going to do things – gave me time limits on things and therefore I got them done (Laura Shipsides, 2007, email to tutor).

WHAT THE RESEARCH SUGGESTS

Professor Colin Harrison's (2002) publication on behalf of the Key Stage 3 National Strategy reviewed research evidence to evaluate the approach to teaching and learning advocated by the Strategy. Harrison, of the University of Nottingham's School of Education, concluded that the research evidence supported the Strategy, in the main; for the rest, his conclusion was that there was insufficient research evidence to either support or refute it. Section four of the publication, *The Teaching Sequence: Has the Strategy Got It Right?*, (Harrison, 2002) relates most closely to the topic of planning, and is well worth reading. Though some practitioners, have been less convinced by aspects of Harrison's conclusions, his survey was broadly welcomed. His bibliography is an excellent starting point for your further, reflective research reading.

Professor Debra Myhill and Dr Rosalind Fisher (2005), of Exeter University, also surveyed a range of research publications as a commissioned work which informed Ofsted's (2005) *English 2000–05: A Review of Inspection Evidence*. Both of these publications go beyond the topic of planning, but have strong bearings on it, in relation to the overall structuring of learning experiences, and would be beneficial in developing your understanding of the issues involved in planning for learning in the diverse and fast-changing world of education.

Key points from this chapter

- The need for thoughtful, careful, imaginative planning, in order to ensure that pupils' learning is engaging and progressive rather than repetitive or disjointed. This goes hand in hand with creativity in *teaching*, to encourage creativity in *learning*.
- The link between the *Every Child Matters* (DfES, 2004) outcomes and planning for learning – more about how you can cater for every child's best interests and individual needs appears in Chapters 3 and 6.
- The need to remember that planning goes hand in hand with preparation, which is also connected to your own subject knowledge and your understanding of curriculum requirements.
- The impact that good planning can have on pupils' behaviour and motivation.
- The fact that planning can have many starting points and various templates, but plans should always be seen as fluid, and may well be changed as you respond to pupil feedback and your own, reflective evaluation.

 Further reading

Any of the books mentioned in this chapter will give you further guidance on your planning and help you to reflect further on your own beliefs and practices. You might start with the suggestions listed below.

Bowkett, S. (2007) *100+ Ideas for Teaching Creativity*. 2nd edn. London: Continuum.
This is an interesting book which will develop your ideas about using creativity and creative thinking as a stimulus for lessons – not just in English. Trainees of mine who have used this book find it helpful in moving beyond the 'default' teaching methods that they may be tempted to stick with. It certainly links practical activities with learning theory.

Davison, J. and Dowson, J. (2003) *Learning to Teach English in the Secondary School: A Companion to School Experience*. 2nd edn. London: Routledge.

Gives a range of advice, planning ideas and templates for schemes of work and lessons. The text takes a topic approach, with chapters on, for example, speaking and listening, reading, writing, approaching Shakespeare and drama, each contributed by authoritative practitioners and researchers. There are also activities, such as those in this chapter, for you to try.

Pike, M. (2004) *Teaching Secondary English.* London: Paul Chapman Publishing.
Adopts a thematic approach, so that Chapter 2, '"Operational" lesson planning', for example, will be helpful as a further review of strategies and issues concerning planning. Chapter 9, 'Differentiation and the individual: gender, ethnicity and special needs', also offers some interesting points for reflection as you consider the individuals in your classes, and what might serve their learning needs best.

Wright, T. (2005) *How to be a Brilliant English Teacher.* Oxford: Routledge.
A lively and realistic approach, which combines practical strategies for implementing the statutory curriculum and is as entertaining as it is stimulating. Wright offers personal anecdotes which highlight, in an accessible style, both commonly felt concerns and how they might be resolved.

Useful websites

Live links to these websites can be found on the companion website www.sagepub.co.uk/secondary.

www.standards.dfes.gov.uk/secondary/
The Standards site is a government produced site, where National Strategy publications are housed. The secondary forum subdivides into Key Stages 3 and 4, and you can follow links to many of the topics covered in this chapter. You will always need to weigh suggestions and advice against your developing awareness of what works best for your pupils.

www.teachernet.gov.uk/teachingandlearning/subjects/english/
The Teachernet is a huge site with many ready-made plans and resources, which you can use, adapt, review and critique in relation to your planning needs and your pupils' learning needs. Suggested approaches and links to other websites also abound.

3

MORE THAN ONE WAY TO TEACH A LESSON

Peter Woolnough

This chapter considers:

- the simple, but important fact that there is no right or wrong way to approach teaching a particular topic
- a range of teaching and learning strategies that you might wish to consider in your own practice.

To this end, the chapter is based on two specific lessons; both aimed at Key Stage 3 (KS3) Year 7 middle-ability English classes. The basic stimulus material was common to both lessons, and the lessons shared the same teaching focus. However, the teachers delivering the lessons adopted different approaches to the subject matter. The lessons themselves are presented in this chapter, in the form of:

- lesson plan templates
- commentary, transcripts and annotated extracts
- personal evaluation/reflection by the teachers.

 You can also access filmed extracts from the lessons on the companion website www.sagepub.co.uk/secondary, with an interview in which one of the teachers explains, in some detail, what he intended to achieve in the lesson and whether he felt the lesson was successful (1, 2, 3). It is important to note here that the lessons were planned and delivered without editorial interference, rehearsal or pre-review by any third party. Far too often, exemplar material of this kind is created in a 'quality controlled' environment which inevitably limits its value for trainees. In the Department for Education and Skills (DfES) videos and DVDs that accompany their vast array of training materials, pens never run out, pupils always seem to know the answers and the lessons themselves have been harshly, but wittily, stereotyped as, 'The Stepford Wives teaching the Midwich Cuckoos!' We very much wanted to present you with lessons rooted in a realistic context, delivered by colleagues brave enough to submit themselves to public scrutiny, in a kind of 'warts and all' atmosphere.

Points for reflection

When you read this chapter, you should think carefully about the purpose and context of an individual lesson. What would you, as a teacher in similar circumstances, be trying to achieve and what would be your most important objectives? How important would it be to follow the lesson structure commonly accepted as 'best practice'? Or would you want to have the freedom to organize the lesson in a different way?

THE CONTEXT

The lessons took place at Sutton High Sports College, St Helens, and were taught by Ian Jackson, an English PGCE trainee on placement, and Monika Maloszyk, the school's acting Head of English. At the time of filming, Ian was several weeks into his placement and had developed a good working relationship with his Year 7 class. Monika, originally from Poland, gained her PGCE at Edge Hill and was in her fourth year of teaching. The two classes participating were Year 7 groups of broadly comparable ability.

THE STIMULUS MATERIAL

Both teachers were given copies of the poem, 'Testing Time', written by Isobel Browett (see Figure 3.1). The poem was selected for a number of reasons:

- Interest and engagement – the theme was likely to evoke personal response in the pupils.
- Poetic features – the poem offered wide scope for exploration of imagery, verse form and rhythm.
- Opportunities for creativity – the poem could be approached in a variety of ways, with a range of different outcomes in mind.
- Framework coverage – the poem could be used to address specific Framework objectives and be integrated within a medium-term plan.

In the broader context of this publication, we also felt that analysis of a 'one-off' poem could be useful to ITT trainees, because schools often ask job applicants to teach a sample lesson as part of the interview process, and the remit for such lessons often involves analysis of a poem or consideration of poetic devices.

THE LESSON FOCUS

Ian and Monika decided that, for their lessons, the agreed *focus* should be on *imagery*, notably *simile and metaphor*. Both teachers had done some prior work on these features with their respective classes, and they felt that, in addition to the consolidation of learning that the activity would afford, it would be interesting to compare two different approaches to a relatively narrow focus. Later in this chapter, we will exemplify the range of activities and varied approaches that a poem such as this might generate, because it is important that you do not

Testing Time

Jamie sits in the silent Hall,
Hunched at his desk like a hutchless rabbit,
But clearly less comfortable.
Pen gripped vice-tight in a sweaty palm
And in his head, alarm.
4b in this, 3a in that,
Under-achievement in three Practice SATs,
But now for the real thing,
The ultimate test,
Confirming his place way behind all the rest.
Despite the revision, the study guides bought,
He knows he can't grasp
All the things he's been taught.

It's testing time.

Well-meaning Mums speak with smiles, but compare,
And fret about setting
In High School next year.
Will Ellie still be with Sarah and Jess
If she messes up Maths
Or the tough Spelling Test?
And why must they have them, these odious SATs
Making Year 6 so grim; unlike the past
When the kids learned for fun
And they raced home each day:
Babbling, excited and eager to say
What they'd done, how they did it and what they liked best,
With barely a mention of Standardised Tests.

It's testing time.

With the Head on his back and Results on his tail,
The Y6 class teacher's the hunted, the whale.
Inspiring and awesome when he can roam free
Now he's tied down by Targets
And all he can be
Is the box ticking prompter
Who points out the flaws, advises on shortcuts
And frequently bores.
And then there's the Marker, with hundreds to do,
Wearily working her tedious way through
Without time to consider the children, the names,
The faces, the hopes, the fears, the pain.

It's testing time.

Isobel Browett

Figure 3.1   Testing Time: poem

view the chapter as a study of one focus. As trainees, you need to develop the skill of taking, adapting and developing source material in a variety of imaginative ways, and we hope to prove to you that a single source can have multitudinous uses! In order to contextualize and clarify the activities that actually took place in our two lessons, we will consider each lesson, in turn. To support the analysis of the lessons, we have included the formal lesson planning documents – with annotation, transcripts from the lessons and the reflections of the partici- pating teachers. Substantial filmed excerpts from the lessons and an interview with Ian Jackson can be found at www.sagepub.co.uk/secondary.

MONIKA'S LESSON: COMMENTARY AND TRANSCRIPTS

As Monika's lesson planning documents clearly show (Figure 3.2), she decided to use a *detailed study* of the poem to consolidate the pupils' understanding of simile, metaphor and personification. She also wanted to illustrate how these devices can be used for specific effects and to create atmosphere. So it would appear that the lesson, to a large extent, has a Reading focus. However, the activities also created substantial Writing and Speaking and Listening opportunities; and these are fully reflected in the learning objectives. The end product is a varied, challenging lesson that manages to secure prior knowledge and encour- ages the pupils to actively display their writing and presentational skills. The lesson, in its entirety, can be found on the companion website at www.sagepub.co.uk/secondary.

Content and structure

Monika structured the lesson (as did Ian) using the Framework's recommended format (DfEE, 2001: 17):

- starter
- introduction
- development/further development
- plenary.

Points for reflection

Should all lessons follow this format? Can you think of instances where a different approach or structure would be more appropriate? Also, why is it regarded as essential that all lessons should begin with a statement of the objectives? Can this lead to a formulaic approach that actually disengages pupils?

Monika's *starter* commenced with immediate reference to the three learning objectives on the board. Through effective question and answer, a definition of imagery was swiftly arrived at, and throughout this phase of the lesson Monika adopted a very gentle and encouraging tone to elicit response and secure meaning. The following transcript extracts illustrate the effective- ness of this approach. Having established that a timid girl could be metaphorically referred to as, 'a mouse', Monika ensured that all the pupils understood why this was a metaphor:

Monika's Lesson: Formal Planning Documents

PGCE Secondary English: **Lesson plan template**

Date: 4th July 2007
Class (including ability range): Year 7,
V – 9   A – 4   K – 8
Location: Sutton High Sports College
Length of Lesson: 60 mins

Topic: POETIC IMAGERY

Aims *(What is your overall teaching aim?)*
To familiarise the pupils with poetic imagery and provide them with opportunities to develop their skills to use the devices.

Learning Objectives *(What do you want pupils to learn in this lesson?)*
by the end of the lesson, pupils will:
– understand what similes, metaphors and personification are,
– know how they are used to create effect,
– be able to use them (similes, metaphors, personification, imagery) to describe.

Differentiation *(how will you cater for differences in your pupils' abilities/learning styles?)*
– by questioning: a range of questions will be asked (Bloom's taxonomy),
– by stimulus: a range of resources, activities; support sheet with examples of poetic devices,
– by outcome: pupils' work will be evaluated,
– by support: provided throughout the lesson,
– by grouping: pair work, peer support and assessment,
– by extension task (G&T),
– by catering for a range of learning styles (Auditory in the starter, Kinaesthetic – starter and development, Visual – use of colours and pictures).
      There are no pupils with special needs/learning difficulties in this class.

Assessment *(How will you evaluate how far your stated learning objectives have been achieved by each pupil?)*
– through questioning: whole class discussions, feedback, etc,
– prior understanding will be established during an introduction,
– pupils' work will be evaluated/assessed against NC criteria,
– A4L: peer assessment, self assessment,
– plenary: open and closed questions,
– homework will be set, marked (using NC Levels) and discussed.

Resources Needed
– cards (three colours – simile, metaphor, personification)
– Testing Time (2 pages: WS, copy of the poem)
– Similes, Metaphors, Personification (introduction & support sheet)
– Poetic Imagery: Extension Task

Key NC/Literacy Objective References

National Curriculum: Speaking and Listening 2.1a, 3.1b
                            Reading 2.2b, 2.2f, 2.2j, 2.2m
                            Writing 2.3a, 2.3b, 2.3f

Framework: Word Level 21
                            Reading 6, 8, 12, 14
                            Writing 6, 8
                            Speaking and Listening 5, 8, 15, 16, 19

Figure 3.2   Monika's Lesson: Formal Planning Documents

Content, including **introduction,** teaching and learning **methods** and **activities, timings** and **review** session:

Timing	Teacher activity	Learner activity	Notes
8 mins	**Starter** • settle the group and take the register, • introduce the objectives to the class, • establish pupils' familiarity with the terms; refresh them, give examples and put on board for reference, • pupils copy definitions onto coloured cards (visual learning).	• pupils take their equipment out and prepare for the lesson – atmosphere centred around learning is established, • pupils are told what they will learn throughout the lesson – learning becomes purposeful, • pupils recall their prior learning (hooking) and refresh or familiarize themselves with the terminology (coloured cards are used to facilitate learning).	Teacher will give some examples and ensure that all pupils are familiar with the terms before the lesson proceeds.
10 mins	**Introduction** Teacher reads out 10 sentences that are examples of simile, metaphor and personification.	Pupils identify the devices through lifting the relevant cards up (yellow for simile, etc). Modelling and securing pupils' understanding of the concepts/terms.	Cards are used to reduce barriers to learning and create a safer/more confident learning atmosphere (pupils lift the cards up and are not put on the spot).
10 mins	**Development** 1. Pupils read the poem 'Testing Time'.	1. Reading: Pupils read the poem. Short whole class discussion follows to ensure all pupils understand the poem. 2. Individual work: Pupils answer questions on the poem. 3. Pair work (A4L): pupils work in pairs checking and comparing their answers. Pupils improve their work further.	Teacher assesses pupils' progress and understanding by listening to their discussions and asking open questions to encourage exchanges of more complex ideas/opinions.

(Continued)

Figure 3.2 (Continued)

Timing	Teacher activity	Learner activity	Notes
15–20 mins	**Further development** Writing a script using poetic devices for effect.	1. Writing: Pair work. Pupils write a script of a conversation between a parent and a child who's just had an exam. They use as many poetic devices as they can. A support sheet is handed out (differentiation). 2. Drama/Speaking and listening: pupils present their work to the rest of the class. The class evaluate their peers' work; they make note of some effective/interesting examples of imagery.	Teacher supports the class by asking questions, making suggestions, discussing and challenging pupils' choices. More able pupils will come up with their own ideas; less able ones will refer to the support sheet.
10 mins	**Plenary** 1. Elements of peer assessment (A4) – pupils evaluate examples created by their peers. They comment on the effect created. 2. Definitions of the devices are revisited through questioning.	1. A4L/Speaking and Listening: pupils comment on others' work and practise expressing their opinion. Further examples of imagery and the effect they create – as used by pupils in their presentations – are discussed. 2. Whole class: Pupils answer questions about the devices/poetic imagery (both open and closed questions).	Teacher will welcome and praise pupils' evaluations. Some pupils – whose progress the teacher is uncertain of – might be asked direct questions to enable the teacher to assess their understanding of the objectives.
2 mins	**Closing routines/instructions/homework etc**	Write a diary entry describing the way you felt last time you had a test. Include poetic imagery.	

To be completed after each lesson:

1. Evaluation of pupils'/students' learning

- How far were your stated learning objectives in English achieved? What is your evidence for this judgement? (Specify: LO1, LO2 etc...)

LO 1-3 were achieved in the lesson as all pupils demonstrated their clear understanding of poetic devices and ability to create their own examples. The progress has been checked through pupils' work, teacher's questioning and whole class discussion.

- Did any pupils (be specific) not achieve the stated learning outcomes? (Be specific.)

All pupils achieved the objectives. The skills will be further reinforced through homework that will be marked by the teacher and future tasks completed in the following lessons.

- What do you need to do next to reinforce/ develop this learning in all or particular pupils? (Consider how this will affect your next / later lesson plan(s).)

The pupils can identify the poetic devices and create their own examples of poetic imagery. In the next lesson, I intend to read a piece of prose in which similar devices are used (for example, a descriptive extract from Of Mice and Men) to ensure that pupils are able to recognise and comment on poetic devices in prose. Then, pupils will write their own descriptions and attempt to create a powerful atmosphere/effect. The PEE structure will be introduced.

2. Evaluation of your teaching

- What were you pleased with? (Think about previous targets.)

The lesson was well structured and delivered effectively (all pupils have achieved the objectives). Pupils enjoyed the learning and found the lesson engaging. Some of them were slightly intimidated by the camera. Kinaesthetic activity, visual stimulus and pair work facilitated learning.

- If you taught this lesson again, would you change any aspect of the plan?

I would try to accommodate more time for the evaluation of the dialogues that the pupils created/ performed. More focused target setting would be beneficial.

- When you teach this class next time, will you change any aspect of your teaching method/behaviour management strategy?

Develop more challenging questioning techniques further.

M   Is she grey? No. Has she got whiskers? No. Has she got little ears? No ... but she is timid and sounds like a mouse ... And the last one (*referring to poetic devices*) is personification. What's that? Can you remember what that was about? It's got this magic word in it (*she circles the 'person' part of personification on the board*) ... Anyone else? (*making sure that it's not always the same pupil who responds*)

Pupil Taking an object that's not alive and describing it as something that's alive.

M   Brilliant! (*writing on the board*) Describing an object as if it was a person. (*note how the answer is slightly refined*) Any examples?

Pupil The sun is smiling.

M   Brilliant! Yes! Because the sun ... it hasn't got a mouth, it's not a face — and only faces smile, but ... we think of it as cheerful.

The *introduction* phase of the lesson was a *card exercise*. Pupils copied the three definitions of the poetic devices on to coloured cards, and as Monika read out a series of 10 sentences, the pupils had to hold up the cards, indicating the figures of speech featured in each sentence. This kept the lesson active and guaranteed that pupils who were unsure of certain answers would be identified only by the teacher. Monika astutely used every opportunity to boost confidence and understanding. When all the pupils correctly raised yellow cards, identifying a metaphor, she said, 'A forest of yellow cards! That's a metaphor itself, isn't it?' At the end of the starter, Monika employed what was, in effect, a *mini plenary* (DfES, 2004: 12) by saying, in relation to the first learning objective on the board,

> Have we achieved the objective? If you're uncertain, put your hand on your head (no one does) … Excellent! Then we can tick that one off.

In the *development* phase of the lesson, Monika focused on the second learning objective. Pupils read out sections of the poem and in the discussion about pupils' attitudes to testing which followed, the class came up with a list of emotional responses (worried, upset, anxious, nervous, petrified) very much like the list generated in Ian's lesson. A series of questions about the poem, on a worksheet, followed. These questions demanded that the pupils established the poem's meaning, explored the atmosphere created by the poem, spotted and underlined examples of simile, metaphor and personification and explained (with reasons) which image they thought was most successful. In effect, the questions led the pupils through the process of an *individual*, critical reading of the poem.

The *feedback* session which followed was particularly well conceived. Pupils were given a few minutes to compare answers and *talk in pairs* about what they had come up with. This generated qualitative discussion and shared learning, as Monika's next instruction indicated:

> Can someone suggest some very good answers that you found on your sheet — let's be proud of our work, it's good to be proud of one's work — or on your friend's sheet? … Put your hand up and let others hear it, as well.

The *further development* section of the lesson gave the pupils the opportunity to apply the skills and knowledge they had developed, in a practical context. Again working in pairs, the pupils had to *write a script* of a conversation between a parent and a pupil who has just had an examination. The script had to be heavily metaphorical, and the writing activity provided variety for the pupils and a new assessment focus for the teacher. The culmination of this phase of the lesson was a *drama activity*, during which some of the pupils 'performed' their scripts. This activity amplified the already substantial *speaking and listening* focus of the lesson and highlighted the fact that an individual piece of stimulus material can be both approached and exploited in a variety of ways. Advice was given regarding the actual performance and the pupils were patently aware that the task had an additional focus. Although some of the participants were nervous in the glare of the cameras, one or two splendid images were conjured up:

> 'I glided through it (the test) … the teachers were perched like vultures …'

The *plenary* included some discussion about what the class had observed and a final revisiting, through question and answer, of the learning objectives, which were summarily ticked off on the board. A *homework* task was set, which involved the pupils writing a diary entry describing their response to doing a test. This activity meant that the pupils would be able to further develop their use of imagery in a different writing context, and it maximized the empathetic potential of the topic. Again, this illustrates how material can be developed to meet a range of objectives and to develop pupils in an holistic way.

Summary of the lesson's key features

In my view, Monika's lesson had:

- extremely clear objectives that were shared, revisited and achieved
- focused links to National Curriculum/the Framework
- an effective structure and excellent management of phases
- pace, variety and challenge
- a supportive, relaxed atmosphere
- imaginative and productive resources/stimulating activities
- thorough consideration of prior learning/learning styles
- productive use of questions and answers (Q&A)/feedback.

INTERVIEW WITH MONIKA ABOUT HER LESSON

1. *In general terms, what are your main priorities when you plan individual lessons?*
    The main priorities while planning lessons would be effective delivery of the objectives and facilitating pupils' progress. I believe that this can be achieved by addressing pupils' needs — special educational needs, learning styles, appropriate pace and challenge — and making learning enjoyable. Only through participation and engagement can pupils achieve and raise their own attainment. This is why I try to include a range of active tasks that evoke interest and create an exciting, sometimes slightly competitive, atmosphere.

2. *Clearly, this was a one-off task. What factors influenced your planning decisions for this particular lesson?*
    The majority of pupils in that class are visual or kinaesthetic learners. Therefore, I planned some reading and active tasks. Auditory learners engaged in class discussions and progressed through expressing their ideas verbally.
    To make the lesson fast paced, I decided to create a variety of shorter tasks (chunking). Through a range of open questions and an extension task I aimed to stimulate the more able pupils (challenge).

3. *What other ideas did you come up with for the lesson, and why did you decide, ultimately, to run with your final plan?*
    I considered making the lesson more reading based but, as a high percentage of pupils display kinaesthetic preferences, I endeavoured to make the activities more active.
    Another idea was to make the lesson more drama based — after reading the poem, using an extract from a play showing strong emotions (for example, from *An Inspector Calls*, one of the conversations between the Inspector and Sheila). Pupils would practise reading it out, adding more poetic devices to make the emotions expressed and atmosphere created stronger.
    However, in the end I decided that referring to their own experience — taking a test/examination — will make the pupils understand and achieve the set objectives more confidently.

4. *How easy would it be to adapt this plan or include the lesson in a SOW [scheme of work] for this group, and what kind of scheme would it fit into?*
    The lesson would be very appropriate for a poetry-based scheme of work. It would be suitable for a range of abilities: the teacher would need to differentiate the activities and shift the emphasis to other learning styles, depending on the composition of the group.

5. *Describe briefly any specific considerations you had when creating the lesson plan (for example, objectives/timing/classroom management and so on).*

The group consists of quite able pupils who are enthusiastic and willing to learn. To engage them fully, I aimed to create fast-paced and challenging activities. The pupils were slightly intimidated by the cameras and did not show as much enthusiasm as they normally display in the lessons. As far as the objectives are concerned, I wished for the pupils to have an opportunity to make the poetic devices 'real' and applicable: pupils described their own experiences and realized that similes, metaphors and personification are used by all of us in everyday conversations.

There are no classroom management issues with the group; sometimes they can get too lively and vocal in expressing their excitement, but that's the beauty of teaching.

6. *How does being observed affect you? Have you any tips for trainees in this position?*
   I believe that it works well to announce to the class that it is the lesson that will be observed, not the way they perform. However, their behaviour will affect the final outcome of the lesson — the achievement of objectives. In that way, pupils develop a sense of responsibility for their learning and behaviour and, at the same time, do not perceive the observation as their personal evaluation.

7. *What of the planning process itself? Can you think of ways in which the process can be improved/(format of pro formas and so on)?*
   Having taught for a few years, I have used a range of lesson plans. The Edge Hill University pro forma is quite accessible (the table is easy to fill in, the details on the front page are relevant). The evaluation sheet seems to be too detailed; however, the truth is that any teacher will answer those questions after every single lesson, not in a written form, but in their head.

Points for reflection

Consider the number of 'audiences' your lessons are aimed at. You are trying to engage and inspire the pupils, but in terms of planning and delivery you also have to take into account all the people who might be monitoring and passing judgement on you: university tutors, heads of department, class teachers, Ofsted inspectors. How do you balance these demands? What organizational and personal pressures will you be subjected to?

IAN'S LESSON: COMMENTARY AND TRANSCRIPTS

As indicated in his lesson planning documents (Figure 3.3), Ian decided to use the poem as a vehicle for consolidating the pupils' ability to understand the use of imagery, and to develop their ability to use similes and metaphors in their own writing. He also wanted the pupils to empathetically engage with the emotive nature of the subject matter. These objectives were referenced directly to National Curriculum and Framework coverage in his plan. A comparative study of Ian's and Monika's lesson plans reveals that, although the essential lesson focus is similar, the actual approaches and activities are quite different. A summary of these differences is provided towards the end of the chapter. Extracts from the lesson can be viewed on the companion website.

When Ian was interviewed about various aspects of his lesson, he said:

Ian's Lesson: Formal Planning Documents

PGCE Secondary English: Lesson plan template

Date: 29 June 2007
Class (including ability range): Year 7 Set 3 (CAT Scores: 87–104)
Location: Sutton High Sports College
Length of Lesson: 60 minutes

Topic: Exploring similes, metaphors and imagery in the poem 'Testing Time'

Aims *(What is your overall teaching aim?)*
To explore the poem, focusing mainly on the use of similes, metaphors and imagery. The pupils will reflect on what testing means to them, and create a final verse for the poem, featuring the poetic devices listed.

Learning Objectives *(What do you want pupils to learn in this lesson?) by the end of the lesson, pupils will:*

LO1.   Review and develop ways of exploring similes, metaphors and imagery.
LO2.   Be able to analyse and express attitudes and feelings towards tests and testing.
LO3.   Demonstrate the ability to effectively use poetic devices and create an additional verse for the poem

Differentiation *(how will you cater for differences in your pupils' abilities/learning styles?)*

By Stimulus:

– use of WB, OHP, worksheets, writing frame (visual learners)
– use of teacher instruction, peer feedback/discussion (auditory learners)
– use of mini WBs, kinaesthetic learning activities (kinaesthetic learners)

By Peer Support: pair work

Assessment *(How will you evaluate how far your stated learning objectives have been achieved by each pupil?)*

Starter: analyse pupils' thoughts, feelings and impressions regarding testing;

Introduction: establish pupils' prior knowledge of poetic devices and ability to apply them (using a picture as stimulus);

Development: monitor pupils' ability to retain information and ability to complete similes, metaphors and imagery using abstract ideas;

Plenary: analyse pupils' completed verses for understanding and ability to express their own ideas using poetic devices.

Resources Needed

WB, WB marker, OHP, OHT Picture (boy taking a test)
'Testing Time' – full version, one copy per pupil.
Verse 1 Cloze procedure – one copy per pupil
Final verse writing frame – one copy per pupil

Key NC/Literacy Objective/Exam Syllabus References
Include both English and cross-curricular objectives, as appropriate.

NC: S+L – 2.1g, Reading – 2.2b , 2.2l, Writing – 2.3c, 2.3f

Framework: Reading 8, 14
               Writing 8
               Speaking/Listening 4, 7

Figure 3.3   Ian's Lesson: Formal Planning Documents

Content, including introduction, teaching and learning methods and activities, timings and review session:

Timing	Teacher activity	Learner activity	Notes
10 mins for starter	**Starter** **Pre-starter:** Put "Silence .. Test in Progress" signs around the class. When pupils ask if we are having a test, say yes and gauge reaction. Then tell them we are not having a test – but the lesson will be about tests. **Starter:** Put picture on OHP of a boy nervously seated behind a desk, waiting to take a test. (Cartoon) On WB ask pupils to write down their initial thoughts, feelings and impressions about this picture. Ask pupils to write down their feelings about tests, for use later in the lesson. Two minutes for the picture task. Ask for feedback and put it on WB.	Pupils enter and are greeted quite officiously by the teacher. Pupils go to seats and immediately get on with starter. Pupils look at picture on OHP/WB and write down their thoughts/feelings on mini WBs or paper. When asked, pupils feed back info.	Put mini WBs and marker pens on pupils' desks before lesson begins. Have pupils use them to write on in the Starter/Intro. If no mini WBs are available, use blank sheets of plain A4.
Then 15 on intro	**Introduction :** Outline LOs and put sentences on the WB, leaving blank spaces for the pupils to fill in missing words on their mini WBs. The sentences create similes, metaphors and images based on the picture on the WB. Get pupils to complete each sentence on their MWBs separately, then take feedback on each one. After each sentence, explain if it is a simile, metaphor or other image. Ask pupils to write one example of each on their paper.	When asked, pupils write their own ideas for missing words on their MWBs to create their own similes, metaphors and imagery based sentences relating to the picture. Each sentence is completed, one at a time, with FB from pupils after each one. Pupils hold up MWBs and explain what they have written. Pupils write down examples of each device, on paper.	Put MWBs and marker pens on front desk, and hand out at start of Intro. Don't hand out before this, to prevent pupils messing with them during Starter. Or, use MWBs in Starter? SIMILE, METAPHOR AND IMAGERY SENTENCES FOR THE WB: • The boy scratches his head like a _____ (simile) • The boy looks confused as _____ (simile) • The test is a _____ to the confused boy (metaphor) • The boy _____ on his pencil as he stares blankly at the test (imagery)

Timing	Teacher activity	Learner activity	Notes
15 mins	**Development :** Hand out copies of the first verse of the poem, "Testing Time", with some of the key words missing. Ask pupils to complete the verse, filling in the missing words (Cloze style activity). Ask pupils to feed back their completed versions of the verse.	Pupils complete "Testing Time" first verse cloze procedure worksheet by filling in the blank spaces. Pupils feed back and discuss responses.	
15 mins	**Further development:** Hand out full copies of the poem and read through as a class. Ask pupils for their comments and relate them to the words they came up with in the Starter. Tell pupils they are going to write a final verse for the poem from their own perspective. (The nerves, sleeplessness and anxiety they might feel the night before a big test.) Tell pupils not to worry about rhyme scheme etc., but they must include examples of the features covered in the lesson. Circulate, offering support/guidance	Pupils read through and listen to teacher reading the poem. Pupils feed back reponses. Pupils listen to teacher instruction and create their own final verse. Using the frame provided, pupils incorporate similes, metaphors etc.	Provide sample lines for those who need them, as a starting point: E.G. So here I am, sweating in bed, Tossing and turning like the sea, Wishing I was dead . . .
5 mins	**Plenary:** Selected pupils read their own versions to the class. Q&A analysis of effectiveness of the devices used. Use of Q&A to secure understanding of the meaning of the poetic devices.	Selected pupils read their compositions.	

I wanted the pupils to enjoy the lesson and to gain something significant educationally ... The idea of tests and testing affects teachers, pupils and parents, and this is well brought out in the poem; looking at the idea of testing from different perspectives ... The pupils I was working with had recently done SATs, and I wanted to get their reaction. So, as well as looking at imagery, similes and metaphors, I wanted to gauge what the pupils thought about tests and testing. That's what I found most interesting: getting their opinions, feelings and ideas. ... I had considered looking at other poetic features such as structure, rhyme scheme and rhythm, but this class had done prior work on 'Spooky Stories', and I wanted them to look at how they could use figurative devices in their own writing.

Points for reflection

It is worth noting here that Ian and Monika have very different personalities, and they each have a distinctive classroom presence. Ian is confident and assertive, and his pupils certainly don't view him as the stereotypical 'student' who is there for the taking! As teacher, he makes it very clear to the pupils what he expects of them, in terms of behaviour and commitment, and the pupils obviously respect him. Monika has a different approach, using a very relaxed, almost gentle style to enthuse her charges. Looking at the two filmed lessons should prompt you to consider what style or approach best suits your own personality and nature. It is certainly worth reflecting on this question if you are about to start on a career in teaching. Most 'successful' teachers have the ability, where necessary, to adopt different personae, but much of the time they have the luxury of being themselves.

Content and structure

Having decided to focus on empathy, knowledge of certain poetic devices and the application of these devices, Ian structured the lesson using the now standard four-part lesson.

In this instance, the *starter* included a clever element which exemplified the commonly accepted principal purpose of starter activities (DfES, 2004: 4) particularly well. Lining the pupils up, telling them they were going to have an unexpected test and strategically placing 'Test in Progress' signs around the classroom certainly had an emotional impact on the pupils – as did the subsequent admission that he was lying!

To exploit the pupils' emotional turmoil to the full, Ian then showed a cartoon on overhead transparency (OHT) of a fretful boy attempting a test. The pupils then had two minutes to write on their whiteboards five words that they personally associated with tests. Ian felt that this strategy would be successful because:

I wanted to meet different learning styles, using visual, auditory and kinaesthetic approaches ... The use of mini whiteboards in the starter meant that individuals could contribute without fear, and when the pupils fed back their responses I tried a technique that I had used before with the class, but had not put in my formal plan. As each person read out a word, I asked anyone else who had also written that word to stand up. This had the effect of keeping it all active, and it also aided the discussion because it made us all aware of widely held fears about tests.

The efficacy of this approach was immediately apparent in the engagement of the class and the list of words that the exercise generated:

- annoyed
- confused
- nervous
- disappointed
- shocked
- frustrated
- scared
- betrayed.

In effect, the starter had toyed with the pupils' emotions and drawn the pupils in to the major theme of the lesson.

The *introduction* section of the lesson included a review of the lesson objectives, which had been written on the board, and an exercise designed to secure prior knowledge of similes and metaphors. Using their mini whiteboards again, the pupils had to create and identify images that would fit successfully into four incomplete sentences. This activity was effective, because it provided *scaffolding* (DfEE, 2001: 16) for the main activity to follow. It also generated some discussion about the effectiveness, suitability and imagination of the pupils' offerings.

The *development* section of the lesson was based on a *cloze* activity. This is another strategy widely held to be useful in developing pupils' predictive *reading skills* (DfES, 2004: unit 13). The first verse of the poem, with key omissions, was handed out and the pupils had to work in pairs to fill in the blanks, feed back and discuss responses. Ian maintained a challenging *pace* during this activity and was able to circulate and support pupils who were uncertain of what to do. The collaborative nature of the exercise and the move from using mini whiteboards to worksheets added some variety for the pupils. The feedback generated a range of responses which were praised and evaluated in some depth. Throughout, there was a sense of all pupils being actively involved.

For *further development*, Ian moved on to the poem itself. His intention was to read the poem, have a class discussion about it and them move pupils on to the final major task: *writing* their own final verse for the poem, expressing their own feelings about tests and utilizing the poetic devices that formed the reading focus of the earlier part of the lesson. Ian again provided support, in the form of an example to kick-start those who might be struggling, and he circulated effectively during the activity. Sensibly, in my view, Ian advised the pupils not to be too concerned on this occasion with poetic features that had not been part of the lesson's focus, but to ensure that imagery was a dominant feature in their verses. Looking back, Ian felt that this section of the lesson had merit, but some weaknesses, too:

> This is a class I know. The kids have got fantastic imaginations, and the idea of writing poetry themselves and drawing on their own experiences is something I know they can do and get some good results ... One of the aims of the lesson was to analyse the poem in detail — and, to be honest, I think that was a mistake on my part. I don't think I really allowed time to analyse the poem. In the lesson we briefly read through it, but this hardly matched the lesson's stated aim. We could have taken a more structured, analytical approach to the poem, but I chose to use it mainly as a vehicle for creative writing.

Point for reflection

This is an important point. It is quite rare for lessons to go exactly as planned, and timing is often an issue. The crucial thing is that you, as the teacher, try to clarify and prioritize in your own mind the key elements of the lesson, then hope for the best. Sometimes, the very fact that stimulus material can be approached in numerous ways is, of itself, a planning headache. Setting clear priorities and, if need be, spreading the key learning objectives over subsequent lessons are probably the best responses to this problem.

The *plenary*, to a certain extent, suffered from timing problems. There was the opportunity for productive feedback, and pupils did both produce and read out some impressive contributions. However, there was no real opportunity to deliver the key outcomes expected of a plenary session (DFES, 2004: unit 5). Had time allowed, it might have been useful if each pupil had been asked to produce a statement explaining the importance of imagery in evoking mood, or something similar, so that the teacher could say with certainty that the learning objectives had been met.

Summary of the lesson's key features

In my view, Ian's lesson had:

- clear objectives and aims that were shared with the pupils
- appropriate structure and management of phases
- focused links to National Curriculum and Framework imperatives
- pace, variety and challenge
- effective classroom management
- appropriate and well-organized resources
- due consideration of pupils' learning styles
- effective use of questions and feedback sessions
- the capacity to engage and stimulate the pupils.

Areas to develop would be:

- timing of the phases
- use and structure of the plenary
- consideration of formal assessment opportunities
- prioritizing key objectives.

SIMILARITIES AND DIFFERENCES IN THE WAYS THE TWO LESSONS APPROACHED A COMMON FOCUS

A poem based on a topic so close to the hearts of pupils, teachers and parents inevitably lends itself to some sort of empathetic response or study, and both teachers exploited this aspect of the stimulus material. The fact that it was actually a poem, replete with a range of images and some kind of rhythm and rhyme scheme also pointed our two colleagues in a similar direction. However, there were substantive differences in terms of their use of the poem and the activities they devised.

Use of the stimulus material

Ian and Monika both agreed to focus on imagery, but they came at the focus from different angles. Monika employed a detailed reading and analysis of 'Testing Time', and these activities constituted a substantial part of the lesson. In contrast, Ian used a section of the poem and only chose to engage briefly with the whole text. This was appropriate because one of his main objectives was to gauge and exploit the pupils' emotional responses to the theme, in general, rather than the poem, in particular. Monika tended to focus on the poetic devices and the empathetic potential of the poem was used mainly to develop pupils' abilities to comprehend and use those devices.

Lesson structures and phases

Both lessons followed basically the same formal structure. Linked, progressive phases were employed, supported by clear instructions to the pupils regarding the time allocated to each activity. Monika managed to complete all phases comfortably, and the only structural element of Ian's lesson that needed development was the plenary.

Nature of the activities

This is the area in which the main differences emerge. Ian's starter was very much driven by the emotional impact of the topic, and the skills work related directly to the pupils' emotional engagement. In contrast, Monika chose to lead with definitions of concepts and a card exercise to secure pupils' understanding. However, it is worth noting that the teachers' use of mini whiteboards and cards, respectively, led to quite similar activities in terms of what the pupils actually had to do in the opening minutes of the lessons. Both lessons also reflected a range of whole-class, individual and paired work, with important feedback and discussion sessions punctuating the phases. Recapping and consolidation were also prominent features in both lessons. When we look at the development/further development sections of the lessons, we can see a clear difference in emphasis and approach. Monika chose to employ a detailed analysis of the poem, leading to a script-based writing task and performance. In essence, this meant that her pupils had to apply the 'poetic' devices in a totally different context and also consider the technical demands of performance. This elevated the importance of speaking and listening as a discrete, assessable skill and also gave prominence to the act of script writing. The writing demands were diversified still further by the inclusion of a diary writing homework task. Ian's choice of writing task – to produce a final verse for the poem, based on personal feelings about testing – was narrower, but no less valid.

WHAT ELSE COULD BE DONE WITH THIS POEM?

English teachers should always be on the lookout for stimulus material that will enthuse and interest their pupils. They should also give serious consideration to the many different approaches and potential outcomes that good source materials make possible. Many teachers, when devising schemes of work or medium-term plans, start with the National Curriculum, the Framework or GCSE criteria and seek out materials and tasks to meet specific criteria. This approach is strongly commended in the Framework: 'Most important is the need to organise teaching around specific objectives in the Framework' (DfEE, 2001: 19) – and it certainly provides a sense of security, continuity and appropriate coverage of key learning objectives. Others – and I confess to being of this mind – prefer to approach much of their planning through searching for what they think will be fantastic stimulus materials, devising what they hope will be interesting tasks and then mapping those tasks against objectives to see what they will cover. The tasks are then tweaked to meet curriculum imperatives and the realities of the attainment of particular groups and individuals. For what it is worth, my recommendation would be to try both methods, and adopt the approach you, personally, feel most comfortable with (see Chapter 2 on planning).

The suggestions that follow, based on 'Testing Time', are general pointers to how it could be used with a KS3 class. It is not my purpose here to go into great detail, because the tasks are not designed for a specific age, ability or grouping. I am merely trying to illustrate the broad range of activities and outcomes that could be considered and planned for.

Reading activities

- Cut up the poem and do a sequencing exercise (DARTs).
- Cloze procedure exercises, focusing on specific elements (DARTs).
- Getting pupils to highlight/annotate key devices, themes and attitudes.
- Divide the class into groups and ask them to discuss/feed back responses to set questions.
- Use groups to conduct and summarize verse by verse analysis.
- Predictive exercise: omit a verse or sections of the poem and ask groups to compose their own versions.
- Scaffold the process of 'How to Analyse a Poem' with another text, then ask the pupils to attempt the same task using 'Testing Time'.
- Ask the class, in pairs, to devise test questions based on the theme, mood, voice and poetic devices in the poem.
- Use the poem to formally scaffold approaches to any of the following: verse form, rhythm, rhyme, figures of speech, style.
- Devise SATs style questions focusing on language use, meaning and effect.

Writing activities

- Use the poem, or aspects of it, to stimulate pupils' own verse writing.
- Use the poem as a vehicle for other types of *creative writing* – diaries, letters, playscripts, detailed descriptions and narratives from the perspective of pupils, parents and teachers featured in the poem – or exploring themes and emotions evident in the poem;
- Use it to stimulate *informational* and *explanatory writing*, such as: a pupil/parent/teacher guide to coping with examinations; a poster or leaflet showing how to revise; a problem page for worried pupils; an article written by the poet explaining her motivation;

- Use it to stimulate *persuasive* or *discursive writing*: a letter to a government minister about testing; a discursive essay based on the pros and cons of SATs; a magazine article attacking or defending the current testing regime in schools; a letter to a newspaper debating the effects of tests on pupils, teachers and parents; reports, letters and articles written from the perspective of parents, teachers or politicians; interviews with characters in the poem, or the poet.

Speaking and listening activities

- Role-playing activities based on situations arising from the poem and involving pupils, parents, teachers, the marker and the poet.
- Hot-seating pupils, parents and teachers featured in the poem.
- Having a formal class debate on testing.
- Writing and acting out scripts or monologues based on the poem's themes.
- Scripting, then filming or audio recording the outcomes.
- Organizing group or paired discussion of the poem's key features, impact or effectiveness.
- Constructing a small group problem-solving activity, based on the poem.
- Getting different groups in the class to create presentations (using OHT, flip chart, PowerPoint, video) of a reading/analysis of the poem.
- Organizing small group performances of the poem – poetry reading.
- Running a competition – who can do the best reading of the poem?
- Conducting an interview – with someone featured in the poem, or the poet herself.

These are just suggestions. Doubtless, you could come up with many more. The ideas obviously need contextualizing to meet the specific needs, interests and abilities of your pupils, and resultant lessons have to be carefully structured. But I hope the list does, if nothing else, illustrate the fact that material as slight as a short poem can have terrific potential for generating a wide range of activities.

Point for reflection

How would you set about the creation of a medium-term plan? What would you take into account before beginning and how would you map out content and coverage? Consider the advice offered in Chapter 2.

WIDER ISSUES: BEYOND OUR TWO LESSONS

This chapter has largely concerned itself with the issues relating to delivery of two specific lessons. It is worthwhile, additionally, considering some of the broader issues that the lessons raise, in terms of your general approach. I am thinking here of such issues as when you should consider breaking the mould of the common lesson structure, and what to do when spontaneous teaching and learning opportunities arise.

Breaking the mould of the lesson structure

The four-part lesson – or a variation on it – has become the norm in recent years. As a result, teachers are extremely reluctant to employ more flexible lesson structures, particularly when they are being observed and assessed. I would not advise colleagues to 'break the mould' in situations where they are under scrutiny, but I would strongly advocate a more flexible approach in other common contexts. Here, in no particular order, is a list of situations where absolute adherence to the four-part lesson would be, in my view, inappropriate:

- when classes or groups are undertaking an ongoing project that lasts for several lessons or weeks. Pupils, in this context, are often working at their own rate and are not all attempting the same tasks at the same time
- when groups or classes are making presentations, over a number of lessons
- when classes are undertaking substantial research or problem-solving activities
- when timed essay work or examination practice is the main activity
- when a specific, single activity (for example, independent annotating and note making based on GCSE literary criticism) dominates a lesson
- when reading a text or viewing a DVD dominate the lesson.

The important thing to note is that, sometimes, particular tasks need *time* and *focus* to do them justice. Artificially compartmentalizing the lesson can actually impede effective learning, and you must exercise your professional judgement to select the most effective vehicle for each lesson. This does not mean to say that you should have lessons without a clear focus, or that consolidation of learning is not important. What it does mean is that you must feel free to select the most appropriate structure for each lesson – except when you are being observed!

Responding to spontaneous learning opportunities

One of the main reasons many colleagues choose to become English teachers lies in the arguably unique potential of the subject to explore ideas, feelings, experiences and culture. As English teachers, we have a particular responsibility to develop pupils' transactional skills – but we also have an unrivalled opportunity to develop pupils' sensibilities. So when, for example, we are studying the ubiquitous *Of Mice and Men* for GCSE, we view it as an examination text, certainly – but we also view it as an opportunity to get the pupils to reflect on their own attitudes and experiences relating to *friendship*, *loneliness*, *racism* and *dreams*.

There will be countless occasions, in class, where something is said that will trigger or provoke an interesting debate/response. A casual sexist or homophobic comment, a surprising personal revelation, a particularly entrenched view; all of these, if pursued, could set your lesson off at a very interesting tangent. But what do you do? You have your tightly structured lesson plan … allowing the digression might mean that important objectives are not met. The simple answer is that you make a judgement, there and then. If you see that the 'digression' has really engaged the thoughts and feelings of the pupils, then pursue it. Spontaneous reflection, debate or argument can have a powerful effect on what and how children think. Worry about your objectives after the lesson has finished and be pleased that something memorable has happened in your classroom.

Better still, try to *plan for spontaneous learning opportunities*. I realize that this sounds somewhat paradoxical, but in reality, it is not. When you know that your lesson content or subject matter will evoke particular responses in your pupils, plan to exploit and maximize them. In *Of Mice and Men*, the glib references to Crooks as 'the nigger', or the fact that Curley's wife has no name, or the childlike mentality of Lennie – any or all of these things could provoke some kind of response from your pupils. Be ready with activities that demand reflection, draw out feelings, challenge preconceptions or confront intolerance.

WHAT THE RESEARCH SUGGESTS

The introduction of the Key Stage 3 National Strategy, incorporating the *Framework for Teaching English: Years 7, 8 and 9* (DfEE, 2001), created a sea change in the structuring of lessons and teaching approaches at KS3. The 'Recommended' status of the Strategy soon evolved into 'compulsory' in the sense that local education authorities (LEAs) and the Inspectorate almost immediately came to judge teachers and their lessons largely on the degree to which Strategy imperatives were being met. Virtually all the important Strategy and support documents can be accessed at the English Resources and Publications section of the DFES Standards website, a link to which can be found on the companion website, where the rationale for the key elements of the Strategy is expounded fully, in downloadable form. Of course, many researchers, teachers and critics of the Strategy (now termed the secondary National Strategy) have voiced concerns about the way the Strategy was introduced and the impact it has had on teaching. Westbrook (2004: 69) rightly points out that: 'the pilot was very short, with little time to either learn from the three years of the primary experience of the NLS, or to evaluate what had worked best in secondary schools'. She also argues against rigid adherence to all aspects of the Strategy's suggested lesson structure: 'You may find that not every lesson needs a starter: if pupils are busily engaged in the writing of a lengthy story, stretching over two or three lessons, a starter may distract them from the task in hand' (Davison and Dowson, 2004: 78).

Implicit concern regarding teachers' over-reliance on the structure of the Strategy has also emerged in Ofsted findings. In a review of inspection evidence 2000–05 (Ofsted, in DfES, 2006: 3), it was stated that schools need to, 'develop varied and engaging approaches to learning in the classroom that are flexible enough to stimulate and meet the needs of pupils'. With specific reference to reading, Ofsted found that schools need to review the approach to the whole-class study of texts and authors to ensure that it contributes more powerfully to promoting positive attitudes to reading. In effect, research and teachers' own experiences have revealed a worrying tension between the prescriptive thrust of the Strategy and the need to maximize and exploit pupils' enthusiasm. The renewed Framework (DCSF, 2008), coupled with the 2007 revision of the National Curriculum, should afford teachers greater flexibility and actively encourage a move away from the rigidity which their predecessors imposed.

Research material relating to the understanding of poetry and pedagogical approaches to poetry teaching is wide and diverse. An effective teaching guide can be found in Gabrielle Cliff Hodges' chapter in Davison and Dowson (2004: 239–61), while a philosophical approach to the topic can be found in Terry Eagleton's *How to Read a Poem* (2006). A favourite practical teaching resource is *The Poetry Book* (Bleiman, 2001).

Key points from this chapter

In this chapter we have established that:

- there is no single right or wrong way to approach a topic
- a wide range of tailored teaching and learning strategies can be employed, despite the apparent prescription of the Secondary National Strategy (SNS)
- effective teaching is the product of imaginative, contextualized planning and delivery.

Further reading

Brownjohn, S. (1994) *To Rhyme or Not to Rhyme*? *Teaching Children to Write Poetry*. London: Hodder & Stoughton.
Perhaps a little more academic than Corbett's offering on poetry writing, but still a useful source for ideas.

Corbett, P. (2002) *How to Teach Poetry Writing at Key Stage 3*. London: Fulton.
This is full of practical ways to get children writing poetry. Too often the emphasis in schools is on analysis of poems, to the exclusion of creating poetry. Corbett's book offers a useful antidote.

Corbett, P. (2004) *Jumpstart: Literacy Games*. London: Fulton.
Lots of short, snappy literacy games for Year 7 and older, lower ability children. The book offers the chance to create fun starters.

Clark, C. and Rumbold, K. (2006) *Reading for Pleasure: A Research Overview*. London: National Literacy Trust.
A reminder that reading is supposed to be a pleasurable activity – not just a vehicle for skills development and objective coverage.

Yates, C. (1999) *Jumpstart Poetry in the Secondary School*. London: Poetry Society.
A helpful blend of poetry analysis and poetry writing. Practical and accessible.

Useful websites

Live links to these websites can be found on the companion website www.sagepub.co.uk/secondary.

www.standards.dfes.gov.uk
www.qca.org
www.poetryclass.net
www.teachit.co.uk
www.poetrysociety.org.uk
www.teachernet.gov.uk
www.curriculumonline.gov.uk
www.teachernet.gov.uk
www.literacytrust.org.uk

4 MANAGING LEARNING, MANAGING LEARNERS

Lynne Warham

This chapter considers:

- the basic principles of effective classroom management
- how to generate ownership of your classroom, while establishing a positive learning environment
- how to organize pupils effectively to facilitate different task types
- basic teaching strategies that lead to successful English lessons
- how to implement these strategies in approaching Shakespeare at Key Stage 3 and Poetry at Key Stage 4.

WHAT IS CLASS MANAGEMENT?

The word 'management' might not be the first that springs to mind when you contemplate a career in teaching. No doubt many of you will have been influenced in your decision to pursue a teaching career by your own personal experiences with teachers – possibly by those who instil with apparent ease a love of their subject in others, who engage their classes and inspire their pupils without so much as breaking into a metaphorical sweat.

However, it does not take much time in the classroom, on the other side of the desk, to realize just how essential 'management' is to effective teaching. There are clearly a number of issues which must be carefully considered in order for you to become a skilful manager of the classroom environment. Such things might include:

- time and how it is organized, divided, and allocated to tasks appropriately
- resources and materials essential to teaching and learning, such as paper resources, ICT (IWBs, laptops, and so on), audio-visual equipment
- the physical environment, including the organization of seating suited to different pupil groupings and task types
- pupils, their safety, managing their behaviour, and pupil interactions
- other adults such as learning support assistants, teaching assistants and parents.

Simply put, 'class management is what teachers do to ensure that children engage in the task in hand, whatever that may be' (Wragg, 2001: 7).

As an English teacher, this becomes all the more challenging given the range of learning objectives you must address and the diverse range of texts you will potentially teach. However, the English lesson can, in itself, assist in effective class management. By their very nature, English lessons have the scope to be creative, challenging and highly engaging – and it is such qualities that prove extremely helpful in minimizing disruption and encouraging pupil participation and co-operation on every level.

Thus classroom management is mainly concerned with the *positive* aspects of managing pupils and the learning environment, with less emphasis being placed on the negatives that the term more commonly conjures up, such as pupil misbehaviour.

MANAGING PEOPLE, MANAGING SPACE

Making an effective start

To make an English lesson truly effective you need to have not only a well-planned sequence of activities, but a range of positive strategies to put these into action in an organized and efficient way. This practical ability to implement plans successfully is crucial in engaging all pupils in the learning process. Alongside this, you also have a professional commitment to:

> Establish a purposeful and safe learning environment conducive to learning and identify opportunities for learners to learn in out-of-school contexts. (Q30)

> Establish a clear framework for classroom discipline to manage learners' behaviour constructively and promote their self-control and independence. (Q31)

Meeting these professional standards ensures that you, as a teacher, create an environment in which pupils feel safe and secure enough to participate fully in learning, as highlighted in *Every Child Matters* (DfES, 2004), and to take the 'risks' necessary to becoming increasingly creative and independent. Such an environment does not emerge by chance, but must be actively created and maintained by you.

As other chapters in this book highlight, careful and thorough planning is the first step to achieving successful teaching and learning; then comes the time to put your plan into action. This is when your role as a 'manager' begins. From the very first moment of your first lesson with a class, you should be consciously selecting and applying a set of predetermined practical routines which you intend to use regularly, in effect 'drilling' your pupils, and establishing clear and purposeful expectations.

However, as Pollard points out: 'Having a clearly organised and managed classroom should not be taken to imply rigidity, for if the rules and routines of the classroom are made clear and agreed, good organisation can increase freedom for the teacher to teach and the learner to learn' (2005: 228). This 'freedom' can be generated by taking even the smallest and most basic of steps. For instance, establishing a set of opening routines with which to start each lesson saves valuable time while also helping to create an orderly and settled classroom environment. One English curriculum mentor in a Liverpool comprehensive school explained that such routines had become an essential tool in managing her classes:

Whenever possible I stand at my classroom door and greet pupils as they enter the room. This helps me to pick up on minor issues and to sort them out before they get into the classroom — for example, pupils might be chewing or messing about with a friend. A quiet word as they come through the door really does make all the difference ... your pupils realize that you're aware of them, that you're paying attention, so they settle into classroom mode much more quickly.

Not only can this type of entrance routine benefit you in terms of pre-empting behavioural issues, the mentor also states that it allows her to forge stronger and more positive relationships with her pupils:

It's a good way to learn pupils' names at the beginning of the year — as they come in, you can greet them as individuals, ask how they are, engage with them on a personal level. Pupils really love you taking an interest in them and this often translates into a willingness to co-operate and to engage with you during lessons.

Of course, these informal interactions also encourage pupils to open up to you, to talk to you about themselves and the things that interest and affect them. Such information can be useful to you when it comes to engaging them. So if, for example, you know a pupil is interested in martial arts you could bear this in mind when selecting stimulus materials or when recommending reading material.

Points for reflection

- What other strategies could you use to learn pupils' names and get to know them as individuals?
- What routines could you establish to ensure time-efficient lessons? (For example, systems for distributing and collecting resources, reorganizing furniture to accommodate group work or drama activities.)
- What closing routines might assist you in creating an orderly and calm end to your lessons?

Making it yours: owning your classroom

One of the most important steps in establishing an effective learning environment is taking ownership of your classroom. If pupils are to take you seriously, are to follow your lead, you must make the space in which you teach *yours*. This will involve a range of things:

1. *Creating an environment which reflects your expectations*:
   Spend some time making your mark on your teaching space. Make it somewhere you feel comfortable by surrounding yourself with things of positive significance to yourself. This will have the benefit of enabling you to operate with more confidence and authority.

   This, in turn, leads to the creation of the right visual impact. A well-organized, well-presented room suggests a teacher who takes pride in their work, thus creating a positive impression when pupils enter the classroom.

   You can also use display and visual aids to promote these expectations and to reinforce learning. Having designated displays in the room which are relevant to current pupil learning can play an important role in supporting pupils and reminding them of key learning objectives and outcomes. For instance, if you are delivering a scheme of work on 'Writing to persuade, argue, advise', you might usefully display posters containing helpful information, definitions and conventions, some of which pupils may have produced themselves. These could then be supported by adding examples of pupils' work as and when it is produced, thus ensuring the display evolves alongside developments in pupils' knowledge and application of relevant skills. Such a dynamic use of displays also allows you to rotate pupils' work on a more regular basis, enabling a better range to be displayed and serving as a form of praise which boosts pupils' self-esteem and confidence in their ability.

2. *Creating your own persona in the classroom*:
   One of the challenges for trainee teachers and those entering the classroom as newly qualified teachers is believing in themselves as teachers, as figures of authority who are able to control the pupils in their care. Self-confidence and belief in your own authority is, therefore, paramount. Remember, as an adult and as a socially respected professional, pupils will already have certain expectations of you and of the accepted norms of control. Given that you already possess this 'power', as it were, it is important that you convey it to pupils immediately. Your actions, your body language, facial expressions, use of voice and even your sense of humour will greatly influence the way pupils perceive you and the extent to which they see you as a figure to whom they are answerable.

   Your body language and non-verbal cues speak volumes and provide key information before you utter a single word. Ensure, therefore, that your physical actions and mannerisms suggest *exactly* what you want them to. It may be stating the obvious, but do simple things like:

   - Stand up straight, shoulders back, head up, as this conveys an air of confidence and authority.
   - Make eye contact with your pupils.
   - Make your presence felt by moving around the room, getting in amongst your pupils.
   - When dealing with a behaviour issue, ensure your physical height mirrors your status. In other words, if your pupil is taller than you, sit them down and remain standing.
   - Respect pupils' personal space by keeping an appropriate distance.
   - Smile – approachability makes a real difference to how some pupils respond to you.
   - Wherever possible, use hand and eye gestures to control pupil actions. You can personalize these and use ones you and your pupils are comfortable with. For instance, raising your hand may act as a signal for pupils to stop talking when they're undertaking a speaking and listening task. If you're doing drama work and pupils cannot easily spot a visual clue, you might deem clapping your hands more effective in achieving the same effect.

Similarly, how you use your voice will have more impact than you might initially realize. Pupil noise level will often be influenced by your own volume, tone and pitch. So, if you are a 'shouter' it is likely that your pupils will mirror you by talking more loudly. You also have to be aware of the fact that the more regularly you shout, the less effective a tool your voice becomes in situations when you may really need it. Less frequent really does equal more effective when it comes to this. Furthermore, if you speak calmly and quietly (though at a clearly audible level), pupil noise level will often decrease so that they are able to easily listen to what you are saying. In this way, you can set certain precedents concerning what is and isn't acceptable in terms of volume and the general verbal conduct of pupils in your classroom.

When you're starting out as a teacher it is very likely that you'll have to rehearse your classroom persona, making your role akin to that of an actor/actress. This in itself can actually be a beneficial reflective tool. The more you consciously employ particular strategies, the easier it becomes to evaluate their effectiveness and so refine and hone your technique.

Points for reflection

- Consider your experience in the classroom so far. Which non-verbal cues do you employ?
- Make a list of strategies that you have tried and/or observed under the headings Effective/Ineffective. Do this for each of the classes you teach, as not all strategies will work with different pupils.
- Video record a lesson you teach and then analyse it in terms of the strategies you use to manage pupils. Which work well? Which could be used effectively with other classes? Which are ineffectual? How might you address management issues that aren't successfully dealt with?

3. *Relationships and routines*:
   (a) Be Yourself. Having said all of the above about the teacher's persona, it is also important to be yourself. In the midst of plans, lesson objectives and resources it is easy to lose sight of one of the most powerful tools you have in the classroom – *yourself*. In my 12 years teaching English in a Liverpool comprehensive school, I realized how important it was that I was transparent and genuine with my pupils, that they could see me as a real person, as a human being. Therefore, do not be afraid to let your personality shine through in your teaching and in your interactions with your pupils. Get to know them, know what makes them tick, what makes them passionate, what makes them sit up and pay attention – then exploit this knowledge to engage them in learning.
   (b) Create routines. In addition to creating a genuine relationship with those you teach, it is also essential that you establish basic routines from the outset. Even the simplest of routines and directives are indicators of your control in the classroom. As I mentioned earlier in the chapter, have clear procedures for pupils entering the classroom, getting settled, distributing resources and such. Nominate pupils to undertake certain duties, such as giving out exercise books, and have systems in place to collect them back in. For instance, it is often more effective to ask pupils to pass resources to a nominated person in their row or on their group table than to have one pupil wandering around the room trying to collect everything in. Create a method to your madness and not only will you be more organised, your pupils will too.
   (c) Seating plans. What's in a name? Put simply, control. It is absolutely essential that you learn pupils' names as quickly as possible during the first few weeks of teaching them. Knowing names means that you can deal with disruptive individuals quickly, and signals to pupils that you know who they are. Alongside strategies already mentioned earlier in this chapter, devising a seating

plan is one of the most effective ways of learning pupils' names quickly. It is essential that you keep pupils in the seats you designate (whether this be alphabetical order or friendship driven) until you know who your pupils are. Once you have secured this knowledge, then you can exercise greater flexibility in terms of seating.

It is worth mentioning a common issue for trainee teachers when it comes to seating plans – that you are often located in different classrooms for lessons, even with the same class, thus making a routine seating plan impossible. However, Joe Felce, ex-Deputy Head of Birkdale High School in Merseyside, recently gave PGCE trainees an excellent tip to combat this. Prepare small pieces of laminated card bearing each pupil's name and, as they enter the room, allocate their seat while simultaneously placing the respective name card on the teacher's desk, its position mirroring the location of their seat. Ultimately, you will have your seating plan mapped out on your desk before you, thus enabling you to use names effortlessly.

(d)   Rewards and sanctions. A plethora of rewards and sanctions are at your disposal in the classroom – as the PowerPoint by Katie Unsworth, a PGCE trainee at Edge Hill University, succinctly summarizes (available on the companion website). The consistency with which you apply your classroom rules is crucial to how successfully you manage your learning environment. When rules are broken or pupils overstep certain established boundaries, it is important that you implement sanctions which are proportionate to the misdemeanour. Remember too that sanctions have to be tried and tested, and that not all will be successful with all pupils. Your dealings with misbehaviour must be tailored to the individual pupil. Where you are faced with a particularly challenging or difficult pupil, don't be afraid to try out different combinations of sanctions – and do not be afraid to seek the advice and guidance of colleagues who have a successful working relationship with the pupil concerned. Find out what works for them – then try it.

As important as sanctions are, it is absolutely essential that you remember the power of praise. The more positive your handling of pupils, the more control you will have. Praise affects even the most apparently disaffected and disengaged of pupils to a surprising extent. So, find ways to praise and reward *all* pupils, as this can often prove the starting point of a successful and mutually co-operative relationship with them.

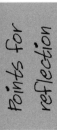

Points for reflection

What sanctions are available in your current placement school and how often/consistently do you employ each of them?

What rewards are available for pupils within your current school? Are these effective? If so, identify what makes them effective. If not, what could be done to improve this?

How might rewards be viewed differently by a Year 7 and Year 10 pupil? How might you adapt your approaches to make rewards more meaningful for different groups of pupils?

Organizing pupils for effective learning

There are a number of different ways of organizing your classroom in order to facilitate the range of activities and approaches to teaching the English curriculum. Aside from the 'rows' of desks traditionally associated with classrooms, there are a number of ways of organizing your room to make for successful paired, group and drama work, and to accommodate whole-class discussion or debate. Given the now-recognized importance of speaking and listening skills in developing both pupils' social skills and enhancing their learning (Vygotsky, 1978), it is crucial that you plan for a range of interactions and collaborative learning. During the planning stages, you should be asking yourself these questions:

- What seating structure might work best for this activity?
- How will I organize pupils?
- Is pupil grouping the most appropriate to the task?
- What changes will I need to make to the physical organization of the classroom in order to accommodate this?
- If a teaching assistant is available, how might I best work with them in order to support teaching and learning?
- What health and safety issues do I need to consider?

So, which groupings are best suited to the diverse range of activities on offer during English lessons? How do you determine whether group work would be more beneficial than pupils working individually? How do you plan for drama within a classroom environment? And how do you organize your seating in order to make your choices successful?

Whole-class teaching and the traditional 'rows' layout
This tends to work best for sections of lessons which involve the well-established 'chalk and talk' method, when you are introducing a topic or recapping work pupils have done previously. This layout ensures that the teacher is the focal point for pupils and that the board is easily observed by all. For instance, if you wanted to facilitate discussion and analysis of a moving image text, the display screen would need to be easily seen by all pupils, meaning that seating them in rows would be beneficial. This, of course, might be preceded or superseded by paired or group discussion, as this would be effective in enabling pupils to 'try out' their responses and ideas on a smaller (and less threatening) scale.

The rows layout is also useful for briefing pupils with key information for a lesson and for task setting such as homework. It is most effective when pupils are required to work independently, but can be appropriate if you want pupils to work in pairs for a significant portion of a lesson.

Bearing this in mind, it is worth considering in advance how you might quickly and safely rearrange tables for group work.

Similarly, paired work can be easily accommodated by such a layout. So, if you were teaching a scheme of work with Year 7 on Persuasive writing, you may decide to use a card sort activity (see later in this chapter for further discussion of DARTS) in order to assess pupils' current knowledge of language and presentational devices. Pupils could be asked to separate presentational devices from linguistic ones, under respective headings, attaching the definition and example(s) for each. This task may be best undertaken in pairs, with the layout as in Figure 4.1,

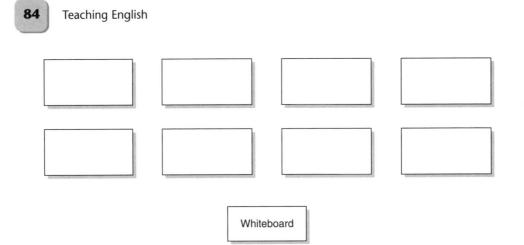

Figure 4.1   Rows layout

so that pupils can support and consolidate each others' learning. If the grouping were any larger than this you would undoubtedly run the risk of some pupils not taking part in the task, thereby undermining its function. As already suggested, such a layout easily lends itself to the grouping of tables later in the lesson if you then wanted pupils to work in larger groups.

Group organization

This type of set-up will serve as the most suitable means of organizing pupils when you want to engage them in collaborative work. Such tasks might include: group reading activities; shared writing; discussion of issues arising from a text (for example characters' motivations and changes); information retrieval and evidence gathering to support a viewpoint or argument; scripting a play or planning for a drama activity.

The layout depicted in Figure 4.2 allows you to create groups selectively, based on some pre-determined criteria (such as ability, friendship or gender). This, in turn, means that you are in a position to provide structured and targeted support to the groupings within the classroom, ensuring that all pupils are able to participate in the set task. Certain support mechanisms may be prepared in advance of the lesson – for instance, writing scaffolds or prompt sheets – and these can prove vital in enabling you to circulate effectively, supporting pupils while they are actually engaged in an activity. Further discussion of the use of such group work and its benefits will appear later in this chapter in the context of two specific lessons at Key Stages 3 and 4.

There are a number of proven strategies which make group work effective, and enable you to approach it with variety and in ways which offer pupils fresh challenges. Effective group work strategies, as outlined in *Raising Standards, English at Key Stage 3, Training 2000: Speaking and Listening* (DfEE, 2000), might include:

- *Pairs to fours* – pupils work in pairs to establish initial ideas, then pairs join to make groups of four to discuss ideas and decide on a collaborative strategy. For example, Year 8 pupils consider a debate topic in pairs. Half the pairs in the class discuss the arguments in favour, while the other half consider the alternative viewpoint. Then pairs from opposing sides join to conduct a mini-debate.
- *Listening triads* – pupils work in groups of three, with each member of the group being assigned the specific roles of talker, questioner and recorder. The talker presents an explanation, argument or such,

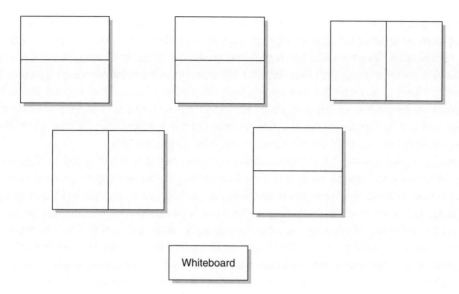

Whiteboard

Figure 4.2   Group layout

while the questioner formulates questions to present to the talker, which further clarify what has been stated. The recorder acts as a scribe, recording key points to feedback at the end of the dialogue. Then roles can be changed, so that each member of the triad has the opportunity to act in each of the roles, thus ensuring all are able to express their views. For example, after discussing the opening scene of Shakespeare's *Macbeth*, Year 7 pupils might be asked how they would present the scene on stage. In threes, they each take turns as talker, questioner and recorder to build up layers of ideas about how they each might approach it. The trio could afterwards collaborate, taking the best of the ideas from this process to present to the rest of the class.

- *Envoys* – after working in groups, pupils select an envoy to visit another group(s) to gather thoughts and ideas. They then return to their home group to feedback their findings. This is a time efficient and effective way of groups sharing ideas and information, without having each group methodically feeding back to the whole class. For example, a Year 10 class have been working in groups researching different aspects of Indian culture and society in preparation for poetry study. Envoys from each group travel to another group to share their key findings and to ask questions they would still like answered. After acquiring additional information, they return to their home group to share this, thus adding to the group's shared knowledge.

- *Snowball* – this involves pupil groupings growing in size at certain stages during a task or discussion, pretty much as a snowball would if it were rolled down a hillside. Pupils begin working in pairs, then join to make fours, then to make eight as and when prompted by you. These groups then come together to create a whole-class grouping, with spokespeople from groups of eight feeding back ideas and opinions. This is an excellent way of preparing pupils for a whole-class discussion or debate, as it enables pupils to try out their ideas in the secure setting of small groups before being exposed to the more risky whole-class forum.

- *Rainbow groups* – this approach to group work ensures that pupils learn to work with a range of others. Groups are organized to work on a task or issue, each member of the group being given a different coloured card. Once the initial task is complete, groups are reorganized based on card colour, all pupils with the same colour card joining together. This ensures that the re-formed groups represent the views and ideas of all within the class, feeding back the combined ideas of their original groups. For example, year 9 pupils were asked, in groups, to research different aspects of Shakespeare's life and times. Each rainbow group researched a different aspect of this topic and, after collating information, reorganized to form groups of the same colour to disseminate their findings.
- *Jigsawing* – after dividing a topic into sections, each member of a 'home' group is allocated a specialist section to focus on. These specialists then regroup to form an 'expert' group in order to explore their particular area. Once this is complete, the specialist groups disperse and 'home' groups are re-formed. Each member of the home group then shares their knowledge with others in the group. This is a sure-fire way of ensuring that all pupils play a part in the task and that they each end up with a good overview of all aspects of the topic under consideration. It does, however, require careful planning and often works best when groups are selected by the teacher. For example, an able Year 11 class worked in groups to prepare for a timed essay on the use of symbolism in John Steinbeck's *Of Mice and Men*. In home groups, each pupil took responsibility for examining one symbolic aspect of the novel (for example, nature, rabbits, the colour red, and so on). These areas formed the basis of expert groups, which collated examples from the novel along with supporting quotations. Experts then returned to their home groups and reported their findings, thus helping to support individual efforts in the essay which followed.

Discussion, debate and drama

When conducting lessons which require a whole class forum or which involve drama, the first things you'll need to consider are:

- how to generate the required space
- health and safety issues generated by moving of furniture
- whether pupils can easily interact with one another.

In the case of whole-class debate or discussion, arranging tables in horseshoe formation (Figure 4.3) is effective in facilitating an open seating forum in which pupils can easily see and hear one another. This arrangement also works well for drama activities such as hot-seating and thought tracking activities, which require only a small active performance area.

Of course, this could also be achieved if you completely remove desks from the discussion area, sitting pupils in a circle. Clearly, moving furniture out of the active working space is something that requires planning and demands that you drill your pupils into a routine for doing this safely and quickly. Before embarking, think carefully about the following:

- How much space will you require?
- Where will desks be moved to?
- Are chairs needed? If not, where will they be stored?
- What will be pupils' individual responsibilities during the move?
- Where will bags, coats and equipment be stored?

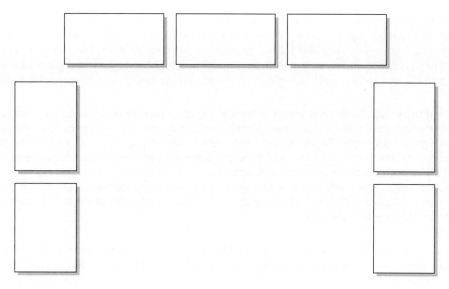

Figure 4.3   Horseshoe layout

These are all crucial issues which will impact on lesson timing and, more importantly, the safety and state of mind of your learners. Get this routine right, and you will find that changing the layout of your room can be done in a time-efficient, organized and effective way, and that your pupils will be ready for the task in hand within a couple of minutes.

Making the right choices when it comes to classroom organization has a significant impact on learning potential and can sometimes 'make or break' a lesson. While on a school placement, one trainee English teacher, Stephanie, realized the importance of setting up the classroom to suit the teaching and learning activities she had planned. After attempting a whole-class debate with pupils seated in rows (Figure 4.1), it soon became clear that such a layout was not conducive to the discussion and drama-based activities she had planned for her Year 10 group. Her follow-up lesson revolved around exploring characters in John Steinbeck's novel *Of Mice and Men*, and included whole-class discussion of George's decision to shoot Lennie, alongside hot-seating of his character:

I knew that working with pupils in rows wouldn't work with what I was trying to achieve ... a couple of lessons earlier I'd used this layout during a class debate. I had pupils turning round as different people spoke ... this meant they had their backs to me and some of them took advantage ... they tried to distract others behind them. So, for my lesson exploring George's character and motivation, I decided to arrange the desks in the shape of a horseshoe (see Figure 4.3). This meant that pupils could make good eye-contact with each other during the discussion task, rather than straining to see each other while they were speaking. The difference it made was really noticeable ... they were more attentive and they actually *interacted* with each other and *responded* to each others' points of view. It made for a much livelier discussion than I'd expected ... it also meant that we could move into the hot-seating activity without any interruption, we simply moved into the space within the desks and were questioning George in no time.

Another PGCE English trainee, Emily Parr, also provides some insightful reflection on the process of organizing pupils in a piece of work produced as part of her professional studies assessment – one which enables trainee teachers to achieve M level. Her 'Critical Incident Reflection' (available in full on the companion website) highlights the importance of making informed choices about pupil groupings when employing creative strategies with a class:

> I planned the groups before the lesson in such a way as to reunite those who had collaborated well in previous lessons and ensure that quieter members of the class would not feel intimidated by more gregarious pupils. To an extent, I considered friendship groups, as I wanted the pupils to feel comfortable with each other and generate a lively atmosphere more conducive to learning (Q30), though I made a point of stipulating that seating to stress it was on my terms, not theirs. Knowing ... how chaos is minimized by rearranging and numbering tables before the lesson, I again allocated each pupil a number at the door and briefly explained arrangements, and monitored the flow into the room.

This element of control is further reinforced by Emily's awareness that three boys in particular might pose a challenge given that she had 'struggled to maintain their attention in previous lessons'. She is clearly mindful of the fact that taking a calculated risk might result in an unsuccessful outcome here – however, given the nature of the task she had planned, the boys were 'enthusiastic' and fully engaged in the dramatic approach to Brontë's *Wuthering Heights*.

KEY TEACHING STRATEGIES FOR SUCCESSFUL ENGLISH LESSONS

This section endeavours not to provide an exhaustive list of teaching strategies which may be used in the teaching of English, but rather to highlight some proven strategies that have been used to deliver aspects of the reading and writing curriculum.

A reading strategy: directed activities related to texts (DARTs)

Directed activities related to texts, developed by Lunzer and Gardner (1979), allow you to get pupils actively engaged the texts they are studying, whether these be hard copy or on screen, by posing them some sort of problem-solving task which, by its very nature, forces them to consider various aspects of a text's meaning, language or structure. There are two categories of DARTs:

1. *Reconstructive activities*: those which require pupils to reconstruct a text which has been modified in some way.
2. *Processing activities*: pupils interrogate or modify an original text in some way.

Of course, the possibilities are endless when it comes to manipulating texts for investigation, and many of these are identified by Moy and Raleigh (1980) in their paper on reinvigorating reading for meaning. However, there are a number of tried and tested favourites such as:

- Cloze procedure – certain words/phrases are removed from the text, forcing pupils to discuss the potential of those missing. In this way, you can force them to consider word choices and the use of certain parts of speech, thus engaging them in a task through which they explore lexical cohesion.
- Prediction – pupils examine a text using contextual clues in order to make informed and calculated guesses as to the next phase or the ending. This can be followed up by pupils comparing their predictions with the actual text, discussing and justifying their views as they do so.
- Sequencing – pupils are presented with a text which has been divided into chunks, the aim being that they reorganize the text in some logical way. This is often an effective way for them to investigate the structural aspects of texts. Prose texts might be divided into paragraphs, while poetry could be divided into stanzas (for longer poems with a narrative focus), or into separate lines (for shorter poems with, for example, a regular rhyme scheme).
- Dramatization – pupils explore texts through the medium of drama, using techniques such as role play, hot-seating, thought tracking and tableaux.
- Text marking – pupils highlight or underline parts of the text with shared meaning, significance or features. Ideas can be colour-coded, making it easier for pupils to group ideas under separate headings. This can be accompanied by annotation, enabling pupils to add comments on the significance of certain marked aspects of the text under scrutiny.

The true benefit of utilizing DARTs is that pupils are engaged in active and collaborative approaches to texts which require independent investigation and reflection on their part. When selected appropriately, they can prove effective in all aspects of a lesson, serving well as either a starter or plenary activity, or playing a central role in the main part of an English lesson. Clearly, it is important that you consider your learning objectives and whether certain DARTs activities will facilitate the appropriate outcome in terms of pupils' achievements. Therefore, if you wanted pupils to engage imaginatively with a character, they might explore this through some form of dramatization. Alternatively, if you wanted pupils to select examples of certain types of language use, you would be better served by text marking.

A writing strategy: using the teaching sequence

The launch of the *Key Stage 3 National Strategy: Framework for Teaching English: Years 7, 8 and 9* (DfEE, 2001a) in 2001 brought with it the now well-established teaching sequence for writing. The sequence is designed to assist teachers in supporting pupils' writing by providing a structured approach to writing which enables pupils to first explore and understand conventions before beginning to apply them to their own writing.

English Department Training (2001), Grammar for Writing (DfEE, 2001b), identifies the five key stages of the teaching sequence:

- Explore the objective.
- Define the convention.
- Demonstrate how it is written.
- Share the composition.
- Scaffold the first attempts.

It is crucial that, when approaching writing for various purposes and audiences, pupils are first able to explore texts for themselves, working out the underlying conventions at work. This enables pupils to work out the 'rules' without there being undue preoccupation with linguistic terminology and labels. The process of then showing how these rules work in one's own writing can be demonstrated by the teacher, who models the key conventions on the whiteboard. The writing process is gradually handed over to pupils as they begin to contribute to the composition of the text, with the teacher prompting discussion about which word choices and structures might be most effective. Having created 'ownership' of rules and collaborative composition, pupils are then better equipped to work more independently of each other and the teacher – though some scaffolding may be necessary at this point (this often taking the form of writing frames, paragraph openers, prompt sheets, vocabulary banks and so on). A good example of this in practice can be seen in Chapter 3, where Ian Jackson skilfully integrates supported writing mechanisms into a Year 7 poetry lesson.

Such an approach would equally apply to the 'writing' or 'production' of a range of media and emerging digital texts such as web logs (explored further in Chapter 9). GCSE pupils involved in media studies might well engage in the creation of moving image texts for instance – hence, the teaching sequence for writing would serve as a useful structural guide for this rather more practical form of text creation.

LESSON STRATEGIES IN ACTION

The next section of this chapter examines potential approaches to teaching lessons at Key Stages 3 and 4, with the focuses being on Shakespeare and multicultural poetry respectively. The section seeks to demonstrate how varied activities and grouping can be effectively employed in order to meet specified learning objectives. The first lesson provides a possible starting point for teaching Shakespeare's *Macbeth* to a Year 7/8 class, and was planned and delivered by PGCE student, Amy.

The Key Stage 3 Shakespeare lesson

Shakespeare and the secondary National Strategy
With the recent revisions to the secondary National Strategy, has come more detailed guidance on the teaching of Shakespeare at Key Stage 3. Notable additions include a range of learning objectives, strategies which could be used to engage pupils with Shakespeare's work, and a series of *progression statements* which outline:

> what pupils can be expected to demonstrate in knowledge, understanding and skills when responding to Shakespeare by the end of Years 7, 8 and 9 in the four main areas of study:
>
> • character and motivation;
> • ideas, themes and issues;
> • the language of the text;
> • text in performance. (DfES, 2007: 1)

Guidelines for Teaching Shakespeare in Key Stage 3 (DfES, 2007) (provided on the companion website) provides a useful summary of the key skills that pupils should have developed at each point during the key stage, with a clear emphasis being placed upon pupils engaging with Shakespeare confidently and exploring issues, characters and language in increasingly creative and analytical ways (Figure 4.4).

	End of Year 7	**End of Year 8**	**End of Year 9**
Character	Describe, both orally and in writing, the characters' feelings and behaviour as shown through speech and actions.	Explain how characters' motivation and behaviour are portrayed through actions and speech with comments on the effects of language on an audience.	Clear analysis of characters' actions, behaviour, attitudes and motivation through appropriate textual references and an appreciation of the impact of language on an audience.
Language	Read Shakespeare aloud with growing confidence. Orally and in writing comment on particular words and phrases to show awareness of some of the features and effects of dramatic and poetic language and devices.	Read Shakespeare aloud with growing confidence, fluency and expression. Orally and in writing demonstrate clear understanding of the features and effects of dramatic and poetic language and devices.	Read Shakespeare aloud with a degree of fluency, confidence and with expression that reflects a personal interpretation. Demonstrate orally and in writing an appreciation of the features and effects of dramatic and poetic language and devices.
Themes	Demonstrate orally and in writing some understanding of the main themes in a play and how they are developed. Identify quotations to support their ideas.	Demonstrate orally and in writing clear understanding of the main themes in a play and how these are presented to an audience. Explain how selected textual references and quotations support their ideas.	Explain, orally and in writing how themes and ideas are presented dramatically, with selected references to the text integrated into well-developed argument.
Performance	Explore plays and scenes through work in role, using voice, gesture and positioning to convey elements of the play (for example, character, theme, setting). Write clearly about productions they have seen and their experiences in role.	Explore plays and scenes through work in role, using a range of dramatic techniques to convey elements of the play. Use the appropriate form of language to articulate insights and understandings into their own performances and those of others.	Select and use appropriate dramatic techniques when exploring plays and scenes through work in role. Write critically about the dramatic impact of scenes by drawing on their own performances and those of others. Show understanding of the potential for differing interpretations.

Figure 4.4   Shakespeare progression statements for Years 7, 8 and 9 (DFES, 2007: 2–3)

These statements clearly point to the teaching of Shakespeare during each of the years at Key Stage 3. While this may seem a daunting prospect, it is important to remember that this does not equate to the study of three whole plays during the key stage. The new 2008 National Curriculum maintains the current statutory requirement for *one* play to be studied during Key Stage 3, albeit there is a much needed emphasis on the need for whole text study. In addition to this, it does in fact widen the scope of Shakespearean study to the *Sonnets*, and discerning English teachers will seize the opportunity to study not just Shakespeare via his plays (in whole or in part) but via his poetry too. (Further information about curriculum requirements can be found in Chapter 7, with some further discussion about approaching texts from an assessment perspective.)

Guidelines for Teaching Shakespeare in Key Stage 3 (DfES, 2007) also highlights key objectives and learning outcomes for each of the four main areas of study, and provides a variety of practical examples of activities that can be undertaken by pupils in their study of different plays. Most importantly, suggested activities offer many practical approaches to Shakespeare (such as DARTs referred to earlier in this chapter), thus reinforcing the need for pupils to experience his texts as performance pieces and engaging with them in imaginative and creative ways. Indeed, the need for such practical interaction with Shakespeare underpins the approaches advocated by Rex Gibson's *Teaching Shakespeare,* in which he quite rightly emphasizes the importance of pupils 'creat[ing] his or her own meaning, rather than passively soak[ing] up information' (1998: 9).

Given that the study of Shakespeare is mandatory in both Key Stages 3 and 4, it is vital that you seek ways for pupils to interact with the text in a proactive and physical way. By bringing Shakespeare to life, transforming the written script into a tangible, visual, audible experience, pupils can better understand the characters, actions and issues in his plays. All the better if you can help pupils to see the ways in which his texts are applicable to them, their lives and the modern world. It is for this reason that 'first contact' with Shakespeare is so crucial, that pupils have some way to relate to him on a personal level. One way of establishing this is to explore a play's key issue(s) from a modern perspective before embarking on study of the text.

These principles are similarly applicable to other texts which might be deemed 'difficult to access', as is clearly highlighted in Emily Parr's 'Critical Incident Reflection' mentioned earlier in which she adopts an active dramatic approach to Emily Brontë's *Wuthering Heights* in order to prepare Year 10 pupils for prose study assessment.

Points for reflection

Points for reflection

- Can you think of any modern-day situations/issues that could be used as starting points for approaching his plays? (See website PowerPoint 'Teaching Shakespeare at Key Stage 3'.)
- Are there parallel story lines in the media or on popular programmes/soap operas?
- Are there any issues which are pertinent to modern-day teenage life, issues which pupils may have personal experience of?
- What resources might you gather to use with a Key Stage 3 class in relation to specific plays?

Such a starting point can lead successfully into study of a play by generating a curiosity within your pupils and by triggering an emotional connection with the issues of Shakespeare's work without them even being aware of it. From here, you can launch into direct contact with Shakespeare's characters and narratives secure in the knowledge that pupils have an empathic starting point.

A sample lesson

Dramatizations of key scenes can be a useful way of exploring characters and dramatic technique as pupils are encouraged to consider the 'active' content of the scenes and how certain characters might be portrayed. This, of course, also opens up the interpretive aspect of such work, allowing pupils to discuss and reflect on the different ways characters might be portrayed and perceived by an audience. A further extension of such an activity could also involve pupils considering the differences in interpretation over time. For example, given the nature of beliefs about witches in Jacobean society, audiences of the time would have viewed their part in play rather differently to a twenty-first-century audience.

Amy, a PGCE trainee, demonstrates (Figure 4.5) how you might usefully begin your study of *Macbeth* by getting pupils to undertake some basic research about the powers attributed to witches in the Jacobean period.

After some initial whole-class discussion about the nature of superstition, which provides a modern frame of reference, Amy then organizes the class into groups as possible with the intention of engaging them in group work. She has already drilled pupils in a routine for moving desks in the classroom she is in, so pupils are able to move from rows (Figure 4.1) into group tables (Figure 4.2) in under two minutes. As mentioned earlier in the chapter, the importance of having a defined routine for this cannot be underestimated and should be planned in advance.

Amy decided to organize the Internet research task on witches as a group activity, allowing pupils to choose their own groups:

I decided to let the class work in friendship groups because I wanted them to enjoy the activity and wanted them to work quickly together given the tight time deadline. It worked really well — especially after I announced there'd be a bit of a competitive activity later in the lesson. It made a difference to the way pupils pulled together in finding information.

When asked why she had chosen to use the envoy approach to enable pupils to share information she stated:

Basically, I knew different groups would pick up different information in the small amount of time they had. Getting one pupil to move around as many of the other groups as possible in that five-minute period puts them under pressure to get as much additional information from each other as they can. The competition gave them a real incentive to get additional information from each other. It was funny to watch some of the envoys ... they actually 'traded' information with other groups ... you give me something and I'll give you something in return.

This group strategy worked extremely well in this situation, as it allowed pupils in the class to access maximum information in a short amount of time. Amy was also able to target groups which had struggled to get information, pointing more able envoys in their

Timing	Teacher activity	Learner activity	Notes
10 min	Starter • Chair whole-class discussion about modern day superstitions and supernatural figures	• Engage in discussion, expressing personal opinion and experiences	• Consider witches – modern-day equivalents? (for example, tarot card readers, mediums, astrologers)
20 min	Introduction • Direct pupils to move tables/form groups • Using laptops, research beliefs about witches during Elizabethan/Jacobean periods • After 10–15 mins, instruct scribes to act as envoys, circulate to share and gather information	• Pupils form groups collating information, one person acting as a scribe for different findings of group members. • Scribe from each group quickly circulates, comparing information and gathering/imparting any findings as necessary	• Move tables from rows into groups, using drilled routine • Assist any groups having difficulty accessing information • Teacher to select scribe/envoy to ensure efficiency
15 min	Development • Settle pupils back into original groups • Read Act 1 Scene 1 aloud – with copy on IWB • Highlight evidence of beliefs about witches as pupils provide it. • Reward group that identifies most attributes	• Groups reconvene, each envoy having collected a bell from teacher • As teacher reads Act 1 Scene 1, groups to 'Spot the Superstition', ringing bell when they recognize an attribute	• Key evidence should include: flying, controlling weather, presence of familiars, power of prediction, speaking in riddles, ability to bring on night, ability to control actions of others
10 min	Plenary • Chair discussion about how *Shakespeare's audience* would have reacted to witches, how *modern audience* would have differences. • What might witches want with Macbeth? • Save class lists to refer and add to again in future lessons	• Contribute to general discussion about witches • Two pupils act as scribes, recording audience reactions to witches on IWB under headings ***Shakespeare's audience*** and ***Modern audience***	

(Continued)

Figure 4.5   (Continued)

5 min	Closing routine • Homework recorded on board: pupils to write paragraph predicting what the witches want from Macbeth and what might happen between them • Organize pupils and room, oversee return of laptops	• Record homework • Pupils move desks back into rows ready for next class • Designated pupils bring laptops back to trolley to put away	

Figure 4.5   Amy's lesson plan

direction to share their findings. This way, all groups had a real chance to contribute to the 'Spot the Superstition' game which followed – something they clearly enjoyed and which proved a successful way of consolidating their newly acquired knowledge.

This also meant that Amy had a natural opening for discussion as to how Shakespeare's audience might have felt about seeing the witches on stage at the beginning of the play, thus introducing them to the social context of *Macbeth*:

> The whole-class discussion in the plenary gave them the chance to speculate about the reactions of a Jacobean audience and to compare them with their own. It also meant I had a really good starting point for my next lesson ... exploring how the witches might be presented on stage or TV ... and getting pupils to dramatize the scene.

As much as Amy's lesson did not involve that all important *performance*, it did enable pupils to engage with *Macbeth* in an active and creative way, providing some essential preparation for further exploratory drama work. This highlights the importance of getting the right groundwork in place if pupils are to successfully engage with Shakespeare as performance text. The lesson also reminds us of the fact that when planning for Shakespeare there are many active and engaging strategies you might adopt, and that not all of these need be drama based as such. On the companion website, you can view another sample lesson plan (Lesson Plan 1) which explores the characters of Macbeth and Lady Macbeth, tracking the changes they undergo during the course of the play. Again, the lesson does not have dramatic performance as its focus, but it does employ pupils in varied tasks which lend themselves to different learning styles, which could either precede or follow dramatic exploration of these characters – via hot-seating, thought tracking, police-type interviews or even a whole-class courtroom trial.

Such a point is further reinforced by the wide range of DARTs activities included in the secondary National Strategy publication mentioned earlier in this chapter, *Guidelines for Teaching Shakespeare in Key Stage 3* (DfES, 2007). Some of these are obviously drama and performance focused. However, activities include other creative approaches such as designing 'Top Trump' cards for key characters, using text marking and annotation to record interpretations of character, creating mood charts/graphs to track changes and high points of emotion, and writing things such as obituaries (after following the teaching sequence for writing mentioned earlier) for characters such as King Duncan or Romeo and Juliet. Teachers TV programmes such as *Shakespeare Shorts: Pupils Plotting* (TV programmes available on companion website), also demonstrate approaches to Shakespeare which promote creative interaction and collaboration – through things such as dance, digital photography and animation.

The Key Stage 4 multicultural poetry lesson

Changes to the programmes of study for English in September 2008 have resulted in greater emphasis being placed on the importance of culture and its place within the National Curriculum as a whole. 'Cultural understanding' now serves as a key thread which runs through the curriculum, reflecting the increasing range of cultural diversity within twenty-first-century British society.

Particularly relevant to the study of multicultural poetry at GCSE, the Key Stage 4 *Key Processes*, paragraph 1.3, directs English teachers to enhance cultural understanding in the following ways:

b) exploring how texts from different cultures and traditions influence values, assumptions and sense of identity.
c) understanding how spoken and written language evolve in response to changes in society and technology and how this process relates to identity and cultural diversity.

Further information on the requirements of the GCSE syllabi in relation to this is available in Chapter 7 of this book, but for our purposes here it is useful to identify the key aspects you need to focus on with classes studying GCSE English.

Regardless of which syllabus you follow, when it comes to the study of poetry from other cultures and traditions, you must prepare your pupils for assessment in these potential areas:

- what the poems reveal about the cultures which they depict
- what the poems reveal about the writers and their attitudes
- how writers use language and structural devices to depict the culture(s) concerned and to convey ideas and attitudes
- how poems may be compared in relation to all of the above.

Given that the curriculum throughout the key stages provides regular opportunities for pupils to develop their knowledge and understanding of literary devices and writers' intentions, in my experience GCSE students often find the first of the above bullet points the most interesting, as it provides an opportunity for real learning about human issues.

How much context?
When teaching multicultural poetry for the first time at this level, you will undoubtedly contemplate just how much 'background' pupils will need in order to understand a

poem's content and meaning. There is no easy answer to this question. You, with the knowledge you have about your pupils, must determine how much contextual knowledge is relevant and appropriate to their ability level. The more able the pupil, the more cultural relevance they will see within a text, meaning that you can encourage more detailed research into relevant aspects of the culture concerned.

It might be argued that, when looking at assessment criteria, much of the study of such poetry need not be concerned with culture at all – as skills are, essentially, what pupils will be assessed on. While this is indeed true to an extent, it is impossible to gain real insight into a poet's attitudes and feelings in a poem such as 'Nothing's Changed', without first understanding apartheid and the history of Johannesburg's District 6. In addition to this, if we remove the 'culture', shift the focus entirely onto poetic technique and structure, surely we are depriving our pupils of a real opportunity to engage in the human issues which these poems raise, to better understand global issues and to become more informed global citizens?

However, at the very least, you must determine the following:

- What do pupils need to know about this culture, its traditions, customs, values and beliefs in order to understand the people depicted within the poems and to understand the poet's attitude towards their subject(s)?
- What knowledge do pupils already have about the culture depicted?

It is often useful to consider aspects of culture in a context more specific to your pupils before introducing them to the poetry itself. For instance, if you were about to embark on the poem 'Blessing', you might first engage pupils in a discussion about personal experiences of times when they have been without water – say when the water supply was cut off due to maintenance work. The initial tales of hardship that ensue are soon put into some sort of context once you get them thinking about this potentially continuing for days, weeks, months or years. The implications, once apparent, provide an excellent way into the poem and help to form pupils' views of the villagers in the poem when the municipal water pipe bursts.

A sample lesson

When introducing students to the study of multicultural poetry at GCSE level, it is essential that you revisit the concept of 'culture' itself, ensuring that they are fully aware of what it entails. While teaching at a comprehensive secondary school in Crosby, Liverpool, I often used this as my starting point with groups of all abilities, getting pupils to reflect on their own lives and the things of cultural value and significance to them and their families.

Lesson Plan 2, which appears in full on the companion website, demonstrates one way of approaching this with an able GCSE class. The lesson starter involves pupils investigating various printed media in order to extract information about the society which it represents. Such an activity creates a group discussion opportunity for pupils to consider the values and beliefs represented within familiar texts, providing useful material from which pupils can begin to form their own definitions of what 'culture' actually is. This starting point also enables you to explicitly highlight the centrality of this concept to this particular part of their GCSE study and the assessment which will take place either by examination or coursework.

Once a working definition of culture is in place, you will have an effective point from which to begin your study of individual poems – and this is something you should revisit regularly, until pupils naturally assimilate it. This can be further reinforced by setting homework which requires pupils to research the key aspects of a culture other than their own – not only will this consolidate their understanding of culture and all it entails, but it also provides a knowledge base for study of poems in the future. You could ensure that pupils engage with the cultural traditions they will need to consider as part of the course by providing a list of possible cultures for research. The collage of information which pupils then generate can form the basis of a display which could be consulted on an ongoing basis as an educational tool as and when specific cultures are considered. With a less able class, such a research activity might best be performed within allocated lesson time, so that you can provide support and appropriate materials for pupils to investigate. This would also facilitate a collaborative approach, enabling pupils to investigate smaller aspects of a certain culture, then combining their knowledge to create a visual resource – such as a Mind Map, PowerPoint presentation or a series of digital still images.

The next step involves moving pupils on to consider some of the issues related to aspects of culture within a poem – in this case, Achebe's 'Vultures'. By presenting pupils with visual images as a starting point for personal reflection and then whole-class discussion, you can begin to assess prior knowledge and opinions of certain key concepts. Thus, by presenting images of a vulture and a German officer on the IWB, you can gauge connotations/associations, simultaneously juxtaposing the two so that pupils, on a subconscious level at least, begin to link the two.

Given that 'Vultures' deals with issues relating to the Holocaust, the choice of a DVD clip here proves highly effective. You might select clips from a range of different films (for example *The Pianist*, *Schindler's List*) or programmes (such as *Band of Brothers*) which present pupils with memorable images of conditions within the Nazi concentration camps. The depiction of skeletal prisoners within the camps proves highly relevant to the references made to the vultures' acts of scavenging in the poem, and the symbolic significance of the birds in relation to serving Nazi officers during the Second World War. By exposing pupils to a range of visual images, you successfully forge a link between the various component parts of 'Vultures' before pupils even read the poem.

This approach is reminiscent of that recommended for the study of Shakespeare earlier in this chapter, in the sense that the best 'way in' to such unfamiliar territory comes via those things that pupils can relate to in some way – and this holds true for other multicultural poetry pupils study.

WHAT THE RESEARCH SUGGESTS

As far back as 1970, Kounin's research identified that pupils' behaviour in the classroom was determined not by the teacher's method of disciplining pupils, but by their classroom management. More recently Muijs et al. (2004) discovered that much of the misbehaviour occurring in modern classrooms was as a result of poor teaching which did not cater to the needs of pupils' abilities and interests. This clearly has repercussions for us as teachers in the English classroom, as it emphasizes the increasing need for us to create meaningful learning experiences for our pupils and to do this in ways which will keep them engaged.

Central to this engagement is the concept of collaborative work. The importance of collaboration in the learning process was clearly identified when Lev Vygotsky (1978) identified the 'zone of proximal development', arguing that children's learning potential could be increased by working together as opposed to working in isolation. Vygotsky further established that talk, being a social and cultural activity, enabled knowledge construction. This has had repercussions for teachers within the classroom environment, as it clearly points to the need for us to plan for collaborative learning opportunities, organizing pupils into various grouping in order to meet learning objectives accordingly.

More recent research has further highlighted the need for teachers to reflect more carefully about the principles which guide them in their choice of pupil groupings. *Grouping Pupils for Success* (DfES, 2006) considers how teachers might effectively organize pupils for learning via a number of key principles: ability, gender, age, need and friendship. However, a key point is made: 'Just organising pupils into ability groups, or single sex groups or friendship groups, or structured mixed-ability groups will not of itself produce positive results' (DfES, 2006: 1). Our knowledge of the pupils we teach is crucial if we are to make groupings successful: we must be aware of their personalities, their individual needs, even their moods at any given moment in time.

The research proves enlightening in terms of identifying advantages and disadvantages of different types of groupings. More importantly, it highlights the need for us to talk explicitly with pupils about the ways in which they are organized and to listen to their views about the 'impact of setting and grouping on motivation, aspiration and self-esteem' (DfES, 2006: 8).

This could, therefore, prove an interesting focus for smaller-scale research, such as that involved in M-level components of PGCE programmes. Such research has the potential to provide highly valuable insights into the mechanisms which drive successful collaborative approaches to learning. This in turn can inform and influence practice in a way which is both formative and meaningful for individual trainee teachers, bringing the best of reflective practice to the forefront.

Key points from this chapter

In this chapter we have established that:

- careful organization and clear routines are essential to effective classroom management
- building positive relationships with pupils creates a meaningful and productive learning environment
- it is important to be yourself
- a variety of pupil groupings and teaching strategies can result in successful learning outcomes
- it is important that learning is meaningful to pupils, and that you make it relevant to them and their lives
- research into your own practices related to collaborative learning could further enhance teaching and learning.

Further reading

Cowley, S. (2006) *Getting the Buggers to Behave.* London: Continuum.
A highly accessible guide to all key aspects of behaviour management.

Gibson, R. (1998) *Teaching Shakespeare*. Cambridge: Cambridge University Press.
The 'standard' text when it comes to the teaching of Shakespeare across the key stages. Accessible and comprehensive, this book (with its accompanying resource pack), provides guidance and ideas for teaching all aspects of teaching Shakespeare's plays. Good for considering performance and related issues.

Kerry, T. and Wilding, M. (2004) *Effective Classroom Teacher: Developing the Skills You Need in Today's Classroom.* London: Pearson Education.
Provides comprehensive coverage of all aspects of classroom organization.

Kyriacou, C. (1998) *Essential Teaching Skills*. (2nd edn). Cheltenham: Nelson Thornes.
A classic text which still proves relevant today. Provides a good starting point for consideration of the generic issues involved in successfully organizing teaching and learning.

 Useful websites

Live links to these websites can be found on the companion website www.sagepub.co.uk/secondary.

www.aqa.org.uk
www.behaviour4learning.ac.uk
www.curriculumonline.gov.uk
www.standards.dfes.gov.uk/secondary/keystage3
www.teachit.co.uk
www.teacherstv.co.uk
www.wjec.co.uk

5 MONITORING PERFORMANCE AND SECURING PROGRESS

Alyson Midgley

This chapter considers:

- the basic differences between formative and summative assessment, allowing you to reflect on the uses of both. Summative assessment is also discussed at greater length in Chapter 7
- practical examples of a Key Stage 3 Year 7 lesson plan and teacher/pupil transcripts, critiquing how both formative and summative assessment operate in the classroom. There is an in-depth discussion of the following particular formative assessment strategies that can be used in the English classroom:

  - targeted oral feedback
  - use of questioning and dialogue
  - written feedback and how this can be best used
  - setting pupil-friendly learning objectives
  - target-setting
  - securing and maintaining progression
  - peer and self-assessment
  - How *Assessing Pupils' Progress* document (DfES, 2005b) is aiding the assessment process.

There are also two written examples of pupils' work at Key Stage 3 (KS3) and Key Stage 4 (KS4). Both written examples also show each pupil's strengths and how the English teacher can set pupil targets for improvement.
This chapter concludes with an overall comment on the importance of assessment.

WHAT DO I DEFINE AS ASSESSMENT?

This chapter is a crucial chapter in understanding why we teach. Teaching and planning a lesson are not just about getting through the lesson; your teaching and planning means making sure all pupils are able to progress and to succeed in their learning.

For you, as an English PGCE trainee, assessment is the hardest part of your day-to-day teaching. You will know that your pupils might have understood, but how far do you know that *all* your pupils have *really* understood? For years, teachers would have relied on gut reaction. But it is only since the introduction of the KS3 strategy (2001) that assessing English has been thought of in terms of managing learning, and only latterly in measuring learning: *managing learning* in the way that each pupil's learning is deliberately planned for and co-ordinated; *measuring learning* in the sense that all learning that takes place in an English classroom must be purposeful and show progress. By the time pupils leave the English classroom, they must each have added to their English skills. But how do you know? How do you measure?

Definitions of formative and summative assessments

Formative assessment or Assessment for Learning is the variety of strategies used by teachers and pupils to recognize and respond to learning, in order to enhance that learning during an activity or task. *Formative assessment or Assessment for Learning* has always existed, though it was mostly carried out automatically. However, in today's classroom, formative assessment is about you being an action researcher, taking a few principles and experimenting with ways of putting them into action. Assessment for Learning is perhaps the most important part of the teaching process, because you will know whether your pupils have achieved and have progressed. Indeed the DfES (2005a: 5) *Assessment for Learning* has defined Assessment for Learning in the classroom as: 'The process of seeking and interpreting evidence of use by learners and their teachers to decide where the learners are in their learning, where they need to go and how best to get there.'

Undoubtedly you will have already noticed that the English classroom environment lends itself to be more personal in sharing and empathizing with concepts and ideas. Not only has the pupil got to trust you, but the pupil must also learn to experiment. It is worth noting that Butler, in Black et al. (2003), comments that the pupil has to trust the teacher; a new teacher, whether a trainee or newly qualified, who comments and simply gives summative grades, can be very demotivating. Using formative assessment strategies builds on that trust. Here are a few strategies that you may wish to use:

- targeted oral feedback
- use of questioning and dialogue
- written feedback and how this can be best used
- setting pupil-friendly learning objectives
- target-setting
- securing and maintaining progression
- peer and self assessment.

Summative assessment is where all the formative information is collated about a pupil and this information is 'summarized' by the result of an external examination such as SATs or GCSE at KS4. Summative assessment is a definitive means to measure learning. With the recent changes in the 11–14 KS 3 SATs in October 2008, it is important to note that some English departments are still using the SATs exams for May 2009 as an internal means of summatively testing pupils at the end of Year 9. These SATs papers will be internally marked and moderated to give a moderated Teacher Assessment level for each pupil. (See Chapter 7 for further discussion.)

Points for reflection

- When observing in the English classroom, note down how many types of formative assessment are used. How are pupils made to feel that they are a part of the learning process?
- What formative assessment strategies do you feel are the most successful and why?
- Also note what is done with the information. Is this formally recorded or just noted by the English teacher?

But before the process of assessment can start in your secondary English classroom, what kind of information do you have on each pupil before planning a lesson? Remember that you are not starting from scratch with a pupil; you are building on previous learning. At the beginning of a school year, you will be given a series of data that will tell you much about your pupils. This information needs to be incorporated into any lesson or medium-term planning.

This example of a Year 7 *Macbeth* class (Figure 5.1) relates to a loosely grouped, mixed-ability class, having attained levels 3 to 5 in KS2 SATs. Broadly, such an ability range suggests a level 3 pupil would need extra support with structuring writing, spelling, use of language and accessing texts, while a level 5 would need further stimulus with incorporating complex sentences, more sophisticated use of paragraphing and just having the extra guidance in boosting confidence when exploring reading and writing. You, as an English teacher, would be given the following:

- KS2 English SATs scores. Summative end of KS2 tests. These are marked externally. A general level would have been awarded, though there will be specific scores for reading, writing and spelling available.
- Social and gender split of the class.
- Teacher assessment level of each pupil. The teacher assessment level has usually been discussed and awarded based on the teacher's ongoing knowledge of the pupil throughout the academic year.
- Separate spelling and reading age scores from the primary school.
- Any need for an Individual Education Plan (IEP) that has identified a problem with acquiring an English skill. An IEP may be specific to the subject or more cross-curricular. If a pupil has a specifically identified English skill problem, then the pupil might have an allocated subject-specific learning support assistant to help;
- Information regarding any necessary provision for pupils with little or no English; the pupil's needs should be identified at the beginning of an academic year. This may include ongoing liaison with the local authority;
- Transition Unit information (DfES, 2001). It was highly recommended that both primary schools and secondary English departments transfer an exemplar body of work. The primary school would complete the DfES[1] written Transition Units then the written work would be transferred

---

[1] DfES is now the Department for Children, Family and Schools. The change of status is to reflect the importance of *Every Child Matters* (DfES, 2004).

Example of a Shakespeare Lesson with suggested Assessment strategies

This lesson has been chosen as a typical example of what might be taught and assessed in the English classroom. The lesson is a speaking and listening lesson using drama techniques. Typically the lesson includes little formal writing and so this lesson begs the question whether this type of lesson is as valid, or indeed tells us as much about a pupil's understanding and general ability. The lesson plan also highlights that there is a lot of information produced on each child in an English lesson, but where does that information go? How is the information recorded?

For simplicity, the lesson plan has been divided into three columns demonstrating teacher input, pupil activity and how the pupil activity is assessed. This lesson shows largely formative assessment strategies and how these formative assessment strategies can be built on in order for a teacher to make a summative assessment of a pupil's ability.
(A detailed breakdown of the SATs paper is discussed in Chapter 8).
The emphasis of this lesson shown is on assessment only.

Outline of the lesson:

Year 7:
Second Set, ability range from levels 3 to 5.
Aim of Scheme of Work:
Introducing a Tragic Shakespearian Character and Mapping His Downfall. The whole scheme of work would be a six week introduction to types of Shakespeare plays, Comic, Tragic and Historical. Edited scenes will be used from various plays.
Using *Macbeth*, Act 1, scene 3.

References to the National Framework:
Reading 7, 8; **Speaking and Listening** 6; **Author's Craft**, 12, 14, 18.

Learning objectives:
- To revise the basic narrative storyline of what happens to Macbeth;
- To discuss Macbeth's experiences when meeting with the witches for the first time;
- To begin to explore what Macbeth might feel as he begins to become more powerful.

Lesson Outcomes:
Pupils will have:
- Arranged the basic outline of the *Macbeth* plot-line
- Explored Macbeth's possible feelings by discussing a series of contrasting video clips
- Explored through question and answer role play, Macbeth's feelings whilst on the Heath.
- Through using Forum Theatre techniques, be able to offer Macbeth advice on his future success.

Figure 5.1   Example of a Shakespeare Lesson with suggested Assessment strategies

Figure 5.1 (Continued)

Transcript

T: This is a simple lesson that should demonstrate how to use some elements of formative assessment. The pupils will have done some level of Shakespeare before. My aim is not to concentrate at this stage on the language, merely to get the pupils involved and to think that Shakespeare did create complex characters. Over the next two lessons I will introduce the idea of tragic hero, but I want them to think that Macbeth did have other alternatives open to him. I want the pupils to be able to empathise with how Macbeth is in a dilemma and that any decision he makes is not an easy one. Should Macbeth be classed as evil?

T: With regards to assessment, you can see that there are a variety of techniques used. It is knowing your class and really putting each pupil in a position that they can really build on their learning. Sometimes you can hear a "click" and you know that something has finally dropped into place. It is then maintaining and building on that knowledge. Still as a teacher, I find that one of the hardest things to do in a lesson. There seems to be so much pupil interaction/information that a teacher wastes in the classroom. How do I record that one pupil has contributed and again how do I gauge the quality and amount?

Teacher Activity	Pupil Activity	Assessment Strategies Formative Assessment Strategies:
Starter: 5 mins Using Interactive White Board, recap on *Macbeth* plot line. Plot statements are arranged ad hoc on the white board.	Teacher targeted pupils to rearrange by dragging plot statements into correct order.	• Targeted teacher questioning. The choice will depend on who the teacher wishes to see interact. Targeted questioning is a definite way to show that the teacher is including all pupils.
Recap on relationship between Macbeth and Banquo. Character statements on Interactive White Board to be sorted into correct column labelled Macbeth and Banquo	Teacher targeted pupils to rearrange by dragging character statements into correct column	• Targeted pupils for activities, also uses the appropriate information/use of statistics that the teacher will have on the class.
2 mins	Individually, each pupil to think of two further statements about each character. Feedback to your pair.	• Individual monitoring while the teacher walks around the class. This is completed continually during a lesson.
Development: 15 mins Setting The Scene: Act 1, scene 3.		• Peer sharing. Teacher can also make judgements whilst listening to the sharing of the learning taking place

(Continued)

Figure 5.1 (Continued)

Activity	Detail	Notes
Using two five min(s) contrasting clips of Macbeth crossing the Heath, pupils to focus on the atmosphere and how Macbeth would have felt after the battle and seeing the Heath and 3 weird sisters for the first time	On handout, pupils to write down their first impressions of how Macbeth might be feeling. (Handout will have comprised of small boxes, enough space for words or phrases to be written down)	• Individual monitoring. These handouts can be stuck into exercise books for future revision.
Each clip may need further showing or explanation on the focus. Teacher to focus or simulate an example by stilling on facial expressions and the atmosphere of the Heath.	Select three pupils to feedback. Teacher and pupils to comment on the first impressions.	• Teacher has planned selectively for specific pupil contribution at this stage.
Possible Questions: 1. Look at the dawn breaking, how does the mist make you feel? 2. What impression do you have of Macbeth? 3. What do you think that Macbeth feels seeing the 3 weird sisters?		
10 mins **Using Interactive White Board. Teacher To Model Selection of Language** Using entrance of Macbeth and Banquo to Witches vanish Act 1, scene 3. Pay attention to the: • Atmosphere; • Tone of voice eg desperation/ordering? • Use of questions.	Targeted pupils to underline on Interactive White Board possible emotive words, phrases that show Macbeth is unsure of himself. For example, *So foul and fair a day I have not seen* and *stay you imperfect speakers.*	• Teacher has planned selectively for specific pupil contribution at this stage. Specific selection and praise go hand in hand here.
Further Development: 10 mins Role Play: What do you want to know most? Teacher to Model Role Play	Pupils to be split into pairs, one pupil to play Macbeth and the other to ask questions. Pupils to be given 5 mins and then swop roles.	• Pair work could be ability arranged, more able with less able. Again teacher to select appropriate pairs to feedback to the class. Pupils may

Figure 5.1 (Continued)

Teacher to choose one pupil. (The pupil may have been primed prior to the lesson) Teacher to play Macbeth, pupil to ask two questions where the Teacher answers in role. Questions should explore how Macbeth feels at this stage and what he should consider doing. **Plenary 10 mins** General Session What have the Pupils Learnt this lesson about Macbeth? Teacher to ask generally who thinks Is Macbeth good or bad at this stage? Who really is at fault? If Macbeth was given a second chance, what might he have done differently?	Teacher to select 2 pairs to demonstrate their understanding of Macbeth. Pupils' comments on the types of questions that have been asked of Macbeth? Pupils to recap using one of the film clips again. Teacher to pause film clip appropriately: • How else could Macbeth have reacted to the scene? • What about Banquo? • How could this have changed the direction of Macbeth's life?	find it useful to write the questions down for future reference. • Opportunity for peer assessment as the pupils will feedback positively on other pupils' contributions. • Whole class assessment. Teacher to target those who have not contributed or to stretch the more able.

Where the lesson feeds into the next lesson.

Learning objectives:
• To be able to explore and consolidate how Macbeth felt when the three weird sisters disappeared;
• To be able to comment on the mood of the Heath;
• To be able to explore Macbeth's possible relationship with his wife;
• To be able to use the formal structures of a letter showing how Macbeth might address his wife.

Possible Activities For the Second Lesson:

Intro:
• Creating an image of Lady Macbeth, matching up the statements to predict what her reaction might be to Macbeth's letter;
• Revising the letter format and looking at possible language a husband might use to his wife. To explore the possible affectionate language that Macbeth might use towards his wife. Would Macbeth being a soldier affect the language used?

Development:
• Demonstrating and creating a writing frame for Macbeth's letter to his wife on the Interactive White Board;

(Continued)

Figure 5.1   (Continued)

- Evaluating what kind of writing frame would more useful to the whole class; pairs to come up with their own writing frame;
- Individually writing the letter using the writing frame

Plenary:

- Exchanging the letters in pairs to peer assess the language and information in Macbeth's letter. For pupils to assign two targets on the end of each letter.
- Teacher to assess the letters and to assign targets and if appropriate a level.

Transcript: (Figure 5.1a)
Teacher Reflection:

After teaching the two lessons, the English teacher was asked whether the learning objectives of the lesson had been met and more importantly, whether the English teacher had learnt more about the pupils' abilities.

Interviewer: How might the assessment have been done better?

T: I said at the beginning of the lesson(s) that the hardest thing really is to keep in mind all of the pupils' abilities. The lesson plan clearly indicates how I assessed the various activities, but there are still pupils in that classroom that I did not speak to personally. I know that they
were engaged with the activities as I walked around the room, but I couldn't feedback positively to all.

I think that the hardest part of the lesson was looking at the language and monitoring whether they had understood Macbeth and
why he reacted as he did. It is the ability to be able to look at a word or a phrase and comment on how that word reflects Macbeth's
feelings or his personality. I only selected those pupils that I know might have had difficulty so that I could gauge whether they had
understood it. The problem seems to me not being able to spend enough time to make sure that all have got the objective.

Interviewer: How might the next lesson be adapted?

Teacher: I am trying to train the pupils to share their work. It is hard in Year 7 at times to train the pupils to share their work because they do not
know each other and may not be in the same class for all of their lessons. The peer assessment takes some time to use successfully,
though it really focuses them on what they are supposed to be learning. Ideally I need a Classroom Support Assistant because I do need
to target the language aspect of the lesson. I need to know how much the less able can glean from the scene and then spend some time
consolidating. Modelling from the front goes some way to demonstrating the knowledge as does spending time with the less able pupils,
but there is not enough of me. I need to know how I can help a pupil progress.

That certainly becomes easier the more you know the class.

Interviewer: Does the pupil perform better in a lesson such as this, compared to a lesson with copious writing?

Teacher: Lesson 2 really consolidated lesson one and made the pupils really think about what Macbeth was feeling and going to do next. I
am not sure that the piece produced was the best example. It did not develop the feel of the Heath or indeed, Macbeth as a soldier.
Certainly the oral responses were at least a quarter of a level better than the written letter response. The letter needs to be
redrafted by using the given targets

to the English department for completion. The DfES premise was that every pupil would have the same starting point in the English classroom. More importantly, each pupil would transfer an exemplar portfolio of English written work that the secondary English teacher could refer to and add to;

- Predicted levels for the end of KS3 and predicted grades for the end of KS4. These are unlikely to change throughout the pupil's school career. These predicted grades give an indication of how each pupil is expected to perform and what each English teacher should do so that the pupil can achieve those predicted outcomes.

And how important is all this information to you? Extremely important! All of the above information is vital so that you do not allow the pupil to regress once they have begun a new key stage. The worst thing that you can do is allow pupils to plateau and stagnate in their learning. You must always provide a fresh challenge in each lesson.

FORMATIVE ASSESSMENT STRATEGIES: MANAGING LEARNING

Oral feedback

The KS3 Year 7 lesson demonstrates where oral assessment has been continually used:

- targeted teacher questions and answers
- targeted pair feedback with expert
- pair peer assessment
- whole-class discussion with more use of general questions to assess overall class learning.

T:	(pupil's name) you are the spokesperson for your pair. What have you decided that Macbeth might feel when he sees the three weird women on the heath?
Pupil:	I would think that he is tired because of the battle that he has fought. We are not sure whether he would believe what he saw.
T:	Why not?
Pupil:	Because he is so tired and the heath would be misty in the morning. We even felt that it might be raining.
T:	Why raining?
Pupil:	Because what is going to happen is bad and it is early in the morning. Dunno really.
T:	Good (pupil's name) you have the right idea, but have you thought …? Can anyone else help?

Figure 5.2   Transcript

Oral feedback is probably the most commonly used form of assessment in the English classroom. You will find that it is the most regular and interactive form of feedback because it is the most immediate. You will know immediately who is responding and who has not understood a main concept. The Qualifications and Curriculum Authority (QCA, 2005), for example, advocates direct oral feedback is more 'effective than written feedback because it is a natural dialogue and provides a genuine response' (2005: 3). Your feedback should always be constructive and positive and will be particularly effective in motivating boys in the English classroom. For example the transcript in Figure 5.2 demonstrates how the English trainee and Year 7 male pupil interacted.

First, the pupil–teacher interaction shows that they have both built up a trusting relationship, though the targeted pupil is unable to develop beyond the pair discussion. The pupil shows that his pair has completed the task, but not applied further thought. Here the teacher knows immediately how to extend the pair's thoughts by asking other pupils to enter the discussion. However, the question could be too general and the teacher may have to specifically rephrase or ask another person. Initially, who the teacher asked had been planned into the lesson's structure; however, in asking for others to contribute, the oral feedback has now become more spontaneous.

What the transcript does not show is that the teacher also paused for effect, or allowed what Clarke (2005) describes as 'waiting time'. Clarke suggests that 'waiting time' is the best way to make sure that the pupil is comfortable with what is being asked of him/her. Importantly, the pupils are given time to reflect independently, to think and formulate ideas before being asked to answer. The teacher may want to too readily 'fill the gap', thus indirectly making pupils feel that they have not given the 'correct' answer. Notably, the teacher has used praise to encourage, but then asks, 'Have you thought?' Such a response can be interpreted in two ways: first, that the teacher wants the child to take a risk, or secondly, that the teacher wants to encourage others to build on the discussion. According to Clarke (2005), the ideal oral feedback is from teacher to pupil, pupil to pupil to teacher.

Use of questions

Questioning should enable some of the following to occur in an English classroom, to:

- recall information
- develop empathy and to perhaps hypothesize and problem solve
- aid pupils' externalizing and verbalizing
- help pupils expand and elaborate their ideas
- help pupils either to link or to apply further ideas, give reasons, summarize or evaluate
- allow the pupils a chance to ask themselves further questions to qualify what the question is actually asking them to explain
- stimulate pupils' imaginations
- allow for pupil differentiation in their responses
- change the direction of a discussion.

The teacher's questions (Figure 5.3) really show two problems. First, the first question is too general. If given a choice, then the same pupils will always respond. Worse still, the pupils may not offer an answer, so the teacher is forced to rephrase the question. The teacher learns effectively nothing about the understanding of most of the pupils. Secondly, the teacher will always end up asking the same pupils or the question will become rhetorical. Asking three questions in quick succession also does not allow the pupil a chance to think and respond or allow the pupil to give a range of differentiated answers. Importantly, however, the transcript shows that the teacher has to be prepared to change the wording or the emphasis of the question. The emphasis on 'how' and 'why' show that the teacher is trying to adapt the questioning and really move away from the narrative plot line. The teacher is trying to make the pupils empathize with the characters and understand why Macbeth is silent through this initial meeting. What the transcript does not explicitly show is how the teacher implicitly prompts or encourages the pupil to answer by using body language (DfES, 2005b)

> T: What do you feel that Macbeth thinks after the three sisters have declared that Macbeth will become King of Scotland? He demands them to stay 'you imperfect speakers'.

Similarly with this question, the teacher demonstrates that Macbeth's mood has suddenly changed and perhaps is more dominant again as he commands them to stay. For the first time in this scene, the emphasis clearly shows Macbeth's frustration. However, the teacher again might have to rephrase the question, because she has led the pupils to the answer by using the word 'demand'. The teacher is trying to get the class to empathize with Macbeth and perhaps spot why he starts to change. For you, it is often very helpful to write down questions so that the right emphasis can be made. Or if a pupil strays from the point, having the questions already there as prompts can help any pupil–teacher dialogue to get back on track.

The key question for you is where does all this information go in an English classroom? How does the teacher record an individual pupil's verbal output and indeed can the quality of the verbal output compare to written output? Who is the best judge and how do you moderate a verbal outcome? Have you therefore enabled all pupils to engage and fulfil their potential in that lesson? Wragg (2004) also raises the point of how feedback in a classroom can remain unbiased. Seating positions, behaviour or merely not knowing the pupil may affect any verbal response you might give. Wragg questions how a teacher can gauge whether the pupil has benefited from the teacher intervention. In many ways, these are impossible questions for you to answer. However, in continually asking these questions, you should make your practice far more reflective about what is happening in your classroom.

Ironically, these decisions that are made throughout a lesson might be more spontaneous than planned. Unless the discussion is going to be assessed for speaking and listening, then such classroom discussion is probably consolidated by written understanding. For example, the next lesson in the scheme of work will consolidate the pupils' understanding of Macbeth's feelings, by setting the task of writing to Lady Macbeth after he has seen and heard the three weird sisters' predictions.

It is very easy to have a departmental system to record formal speaking and listening activities. These records may take the form of an A4 sheet per pupil with key speaking and listening objectives matched to the planned pupil activities. At the end of a formal speaking and listening activity, it may be a combination of the pupil and teacher who assess what the pupil has achieved. This may simply be by highlighting the appropriate speaking and listening assessment objective, or by the teacher and pupil writing more formal comments against the assessment objective.

Nevertheless, such a recording system does not account for the immediate feedback that takes place continually in an English classroom. More realistically, you would be mentally noting what your pupil has understood and build on their knowledge by adapting the lesson accordingly, or change the next lesson's emphasis. This is why targeted questioning plays such an important role in the English classroom. Targeted questioning works best where you have already planned the questions and know which pupils you want to answer the question.

The lesson transcript in Figure 5.3 does not show a thorough, effective use of targeted questioning. The questions are at first deliberately wide-ranging, to enable the English teacher to initiate some thoughts about how Macbeth is feeling. However, once this has been achieved, the ideal is for the English teacher to specifically start asking individual pupils. For example, see Figure 5.4.

The use of the pupil's name definitely personalizes the pupil–teacher exchange and the pupil is also forced out of the comfort zone by having to think beyond what is obvious. By targeting this pupil, the teacher has also demonstrated that the pupil has understood the basic premise of the objective and is beginning to apply understanding. The teacher can now build on that knowledge and plan for extension activities where appropriate. Indeed, the exemplar lesson plan does indicate where the teacher has targeted the pupils through the activities.

The section of the lesson that focuses on the language when Macbeth and Banquo first encounter the three weird sisters:

T: How do you think Macbeth would say the words, 'speak if you can: what are you?' Just imagine your reaction. Would anyone like to come and underline the words on the board and perhaps put a staging note by the side?

(The same hands appeared. The teacher made a decision to specifically ask the same question to another pupil who had not offered an answer.)

T: Why does Macbeth ask 'what are you?' He has Banquo there to ask? Why does he allow Banquo to take the lead?

Figure 5.3   Transcript

T: Good answer, (pupil's name). But why does Macbeth still disbelieve the three weird sisters, when he uses the words, 'Say from whence you owe this strange intelligence? Or why?'
Pupil: Is it too good to be true?
T: How do you mean (pupil's name)?
Pupil: Well, he has just fought a battle, and someone says that he is going to be Thane of Cawdor, when he knows that the Thane of Cawdor is still alive. I wouldn't believe them. It is like a joke.
T: So why do you think that he finally does believe them, (pupil's name)?

Figure 5.4   Transcript

Peer/self Assessment

According to Clarke (2005), pupil peer and self assessment are the way forward. Using peer and self assessment strategies is just another way to continue the pupil–teacher dialogue of how to improve. Importantly, peer and self assessment also focuses the pupil directly onto the learning objective. Just as oral feedback provides a pupil with an immediate response, so does peer and self assessment. The key is to share learning and assessment objectives all the time. The *Macbeth* Year 7 lesson, for example, uses peer assessment at the end of the lesson to draw the strands together. While completing the role play, the pupils will have the focus for the activity and be able to judge if each pair has understood Macbeth's character. Perhaps, after formally focusing their thoughts, the pupils are asked for their opinions, so that the pupils can offer suggestions on how others can improve.

Importantly, the sharing process should be an integral part of teacher planning. The brief outline of the second Year 7 *Macbeth* lesson indicates that the assessment will be far more formal because the pupils are writing a letter from Macbeth to Lady Macbeth, recording what he has felt and seen on the Heath. Instead of you immediately marking the pupils' work and feeding back to them, the class could be split up into pairs and exchange their letters. Each pupil would have the assessment focus linking back to the learning objectives; hence, pupils would be able to make a judgement on their partners. The same applies to self assessment. Pupils would be able to make a judgement on their own work and be able to come up with some strategies for progress in their next piece of work.

However, the use of peer assessment may sound easy to use in the English classroom, but pupils need to be taught the value of collaboration in peer assessment. Pupils need to see that peer assessment has to be positive and you have to engender a positive atmosphere. Pupils need to be taught that they can become more independent learners because they know what they are looking for – more independent, therefore, certainly more motivated. It is up to you to consistently encourage pupils' self-reflection, so that the pupils can take responsibility for their next steps.

In the same way that peer assessment needs to be practised with the pupils, so does target-setting. After reading through this transcript, it would be easy for you to plan additional time for individualized target-setting. Target-setting can be simply defined as pupils and teachers mutually setting targets, which takes the pupil onto the next stage of their learning. With practice, ideally the pupil will be able to set their own learning targets by identifying their individualized needs. Indeed, the whole emphasis is on how formative assessment can inform not only you, but the pupil.

Points for reflection

- How can you, as a trainee, build a positive sharing atmosphere so that peer and self assessment can operate?
- How far can you gauge that peer and self assessment does focus and put pupils in charge of their own learning?
- How far does the pupil know how to set their own targets and learn from them?

WHERE DOES WRITTEN FEEDBACK FIT IN?

Written feedback is part of the formative assessment procedure and can be summative too. However, only in recent years have English teachers learnt that marking books each week does not always highlight a pupil's progress or indeed measure achievement (Henry, 2002). At first you will love marking books; but you have to learn to mark for a purpose – as a reinforcement of the taught learning objectives and not as proof of marking spellings and sentence structure. Once the pupil can see what is supposed to be learnt, practised and therefore understood and applied, then written marking is part of a natural cycle of learning.

Preparation for marking: setting pupil-friendly objectives

The key to marking is having pupil-friendly, broken down, focused learning objectives. Clarke (2005) maintains that it is crucial that all pupils need to know how those learning objectives will be assessed. All pupils need to have well-defined processes of formative assessment otherwise a pupil will become disheartened. Equally, when you share the simple assessment learning objectives, such sharing helps encourage 'consistent pupil esteem' (McCallum, in Black and Wiliam, 1998: 8). Nevertheless, the main question you have to ask is whether written feedback is useful? Or do pupils revert to just looking for the grades or the mistakes? Black, in 'Beyond the black box' (Black and Wiliam, 1999), argues that teachers still have a tendency to assess/mark for quantity and presentation of work and pupils still look for grades or good comments.

For example, the pupil-friendly learning objectives on the Year 7 lesson plan, (Figure 5.1) assesses two clear principles. First, that the pupils do know the plot line of *Macbeth*; and second, that the pupils are beginning to question and explore why Macbeth becomes the man he does in the play. The pupils will have been introduced to these objectives at the beginning of the lesson and, through both teacher guidance and pupil activity, these learning objectives would have been reinforced: see the English teacher's transcript that critiques whether she felt that the learning objectives had provided enough focus (Figure 5.2).

Implications

Any written feedback that you give is arguably a crucial response for the pupil. Pupils do expect some sort of mark, though it is up to you to make that 'marking' as relevant as possible. It is also crucial for you to return the marking as quickly as possible, otherwise the pupil has forgotten the point of the writing task (Tanner and Jones, 2003). For example, it may take over a week for you to return 33 marked and targeted essays. Undoubtedly, the English teacher has carried out this role, but it is questionable as to its relevance, especially when the pupil may have forgotten the purpose of the task. From an English teacher's point of view, 'prompt marking can identify errors before they become engrained through use' (Tanner, 2003: 63).

Butler suggests that 'teacher comments have not been specific enough' (in Clarke, 2005: 45). Certainly, with English teachers it is very easy to write copious amounts or to use private shorthand without providing a structure for improvement. Comments such a 'good effort' or 'you need to look at your spelling' really do not help focus pupil understanding or indeed focus where the pupil should be looking to improve. The English teacher's comment should be giving an example of a spelling that is continually spelt incorrectly. Perhaps it is just one syllable of the spelling that the pupil is writing wrongly. For example, if the pupil is writing a key word by mistake such as 'emosion' then the teacher should target the 'tion' part of the word.

Effective marking should directly address the pupil and specifically bullet point one or two targets for improvement. If you swamp the pupil with too many specific targets then this will also defeat the purpose. Pupils must recognize that 'written feedback is part of the pupil/teacher dialogue' (Butler, in Black et al., 2003: 48). You must also realize that time has to be built into a lesson so that 'marked' work can be seen to be relevant. Using the written piece as a basis for a 10-minute lesson starter might be one way to incorporate marked work into a lesson structure (look at Sarah's lesson for an example of this). Such time would help promote better understanding and certainly engage pupil interaction and self-reflection.

A TYPICAL EXAMPLE OF A YEAR 7 PUPIL'S WRITING

Consolidation in Lesson Two

The letter (Figure 5.5) is a formal consolidation of the KS3 *Macbeth* lesson (Figure 5.1). Not only does the purpose of the letter predict Macbeth's relationship with his wife in Act One, but the letter also reinforces the events on the Heath.

What to mark?

This piece of Year 7 written work (Figure 5.5) is part of the formative teacher assessment. For a short piece of writing, you would have no intention of levelling, though for your purpose

---

Levelled and comments based on the learning objectives:

Learning objectives:
   To be able to explore and consolidate how Macbeth felt when the three weird sisters disappeared;
   To be able to comment on the mood of the Heath;
   To be able to explore Macbeth's possible relationship with his wife;

Learning outcomes:
   To be able to use the formal structures of a letter showing how Macbeth might address his wife.

Dear Wife,

I hope you are well. The battle was hard and I am sorry that I did not write to you before.
I need to tell you about the three witches that we met they was horrible, dressed in some old clothes and they smelt awful like rotting meat. I did not believe my eyes at first. Banquo was the same. The bit of ground was like a heath with nothing on it, it was also misty and the mist was rising off the ground. I couldn't see. They were singing saying things that I did not understand. Banquo got quite cross and I tried to calm him and even I got frustrated.

Do you know what they said to me. That I would be King of Scotland. Do you want to be married to a king I know you do not like me being away at war so much. I have forgotten what you look like. They just disappeared leaving us standing there. What do you think it means?
I am really writing to you so that you know what is going on. We should be home soon.

All my love,

Macbeth.

Figure 5.5   Example of Key Stage 3, Year 7: Macbeth's letter to Lady Macbeth

here, an overall level will be assigned. The question is whether you would merely mark the objectives or correct the sentence structure and use of vocabulary, too. Clearly, the layout of the letter is basically correct, as is its tone. The pupil has understood how Macbeth should address his own wife. This would be an excellent example for peer assessment. The piece of writing is brief and can easily be given two or three targets for improvement. Below are listed the typical kinds of feedback that you might want to give the pupil.

Positive points

- The pupil has knowledge of paragraphing, though this is not used consistently.
- The use of the letter format and how Macbeth addresses his wife.
- Knowledge of the three weird sisters' scene and some indication of what Macbeth felt at the time.
- Indication/prediction of Macbeth's relationship with his wife in Act One. There is an implication that he wants her advice, but does not know how to ask for it.
- Some sense of how the mood of the scene might have affected Macbeth's judgement.

Pupil targets for improvement related to the learning objectives

- More detail about the three weird sisters. You mention smell and clothing, but not what they were doing or perhaps why they were there.
- Get the sense of the Heath, but a better physical description could have been added. For example, the ground, how the mist was swirling and so on.
- How do you feel Banquo felt? What is your relationship with Banquo?

Overall accuracy comments

- Paragraphing: for example, the letter could have described the three sisters and then moved on to some sentences describing the mood of the Heath.
- Full stops: use of full stops needs to be reinforced in a starter, demonstrating that there has to be capital letter and full stop at the end of a sentence and a sentence should be able to stand alone to make sense.
- Overall length: to be levelled, the letter should be longer to give a more sustained demonstration of the pupil's skills.

According to the English National Curriculum (QCA, 2000/DCFS, 2008), this piece of writing would attain a solid level 4. The basics are there, but to attain a level 5, more con-sistent use of complex sentences, for example, use of commas, extension of ideas and more definitive use of paragraphing would be necessary. Obviously there are gradations within assigning a level to a piece of work. In this example, the pupil would be moving towards a top level 4, or, as some English departments differentiate, a level 4a. Ironically, in giving such specific pupil targets does assigning such a general level tell the English teacher any more?

Points for reflection

- When you have begun to mark pupils' work, make sure that you know what you are marking for.
- Have you begun to personalize your learning targets so that pupils feel that you have considered their individual work?
- How are you wording pupils' targets? Are you being specific enough?

RESPONSE TO MULTICULTURAL PAPER

Lesson plan Year 10

Similarly, this KS4 response to the Multicultural examination Paper Two demonstrates how a lesson's discussion can be consolidated (refer to Figure 5.6). The KS4 response has deliberately had little preparation, so that the pupils can see that they need to know how to be taught the structure of the examination. Please note that the examination requires pupils to compare two poems. As this example is a first attempt at answering the question, the comparison requirement has not been introduced (for further reference to GCSE poetry, see Chapter 7).

What to mark?

What you have to notice, with this piece of Year 10 work, is that it is clearly unstructured and really lacks focus. In short, it does not answer the question. Certainly, it responds to the discussion in the first lesson and the pupil has knowledge of what Achebe is trying to achieve in the poem. But the answer needs to be honed to demonstrate skills in an appropriate examination format. This would be an excellent starting point for a pupil to unpick what the examination requires to achieve a grade C.

Also note that the pupils have the clear learning objectives, but they also need to be given a pupil-friendly version of the GCSE mark scheme. Pupils need to see what will achieve a grade C or what will allow them to improve to the next grade. In this case the starting point is as listed below.

Positive points

- The pupil has knowledge of the poem and can articulate what the basis of the poem is about. The pupil has understood the analogy to the German Commandant and the importance of the vultures.
- The response shows some sort of essay structure and really does focus on the question in the first sentence. There is a clear indication of knowing what the first paragraph does for the essay.
- There is some level of personal engagement in the essay with the phrase 'I like'. This shows that the pupil has moved away from perhaps your opinion as a teacher and has really engaged with the poem.
- There is some level of formality in the language; the style also addresses the audience.

Here are the learning objectives for the Multicultural Year 10 lesson. These learning objectives are very specific relating to the details of the poem.

To identify and explain the poet's use of the metaphor of the 'vulture'. L01
How the use of the 'vulture' relates to the other examples used in the poem. L02
How the poetic structure of the two poems enhances the meanings of the poems. For example, enjamb-ment, use of metaphor, ellipsis, rhetoric. L03
How the poet(s) see their own identity and how that identity changes according to the humanity of the society they live in. L04
Compare how the poets reveal their feelings by writing a formal response showing the pupils' under-standing. (Completed for homework). L05
Give a working definition of 'culture' and 'identity'. L06
Comment on the effectiveness of the use of metaphor. L07

Question:
Write down your understanding of the word 'culture' and explain Achebe's purpose in 'Vultures'. Use quotations to support your answer.

Edited Part of a Year 10's Answer to the Mock Question:
The word 'culture' to me really means that we are different. Living in the North is different from living in the South and all regions seem to have things that are typical of the region. For the North it is mushy peas and Manchester United, while in the South, it is posh houses and accents. I have never been further than London.

'Vultures' by C. Achebe seems to suggest that we are all different people. And that we have different things that make up our own personalities. He uses a German Commandant of a concentration camp to show that people are not all bad. They just do things that look bad. Does that make us look bad on the surface. One minute, the German Commandant is killing loads of Jews and the next minute he is going home to his daughter. She does not know what he has been doing that day and doesn't judge him. The same thing is with the vultures. Achebe uses the images of the vultures to show that an ugly thing too has feelings. I like the sense that the vultures are just sitting there waiting, but really somebody loves them. Did you know that the vulture urinates down its legs after feeding to really clean itself.

The poem is written interestingly, but I found it difficult to get into at first. I have never seen a vulture. There is no punctuation and the lines run into each other. That makes it difficult to read, but the second part of the poem is almost like a summary. Achebe is making a point …

Figure 5.6   Learning objectives for multicultural Year 10 lesson

Pupil targets for improvement and progress (to achieve a potential grade C)

- Use of quotations. The rest of the response resorted to narrative explanation. The pupil needs to be able to use quotations appropriately and make them an integral part of the sentence.
- Needs to build on the structure of the essay and make references to examples less sweeping.
- Needs to have a consistent sense of addressing audience and really examine the author's purpose.
- Sustained response throughout the answer. There is evidence that the response is begining to fizzle by the end.
- Definite examples/modelling of how to structure an essay and comment on the language and literary devices that the poet uses. There is almost no comment.
- Commenting on the use of language.

- Introduction – comparing two poems. The emphasis of the exam paper is comparison and how this comparison is structured in the essay. For a grade C, the level of comparison in the essay has to be consistent.
- Importantly, developing personal responses to the poem. Regurgitating the English teacher's personal understanding is not the point of the exam.

At this stage of marking, it would be vital to only give one or two areas for improvement; but as a teacher, you would have made a more in-depth analysis as to the pupils' needs.

IMPORTANCE OF LEVELLING/GRADING

In your classroom, you have to enable your pupils to realize that day-to-day grading of a piece of writing means that it is a summative assessment of their ability; a level or a grade at this stage merely adds to the wider picture of what a pupil might be capable of achieving. The level or grade in itself does not tell you what you want to know. Specifically, analysing and setting targets does. A level or grade only gives you a general idea.

Some pieces of written work will not be graded. Certainly, by giving specific targets as to how a pupil can improve, the pupil will be more focused in how those targets can help to achieve a specific level or grade the next time. It is all about giving the pupils confidence. The question is, does the emphasis of the level or grade detract from the written targets? Indeed, Petty (2000) argues that grading does detract from written comments. Consistently giving low grades can be seen to demotivate low attainers and make high attainers more complacent.

Points for reflection

- When you have levelled or graded a pupil's work, analyse how that pupil reacted to your marking. Did your pupil look at your targets and generally feel rewarded or did your marking demotivate the pupil?
- Interesting to note whether your pupil did realize what their piece of work was being marked for. Was your marking sufficiently linked back to the learning objectives?

Importantly, it is also interesting for you to question who moderates the quality of your day-to-day marking. Who is to say that your – or indeed any English teacher's – judgement is correct? Arguably, English as a subject can be particularly subjective, so one English teacher may be perceived harder at grading, while others may seem more lenient. Unless there is a rigorous underpinning of levelling and grading within an English department, assigning levels and grades debatably has little use. My advice is for you to make sure that your departmental buddy or assigned mentor sees a range of your marking at whatever key stage.

On a wider scale, there should be some level of cross-school moderation, so that a pupil experiences the same quality of marking and 'marking language' in all subjects. Levelling and grading merely provide a simplified overview of a pupil's achievement. Indeed, Clarke (2005) has gone one stage further by suggesting 'that giving grades merely focuses the pupil on what they haven't achieved, compared to others in the class' (2005: 69). Nonetheless, levelling and grading a piece of written work provides a secure written record for the English teacher of how a pupil has progressed.

ASSESSING PUPILS' PROGRESS DOCUMENT

One of the most important formative assessment documents is *Assessing Pupils' Progress* or APP (DfES, 2005b). This document has enabled English departments and pupils to hone and reflect on their understanding of what they are being assessed on. Arguably assessment is the key backbone of the 2007 National Curriculum. Hence, *The Handbook for Assessing Pupils' Progress* of 24 tasks enables you to focus on and track more closely your pupils' progress in reading and writing throughout KS3. The 12 reading tasks offer a range of fiction, non-fiction stimulus, while the 12 writing tasks cover all aspects of the four writing triplets. For example, if a National Curriculum level does not specifically diagnose how a pupil needs to progress to the next level, then the APP document *does* suggest how a pupil can progress. Importantly, the diagnosis also allows you to track each individual pupil's performance at least once per half term. Significantly, APP enables you to be able to analyse and focus on pupils' strengths and areas on which the pupil needs to improve. You are also able to set mutual targets with your pupils and to involve them in their own learning.

The *Assessing Pupils' Progress* document (DfES, 2005b) focuses on EN2 Reading and EN3 Writing. The assessment focuses are as follows:

EN2 Reading

AF1 — Use a range of strategies, including accurate decoding of text, to read for meaning.
AF2 — Understand, describe, select or retrieve information, events or ideas from texts and use quotation and reference to the text.
AF3 — Deduce, infer, or interpret information, events or ideas from texts.
AF4 — Identify and comment on the structure and organization of texts, including grammatical and presentational features at text level.
AF5 — Explain and comment on writers' use of language, including grammatical and literary features at word and sentence level.
AF6 — Identify and comment on writers' purposes and viewpoints, and the overall effect of the text on the reader.
AF7 — Relate texts to their social, cultural and historical contexts and literary heritage.

EN3 Writing

AF1 — Write imaginative, interesting and thoughtful texts.
AF2 — Produce texts which are appropriate to the task, reader and audience.
AF3 — Organize and present whole texts effectively, sequencing and structuring information, ideas and events.
AF4 — Construct paragraphs and use cohesion within and between paragraphs.
AF5 — Vary sentences for clarity, purpose and effect.
AF6 — Write with technical accuracy of syntax and punctuation in phrases, clauses and sentences.
AF7 — Select appropriate and effective vocabulary.
AF8 — Use correct spelling.

A typical reading fiction task would be:

Task outline:

This task requires pupils to read and respond to two extracts from H.G. Wells's *The Red Room* (1896). There is an emphasis on reading strategies as well as exemplar pupil responses to support and promote pupils' independent reading and response. The tasks aims to meet the two assessment focuses of 'infer and deduce meanings using evidence in the text, identifying where and how meanings are implied and secondly how writers convey meaning through word choice and sentence structure'. The task uses a variety of different questions; the first question is: 'The old man tells the young man how to get into the red room … There is a map – (diagram of the map shown in pupils' answer booklets) – complete it by filling in the missing labels'. (www.standards.dfes.} gov.uk/secondary/keystage3/repub/englishpubs/ass_eng/optional_ tasks, PDF download available).

Assessing Pupils' Progress has been seen as an essential progression in focusing pupils on and individualizing their own learning. The use of APP has been particularly successful for a number of reasons, but mostly because it links formative and summative assessment and therefore teachers have become more secure in how they level pupils' work and how they can advise pupils on how to progress to the next level. Crucially, the assessment focuses are so exact that it enables you to identify if a pupil is not progressing and in what area. Moreover, the *Assessing Pupils' Progress* document suggests that it is 'helpful to note where a pupil's level is "low" or "insecure"' (DfES, 2005b: 12). Hence the mark scheme for the assessment tasks divides the levels into 'sub levels' – usually noted as 'level a/b/c'. Once the level has been identified, you can intervene and provide the necessary specific support for the pupil.

However there are key implications for each English department. Each English department would need to allocate time for cross moderation so that the assessment focuses have been addressed and marked uniformly. The *Handbook for Assessing Pupils' Progress* (DfES, 2005b) also suggests that planning or 'schemes of work should not be assessment led … what pupils need to be taught must be the main consideration' (DfES, 2005b: 23). In short, APP material and assessment focuses is another strategy to be used in your wide repertoire of how do you assess whether your pupils are making progress. With the summative KS3 SATs no longer in place, for the forseeable future APP will become particularly crucial in moderating Teacher Assessment levels during and at the end of KS3.

Points for reflection

- How is APP applied in your department?
- List why the APP strategy is advantageous for you as a teacher and for your pupils.
- As a trainee teacher, how does the APP make you feel more secure in your judgement of a pupil's ability?
- How does the APP feed into pupil target setting?

SUMMATIVE ASSESSMENT: WHAT DOES IT MEAN?

This last section is a 'taster' to make you think. (How summative assessment is applied is examined at length in Chapter 7.)

So how do all the day-to-day formative assessment strategies feed into the end of a module or key stage? The ever looming presence of the summative KS3 SATs or assessment objectives of the GSCE papers does drive the requirements of day-to-day marking and what skills the pupils need to practise. Undoubtedly, the nature of the KS3 and KS4 summative assessments need to be prepared for. Chapter 7 also explores the new suggested changes in how KS3 SATs and teaching will be approached.

Point for reflection

- Note how far in advance, pupils are prepared for the summative assessment, for example, KS3 SATs and GCSE examinations; consider how pupils are taught skills, content and particularly format of the summative examinations.

Here, the argument for assessment becomes more controversial. It is important for you to realize that the nature and the format of the questions immediately divides the pupils' ability to attain. Those, for example, with perceived level 5/6/7 attainment ability would cope well with the style and format of what is unquestionably a 'middle class' summative assessment. The fact that at KS3 one paper has to cater for almost all abilities, levels 3 to 8 (although only identified as levels 4 to 7), does suggest that the format and language of the paper will cater for the middle ability. Wragg (2004) argues that an English exam paper will perhaps unconsciously put an emphasis on one word which a pupil from a particular social or ethnic background might not recognize or indeed appreciate its nuance. You have to ask yourself, is the end of the key stage testing skills or the ability to apply the system of assessment? In other words has 'real learning' taken place? Or does the end of a key stage level or grade tell us any more about the pupil?

You also have to question further. Wiliam (2001) raises the point about validity. If a pupil has achieved a level 5 at the end of the summative key stage, would the pupil then achieve that same level 5 after three months, or indeed be able to sit the same examination? Effectively, what does a level 5 mean when it comes to moving into KS4? Level 5 demonstrates that the pupil has achieved the average grade for a 14-year-old, so should be able to achieve the same average grade C at 16. Again, assigning levels and ultimately grades does assume that each pupil learns in a linear fashion – each pupil is able to attain, retain and build on his/her knowledge and skills.

Overall, some English departments would like to move away from the summative, definitive, examination result because at the end, pupils are continually reminded of their achievement and how that achievement is regarded. In his article, Clark (2005) insists that levels and grades merely compound failure and the words 'pass' or 'fail' should be banned from the classroom. Ironically, however positive a formative experience a pupil has had throughout the key stage, ultimately the level or grade will be deemed a pass or fail.

WHAT THE RESEARCH SUGGESTS

At the beginning of the chapter, I said that coming to terms with pupil assessment is perhaps the hardest part of teaching. This chapter has enabled you to ask yourself questions as to what and how you are doing in the English classroom.

Assessing a pupil's achievement must always act as a focus for the English teacher. The chapter has given a taste of an ideal of what should happen in the classroom and how you should always be aware of how and why pupils learn. You should also be aware that the notion of formative assessment is always evolving. Current government funding of £150 million over the next three years (2008–11) indicates that the government takes the issue of pupils' progression very seriously. Schools should be using formative assessment strategies to drive pupil progress. Indeed, the government funding is looking specifically at strengthening pupil tracking and identifying when to provide the appropriate support for intervention. Formative assessment will focus on tackling barriers to learning and closing the attainment gaps.

Indeed, the very fact that the government has raised the average end of KS3 pupil achievement to level 6 in 2009 suggests that they firmly believe in the formative assessment procedures that they are putting in place. The Making Good Progress pilots (2007) in 10 comprehensive schools (www.standards.dfes.gov.uk/secondary/keystage3/ advocates that standards are rising and that formative strategies adopted in English classrooms like the assessing pupils' progress tasks serve to make the teachers' judgements more secure and in line with the summative strategies used at the end of each key stage. Hence the introduction of KS3 single level tests from September 2009 (for further information see Chapter 7).

Consequently, you must always be prepared to engage the pupil, motivate the pupil and hence make sure that learning and progress have taken place. You must also be aware of what learning is taking place in your English classroom. Assessment is about taking note of pupils' potential and how you, as the English teacher, have to make provision for all pupils' potential. Importantly, it is crucial that you see not only formative assessment, but also summative assessment as one informative cycle. Both modes of assessment are intrinsic to each other and potentially enhance your methodology in the classroom.

Key points from this chapter

- The learning needs of the pupils needs to be paramount in the classroom. Pupils' prior learning and individual needs have to be taken continually into account when planning, to allow assessment for learning to be successful. Both short- and medium-term schemes of work need to be adapted to suit pupils' learning.
- You, as a teacher, and your pupils need to be aware at all times of the learning cycle that has taken place in the English classroom. The discussion of formative assessment strategies provides a vital basis for lessons so that you can continually build on your pupils' progress and success.
- Assessment for Learning is a variety of strategies used by you as a teacher and your pupils to recognize and respond to learning consistently from lesson to lesson.
- Teaching, learning and formative assessment strategies are integral in enabling you as teacher to build an in-depth pupil profile; the process also feeds into external summative assessment.
- Hence the *Assessing Pupils' Progress* (APP) document has added to the security of your teacher assessments which feed into the end of key stage summative assessments.

Further reading

Black, P. and Wiliam, D. (1998) 'Assessment and classroom learning', *Assessment in Education*, 5(1): 7–74.

Black, P., Harrison, C., Lee, C., Marshall, B. and Wiliam, D. (2002) *Working Inside the Black Box*. Assessment for Learning in the Classroom. London.
Black and Wiliam are the formative assessment gurus. This journal article was one of the first pieces that advocated that formative assessment in the classroom enabled pupils to take 'control' of their own learning. By taking control, Black and Wiliam believed pupils could assess where they were up to and build on their skills and knowledge.

Clarke, S. (2005) *Formative Assessment in the Secondary Classroom*. London: Hodder Murray.
Shirley Clarke's text on formative assessment is a very practical guide on how teachers can best use formative assessment in the classroom. Originally a researcher in the primary classroom, Shirley Clarke built on her knowledge and provides some excellent strategies in how to engage both teachers and pupils in formative assessment in the classroom.

Wiliam, D. (2001) *Level Best? Levels of Attainment in National Curriculum: Assessment*. London: Association of Teachers and Lecturers.
Wiliam provides an excellent basis for the argument – formative or summative assessment – which is best? *Level Best* (2001) also questions the validity of summative assessment at KS3 and in light of the current climate – how much does a summative level tell the teacher and pupil about attainment at the end of KS3?

Useful websites

English_gcse@aqa.org.uk
www.qca.org.uk
www.standards.dfes.gov.uk.secondary/keystage3//all/repub/en_asspup
www.standards.dfes.gov.uk/secondary/keystage3/repub/englishpubs/ass_eng/optional_tasks/
www.standards.dfes.gov.uk/secondary/keystage3/
www.standards.dfes.gov.uk/personalisedlearning/five/afl/
www.standards.dfes.gov.uk/secondary/keystage4/subjects/english

TEACHING DIFFERENT PUPILS, TEACHING DIFFERENT ABILITIES

Phil Rigby

This chapter considers:

- the principal issues involved in teaching pupils with a wide range of abilities, aptitudes and interests in order to provide for their individual needs
- inclusion in the English classroom
- definitions of different abilities
- differentiation and how we differentiate
- mixed-ability teaching
- creating an atmosphere for learning
- personalized learning.

By focusing on two particular trainee teachers preparing for a teaching placement, you can reflect upon practical approaches to meeting pupils' needs. You also examine medium-term planning documents, considering the ways in which they address the particular abilities, aptitudes and interests of the pupils in the class.

In Chapter 2, you have already been introduced to some of the practicalities of planning in English, including:

- planning from the National Curriculum for English
- using the Framework for secondary English
- moving from medium-term plans to individual lesson plans
- setting clear objectives
- having a clear structure
- planning for assessment
- evaluating learning.

During the process of exploring planning in English, you considered the importance of knowing your pupils as individuals, for example the need to be aware of the specific needs, personalities and learning styles of everyone in the class, and using available achievement data as a baseline from which to measure future performance. This chapter further develops these ideas, exploring in more detail the issues involved in getting to know your pupils and in planning for them as individuals. It introduces and discusses the topics of inclusion and differentiation in the English classroom, reflects upon planning for pupils with different abilities, aptitudes and interests, and considers some of the key considerations in creating an atmosphere for effective learning.

MEET LAURA AND JANE

It is a mid-December afternoon and two trainees, Laura and Jane, have come to speak with me prior to starting their first main teaching placement. Each of them is rather troubled by the practicality of meeting the individual needs of a range of pupils within their Year 8 classes, although for different reasons. For both of them their difficulty arises not from the setting of the school, the social background of the pupils or the individual personal circumstances of the pupils. The issue arises instead from managing the internal classroom dynamics of the particular groups of pupils.

JANE   I've got the whole shooting match in there! It's as if they've decided to create a sample class that includes every known social and psychological issue – a bit like Noah's Ark. And then they've given that class to me! I just can't see how I'm going to teach them anything. I'm going to have 30 different lessons going on at the same time. I feel like I'll spend all my time spinning plates and end up teaching them nothing.

LAURA   When I listen to you I feel really lucky. My Set Two are all exactly like one another and it's really difficult to get them to say anything at all. It's eerie really – it's like trying to run a lesson in a scene from *Shaun of the Dead*. I'm almost tempted to say to them, 'Let's all join hands and see if we can make contact with the living!'

JANE   Mine are certainly nothing like each other, and they're certainly not quiet. For me, it's more like teaching in Billy Smart's Circus!

LAURA   But what I really can't get my head around is the bit on our lesson plans where we have to identify the methods of differentiation that will take place in the lesson. I can't see that there will be any. I just don't need to differentiate – they're all so close in ability anyway.

JANE   And what do I do? With my class it's all about differentiation. Do I really have to plan different lessons for every pupil in the class? I just don't see how I can do that level of planning and then cope with managing all these different things at the same time.

LAURA   Well, could I just write 'Differentiation by outcome' on my lesson plans? I mean, that would be true, wouldn't it? Whatever work I set them, they'd do it at their own particular level, wouldn't they? Then I could say that the work was being differentiated by outcome.

JANE   But with a mixed-ability class like mine, I'm going to have to do a lot more than that. I can't just give them all the same thing to do and say, 'There you are, get on with it'.

In many ways, Laura and Jane are typical of many trainees at this particular stage in their development as teachers, in that the whole issue of planning for the range of pupil abilities seems simply too big or too impractical to manage effectively. Certainly, their individual situations are rather extreme, but they are by no means uncommon. As often happens, they have come to speak with me hoping that I will somehow easily solve their problem or else simply make it go away. Unfortunately, though, life is not like that – at least not in my experience, or that of my trainees!

In fact, this sense of being overwhelmed by the sheer scale of the task is one that many experienced English teachers will share. It seems fairly obvious that, in order for learning to take place effectively, a teacher will need to consider the individual needs of all the pupils in the class, but how can this be achieved either practically or realistically? Take Jane's class, for example; as she says, she has 30 very different pupils, each one with his or her own attitudes, aptitudes, interests, reading age, Cognitive Abilities Tests (CAT) scores and SAT scores – not to mention the events that are occurring away from the classroom, events that Jane herself will be unable to influence or control, and very often outside the influence or control of the pupils themselves. And she is teaching two such classes a day (on her next placement that will rise to three classes a day; next year it will probably be four such classes a day). And yes, although the scale of this task is recognized and acknowledged, it is by no means impossible: using this as an excuse to do nothing is simply not an option. The issue of dealing with children's individual needs is an important one, which needs to be addressed.

There were a number of important points in what Laura and Jane said, for example their comments on mixed-ability teaching and differentiation by outcome are worthy of comment, but that will come later in the chapter. However, for me, two key comments stood out from among their words, comments that I felt needed highlighting and unpicking with them at the very outset. The first came in Laura's words, 'I just don't need to differentiate', and sent an all too familiar shiver down my spine. How often we come across such an approach, not just from trainee teachers but also from more experienced practitioners; and how often it manifests itself in a lack of motivation and engagement, leading to underperformance from the pupils in their charge and, all too frequently, to behavioural problems that could have been avoided with more thorough and appropriate planning. I discussed with Laura the constant need to differentiate, and pointed out that however narrow the span of abilities within a classroom it will still be a mixed-ability class; that ability itself is a very fluid issue; that there will always be pupils who perform better at one aspect of the English curriculum than another or who prefer to learn and express themselves in different ways. The second comment was in Jane's words, 'it's all about differentiation'. For Jane it came almost as a cry of despair at her situation. However, unwittingly, she had stumbled across the answer, or at least an important aspect of it. Well done, Jane – you're getting there!

Our conversation went on to consider practical ways in which Jane's planning and classroom management could become both effective and sustainable. You consider some of these later in the chapter. At the same time we explored with Laura some of the key differences between the pupils in her class, and looked at ways of introducing differentiation into her planning and teaching, which is an appropriate point at which to make a start in considering teaching pupils with different abilities.

Legally, morally and ethically, schools and teachers have a responsibility to provide a broad and balanced curriculum for all pupils, according to their needs. As you begin to explore the practical and realistic methods of addressing the individual abilities, aptitudes, interests and needs of the pupils in your class, you very soon become aware of three key terms that recur with some regularity: 'inclusion', 'differentiation' and, more recently, 'personalized learning'. You will consider the latter two in due course; first, however, you need to consider the first term, inclusion, as in a sense this overarches the whole issue of how to teach pupils with different abilities, aptitudes, interests and needs.

INCLUSION

In order to begin to understand the issue of inclusion within a classroom setting, consider the following three statements, each taken from the National Curriculum:

1. An inclusive curriculum is one where all learners:
    - see the relevance of the curriculum to their own experiences and aspirations
    - have sufficient opportunities to succeed in their learning at the highest standard.

2. Inclusion is about the active presence, participation and achievement of all pupils in a meaningful and relevant set of learning experiences ... One of the main purposes of the whole-school curriculum will be to establish the entitlement to a range of high-quality teaching and learning experiences, irrespective of social background, culture, race, gender, differences in ability and disabilities.

3. Planning for inclusion means thinking about how the curriculum can be designed to match the needs and interests of the full range of learners. These will need to be addressed both inside and outside the classroom.
    The learners may include:

    - the gifted and talented
    - learners with learning difficulties and disabilities
    - learners who are learning English as an additional language
    - the different needs of boys and girls
    - children who are in care
    - learners with social, emotional and behavioural difficulties.

Young people will also bring a range of different cultural perspectives and experiences. These can be reflected in the curriculum and used to further an understanding of the importance of diversity issues. (QCA, 2007, www.qca.org.uk)

Point for reflection

What are the practical challenges that will face you as you address these key inclusion statements within your own classroom practice?

Since the mid-1990s, school environments have become considerably more diverse and wide-ranging; the result of social and educational policy intended to bring a greater proportion of pupils into mainstream classrooms. Although seen by some simply as a pragmatic, cost-cutting measure, such developments have largely been welcomed from a moral viewpoint, as they demonstrate a tangible expression of the way in which society at large is changing: in today's schools, pupils are far more likely to be accepted for what they are rather than being judged and found lacking in particular areas. A further benefit of this development is that the wider range of pupil experience will hopefully bring a variety of cultural perspectives, which can not only be reflected within the curriculum itself but also be used to further all pupils' understanding of the importance of diversity as an issue. Indeed, so crucial is inclusion now felt to be, both socially and educationally, that the National Curriculum incorporates an overarching statutory inclusion statement, which sets out three principles for developing an inclusive curriculum in order to provide all pupils with relevant and challenging learning. In order to provide for the needs of their pupils, schools must:

- set suitable learning challenges
- respond to pupils' diverse learning needs
- overcome potential barriers to learning and assessment for individuals and groups of pupils. (QCA, 2007, www.qca.org.uk)

These three principles of inclusion are particularly important for you as a teacher because, as previously explained in Chapter 1, the National Curriculum itself is a statutory document.

Point for reflection

Planning an inclusive English curriculum involves thinking about shaping the curriculum to match the needs and interests of the full range of learners. What are the particular benefits for you as an English teacher of developing an inclusive approach within your teaching?

Point for reflection

In a recent undergraduate English teacher training session at Edge Hill University, I asked the trainee group to consider the issue of inclusion, and what it meant to them as teachers. Their responses were as follows:

- 'It's about treating each pupil as an individual.'
- 'It's about pupils with different physical impairments or disabilities being taught in mainstream classrooms.'
- 'It's the changes that you have to make in your teaching to take account of this.'
- 'It's fairer.'
- 'Pupils who don't speak English as a first language.'
- 'Pupils who don't speak English.'
- 'It means you need to use teaching assistants.'
- 'It means that you need to adapt your teaching to cope with the demands of pupils with special educational needs.'
- 'It tries to create a more tolerant society, but it doesn't work, so it has the opposite effect to what was intended.'
- 'It means that teachers need to work closely with other teachers and with other professionals who work in children's services.'
- 'It makes things harder for the teacher.'
- 'Pupils with behavioural problems.'
- 'Pupils with learning difficulties.'
- 'Gifted and talented pupils working alongside those who aren't.'
- 'The ones in the middle who don't fit into a specific category and sometimes get forgotten.'

This was quite a representative range of answers, I thought, some quite perceptive, others more cynical. However, all of them had at least an element of truth and accurately reflected the particular stage in their development as teachers that the trainees had reached.

DIFFERENTIATION

Hopefully, by now, you will have begun to understand that the English curriculum is a very broad church, certainly not one that is defined simply within the confines of the Framework for secondary English or even by the National Curriculum for English, although both are vital documents for English teachers. English is a dynamic subject, constantly moving and growing, often with a tendency to develop into areas usually associated with other subject areas, offering real and practical opportunities for meaningful cross-curricular work. The English curriculum, by its very nature, naturally creates opportunities to cater for the particular strengths, interests and preferred learning styles of the full range of pupils. Indeed, it is this very breadth within English, its reach and inclusiveness, which provides the greatest opportunities for differentiation – as a teacher you will constantly be working on different areas and in different ways.

Point for reflection

Think back to earlier chapters, when we have considered the full range of components of the English curriculum. From among that range, which do you remember with particular pleasure from your own English lessons at school? Were there any that you particularly excelled at? Were there any that you particularly disliked or felt uncomfortable with?

Differentiation is a frequently used term, appearing in both medium-term and individual lesson planning documents, but one which is notoriously difficult to understand in practice. One of the principal problems with differentiation is its lack of a commonly accepted definition: it can mean different things to different people. However, in essence, it is the means by which teachers provide for the individual strengths and weaknesses of their pupils. There is a wide range of ways in which such modifications to the planned teaching and learning can be developed. First, it is important to remember that the best differentiation will take place over a period of time, meaning that teachers will consider the shape and structure of an entire scheme of work rather than focusing exclusively on differentiation in individual lesson plans. Teachers will effectively employ a range of differentiation strategies, often in the way they will deliberately structure and express questions for pupils of different abilities. The assessment process is another obvious example of differentiation; teachers will select the most appropriate feedback to individual pupils, based on their knowledge of each pupil's capacity to benefit from the advice provided.

Setting pupils in ability groupings is sometimes seen as a method of differentiation; single-sex groupings, fast-tracking pupils or an accelerated Key Stage 3 curriculum are others. However, in reality, differentiation has nothing to do with whether a class has been constructed as a result of the tightest of setting procedures, as in Laura's case, or whether it is simply a mixed-ability class that has fallen together by chance, as in Jane's. Whatever the class, it will contain a spread of interests, aptitudes and abilities, to say nothing of preferred learning styles. There will be some pupils with a natural interest in and affinity towards English, and others who are diffident at best towards the subject; there will be some who prefer one aspect of the subject and others who prefer another; there will be some who are naturally talented at speaking and listening activities and others who find this element of English completely terrifying. A key aspect of your responsibility as a teacher is to cater for the individual needs of each of those groups of pupils.

Laura's comment that there was no need to differentiate in her planning had failed to take account of the breadth and span of the English curriculum. What she was doing was taking a narrow view of how the pupils first presented themselves, together with their overall National Curriculum levels. By opening out those levels and by looking at how each pupil performed on particular aspects of the English curriculum, together with their interests and preferences for learning in a particular style, a much fuller picture could be grasped of those pupils as individual learners.

Point for reflection

Consider again the breadth of knowledge, understanding, skills, qualities and attitudes covered by the English curriculum. Think too of the many practical ways in which this range is nurtured and developed successfully within the English classroom. Here are 10 as a starter; how many more can you add to the list? You should easily be able to reach 25; now can you double that?

1. working in groups to construct a news bulletin
2. shared planning for a writing task with the whole class
3. prediction activity to develop understanding of a shared text
4. reinforcing a grammar rule, using a starter activity
5. hot-seating as a way of understanding character
6. researching how a central issue from a class text impacted on local life
7. using recorded video material to explore television advertising techniques
8. modelling exercise, representing particular information in a different way
9. redrafting a piece of written work, with a particular focus
10. asking pupils to research, discuss, prepare and present parts of the lesson.

The point of this reflection is to consider the breadth and scope of the English curriculum. With such a huge span of skills, activities and working styles, you can begin to understand that planning for the particular needs of *all* of the pupils *some* of the time can become a practical and realistic task. This point will again hopefully reinforce the crucial importance of your medium-term planning: it is through your medium-term plans that you will monitor your coverage of the full range of the English curriculum; the Framework for secondary English will also prove a useful tool. Indeed, it is through your medium-term planning that you will record and demonstrate that you have offered a range of learning opportunities in order to cater for the needs of all pupils. However, this does not mean that you will be expected to meet the individual needs of every pupil in every lesson all of the time; nor will you be expected to do everything straight away. On the contrary, as a developing professional you should expect to be supported in adopting a practical and realistic approach to the development of a range of appropriately differentiated teaching and learning opportunities over a period of time stretching well beyond your initial teacher training programme and probably over your first few years as a professional.

As already demonstrated through the planning process, there are practical, achievable strategies that are highly effective in the short term and which you can utilize in order to address the issue of differentiation within your teaching. Through changing curriculum focus, changing activities, changing working styles, changing assessment methods, changing pupil groupings, you can begin to manage the issue of catering for your pupils as individuals. Furthermore, as you go on to explore the range of available differentiation practices, you will quickly realize that many of them are simply good classroom practice.

Stradling and Saunders (1993: 13) highlight five major types of differentiation:

- differentiation by *outcome*, where the same general task is set, but it is flexible enough for pupils to work at their own level
- differentiation by *task*, where pupils cover the same content but at different levels
- differentiation by *learning activity*, where pupils are required to address the same task at the same level, but in a different way
- differentiation by *pace*, where pupils can cover the same content at the same level but at a different rate
- differentiation by *dialogue*, where the teacher discusses the work with individual pupils in order to tailor the work to their needs.

Each of these is an area that you as an English teacher can utilize effectively; however, the skill is selecting the appropriate method for each situation. It must be stressed, though, that one of these methods, although valid, does come with something of a health warning. Differentiation by outcome has traditionally been seen as the refuge of the English teacher who has not fully got to grips with differentiation – remember Laura's suggestion that by putting 'differentiation by outcome' into her plans she would be demonstrating that she had addressed this issue. At its simplest level, it means that a teacher can set a class any piece of work to do and that each pupil will complete it according to his or her ability, achieving an appropriate level of outcome. For instance, give a class a story to write and they will all write different stories, each of a different standard, even though the same title has been provided. However, when teachers use the term 'differentiation', the implication is that they actually intend to modify their planning in some way in order to take account of individual pupil difference. In differentiation by outcome this is not the case; it suggests instead that the teacher does not intend to modify their plans at all and that whatever individual progress the pupils achieve will almost be in spite of the teacher's efforts, rather than because of them. Because of this, your use of this method does need to be monitored: if overused, it can develop into an easy way of ducking the practical issues of differentiation.

Another different way of thinking about differentiation, which many teachers find effective, is by considering potential levels of achievement, together with consolidation and extension work as necessary, in any planning activity. For example, tasks could be approached on the basis that:

- most children will …
- some children will not have made so much progress and will …
- some children will have progressed further and will …

Point for reflection

Make a list of the issues which individualize the different pupils entering your class-room, and which might require differences in your teaching approach to maximize their learning (for example, gender, concentration span, and so on). How many others can you think of?

MIXED-ABILITY TEACHING

If you remember, Jane's comment on her class was that she felt that differentiation was particularly important to her because this was a mixed-ability class. Such a comment immediately raises two key points that need to be mentioned here; the first, as already mentioned, is that all classes by their very nature are 'mixed ability'. Each year I encounter trainees who believe, as do a number of more experienced English teachers, that if a class is set then all the pupils are the same in terms of ability. However, remember that no two pupils are the same; each has differing abilities, aptitudes, interests and needs. Secondly, the very concept of 'ability' is controversial in itself. Indeed, a number of educational writers (for example, Gardner, 1993) have questioned whether it makes any sense to talk about generalized ability or intelligence at all, suggesting instead that there are different types of intelligence. In similar vein, other writers have challenged the view that ability is something fixed, arguing instead that it is more fluid, varying with context, level of interest and motivation.

For these reasons, it is important not to become too fixed on the notion of ability, and certainly not in the sense of labelling someone as being 'good at English'. Remember, the very structure of the National Curriculum for English reminds us that it is necessary to distinguish between speaking, listening, reading and writing. In addition, the English-specific section of the statutory statement on inclusion in the National Curriculum also highlights the fact that pupils may have an uneven profile across the attainment targets. For instance, within each of the attainment targets it is possible to distinguish between performance in different reading skills or at different styles of writing. It is also important to recognize that performance can be affected by changing circumstances.

One of the major challenges facing teachers of English is deciding how to make provision for the wide range of abilities and aptitudes likely to be encountered in any one class. However, there are effective strategies and techniques that teachers can utilize in order to make the best of the situation:

1. *Being thoroughly prepared.* Like many of the features within this chapter, the key to successful mixed-ability teaching is the key to successful teaching — the two go hand in hand. It is taken as read that your lessons will have been thoroughly planned and prepared, including visualizing, or 'walking through', particularly key moments in advance. However, this can easily go badly adrift if you are not properly prepared physically for the lesson. On occasion, although still too often, I have seen a lesson that seems really well prepared on paper start to disintegrate because of a lack of organization or the failure to have the necessary resources available at the appropriate time.

2. *Adapting pupil groupings.* Using pupil grouping in a sensitive and supportive way can also make the mixed-ability classroom an extremely effective learning environment. At times, it will make sense to group pupils according to their ability at a particular task, so that they can all work at an appropriate level of challenge and so that your teaching input can be targeted and focused. However, at other times, it will be entirely appropriate to mix more able and less able pupils, particularly if the more able pupil is able to explain a taxing concept successfully — indeed, rather than holding back the progress of such pupils, this type of activity really can consolidate the learning of the more able pupil. Sometimes friendship groupings will produce the best results; at other times boy-girl pairings can change the social dynamic of the class; on occasions, completely random groupings can produce a surprising result. The important thing here is to keep things changing, and to remember that the decision as to who sits and works together is yours.

3. *Varying the questioning style.* This is a really important skill and one that you will need to work at developing. It is important that your questioning style and choice of vocabulary are

carefully selected, that you involve and include all pupils so that they feel that they can contribute and offer their thoughts without fear of failure or ridicule. Also try, if you can, to avoid the situation where you ask a question, get a response and then move on to another question and another pupil. Consider targeting more factual, starter questions to less able or confident pupils, then using their answer to bounce off a more speculative question to a more able or confident pupil across the room. It also keeps them on their toes and it makes them listen.

4. *Signalling the transitions between phases of the lesson and between individual lessons.* Pupils like to know what they are doing and why. For that reason, it is important that you use clear punctuation marks within your lesson structure, particularly in a class with a wide and diverse range of abilities. This gives the pupils a clear signal that things are changing, that we are stopping working in this particular way on this particular task, and that we are going to begin another activity. Let the pupils know, not only how the individual pieces of the lesson fit together, but how this lesson relates to yesterday's lesson and to what they will be doing next week.

5. *Changing pace between different activities.* You know that feeling you get sometimes, early in the afternoon, when the day seems to go rather flat and you start to become sleepy? Sometimes that happens in lessons too. Everything has started well: objectives are crisp and appropriate, pupils are responsive and alert, and resources are fully prepared. Then, inexplicably, in the middle of the lesson things just start to sag and go a bit flabby. The spread of abilities can just amplify this. The important thing here is to be aware that this might happen, anticipate its arrival and then ensure that you have something to move on to that will pick things up and get them moving again.

6. *Knowing the level of difficulty of a text.* The final item on the list is crucial: you need to know the level of challenge that a particular text will offer to the pupils in your class. Many English teachers label some texts as suitable for higher-ability or lower-ability pupils. However, this misses the point that less able readers can tackle quite complex and challenging texts, if they are presented in an approachable, engaging manner; similarly, do not underestimate the mileage that more able readers can get from a less challenging text – indeed, such a text can often give full rein to their creative tendencies which are too often constrained.

PLANNING FOR DIFFERENT PUPILS

The following week Laura returns to see me, this time alone. Since our last conversation she has been back into school and discussed her Year 8 class with her mentor, Louise. Together, they have constructed the outline for a six-week plan based on the novel *Private Peaceful* by Michael Morpurgo. The first sheet is already complete in draft form and she shows it to me (see Figure 6.1). We talk about her plans and how she intends to cater for the different learning needs of the pupils in her class. This time, she is more confident and wants to sound out her ideas before finally committing them to print.

Point for reflection

What six pieces of useful advice would you give Laura, in terms of catering for the individual needs of the pupils in her class? (Remember Laura's description of the class at the beginning of the chapter).

1. Take an overview of the whole six-week unit, rather than just focusing on individual lessons.

2. Use Janet's knowledge of Daniel to assist you in meeting his particular needs; make sure that you communicate both in advance of and after the lesson.
3.
4.
5.
6.

As we talk through Laura's lesson plans, it becomes quite clear what her own preferred learning style is. An avid reader, her teaching file is a model of thoroughness and organization; notes are thorough and meticulously catalogued. She is a clear case of a visual learner (as had become evident earlier in the year when the trainees underwent a learning styles diagnosis) and, as so often happens, her own lesson ideas follow her own preferred style. It is natural, I suppose; people naturally tend towards situations where they feel comfortable, and Laura's

PGCE secondary English

| **Title of scheme**: Private Peaceful
Focusing on language choices and impact created |

Year/class: Year 8 Set 2 (30 pupils: 12 boys 18 girls)	**Dates:** 5 January – 13 February Monday p4 Tuesday p1 Friday p2	**Number of lessons:** 18 (3 1-hour lessons each week)

Nature of pupils
10 pupils at level 5b; 12 pupils at level 5c; 8 pupils at level 4a
Daniel (Asperger's) helped by TA – Janet
Mainly visual and auditory learning styles

Objectives to be addressed in whole scheme:
READING
  6 – Recognize bias and objectivity, distinguishing facts from hypotheses, theories or opinions
 10 – Analyse the overall structure of a text to identify how key ideas are developed
 11 – Investigate the different ways familiar themes are explored and presented by different writers
 13 – Read a substantial text revising and refining interpretations of subject matter, style and technique

WRITING
  1 – Experiment with different approaches to planning, drafting and presenting writing, taking account of the time available
  5 – Develop the use of commentary and description in narrative
  6 – Experiment with figurative language in conveying a sense of character and setting
 17 – Integrate evidence into writing to support analysis or conclusions

SPEAKING AND LISTENING
  2 – Tell a story, recount an experience or develop an idea, choosing and changing the mood, tone and pace of delivery for particular effect
 15 – Explore and develop ideas, issues and relationships through work in role

Learning outcomes
Piece of empathetic writing/analysis of war propaganda

Figure 6.1 Medium term scheme of work

lessons are very text-reliant, with copious amounts of reading followed by a wide range of writing activities. I do not quibble over the variety in writing tasks; in fact I am very impressed at the different opportunities that pupils will have to express their ideas in writing.

However, we do discuss her over-reliance on text-based activities, and the need to introduce a wider range of speaking and listening activities, together with opportunities both for different groupings and to get the children moving away from their desks. She leaves to go and put her scheme of work together before bringing it back to me for approval the following week. Hopefully, this time she is clearer about what she has to do in terms both of coverage of the curriculum and meeting the particular needs of her pupils.

PERSONALIZED LEARNING

> the best way to achieve world class standards is a system in which all children receive teaching tailored to their needs and which is based on their stage, not age. (DCSF, 2007 www.standards.dfes.gov.uk/secondary/framework)

In terms of effectively meeting the needs of individual pupils and raising their levels of achievement, personalized learning has become the most recent addition to the teacher's toolkit. Not a new innovation, like many 'new initiatives' it takes a number of the features at the heart of existing good practice and reshapes them to create a new focus and direction. Personalized learning involves the teaching, curriculum or school organization being tailored in order to reach as many pupils with diverse needs and experiences as possible for as much of the time as possible. Closely allied to the current drive towards personalization throughout all the public services and to the *Every Child Matters* agenda it feels like an idea whose political moment has come (DfES, 2004). A more detailed introduction to the topic of personalized learning can be found in *2020 Vision: The Report of the Teaching and Learning in 2020 Review Group* (DfES, 2006)

As we have already seen in this chapter, it is nothing new for teachers to tailor curriculum and teaching methods in order to meet the individual needs of pupils. However, personalized learning seeks to extend the lengths to which differentiation can be taken and sets high expectations for all pupils. It is built around five core themes:

1. *Assessment for learning* together with planning to objectives, a clear sense of subject progression, oral and written feedback, listening and observing, carefully framed questions to ascertain understanding and pupil peer and self assessment.
2. *Teaching and learning strategies* that develop the competence and confidence of every pupil by actively engaging and stretching them.
3. *Curriculum entitlement and choice* that delivers sufficient breadth of study, personal relevance and flexible learning pathways through the system, with a wide range of subjects, each assessed at appropriate levels.
4. *A student-centred approach to school organization*, with teachers thinking creatively about how to support high-quality teaching and learning.
5. *Strong partnership beyond the school* to drive forward progress in the classroom, to remove barriers to learning and to support pupil well-being.

Proponents of personalized learning point out that, although there are clear links to differentiation, the two are not the same. Personalized learning differs from differentiation in that it provides the learner with some degree of choice about what is learned, when it is learned and how it is learned. It is not intended to provide pupils with unlimited choice, since they will still have targets to be met. However, it does give pupils opportunities to learn in ways that suit their individual learning styles. Personalized learning is an approach to teaching and learning that stresses deep learning as an active, social process and which is explicit about learning skills, processes and strategies. It is not about individualized learning, but about building independence through interaction, intervention, stimulation and collaboration.

> The term 'personalized learning' means maintaining a focus on individual progress, in order to maximize all learners' capacity to learn, achieve and participate. This means supporting and challenging each learner to achieve national standards and gain the skills they need to thrive and succeed throughout their lives. 'Personalizing learning' is not about individual lesson plans or individualization (where learners are taught separately or through a one-to-one approach). (Thomas, 2007: 5)

At the time of writing it is too early to say whether personalized learning will become fully established, a central feature of every school and of every teacher's practice, or whether it will become a victim of fashion, superseded by newer and fresher initiatives. It also needs to be pointed out that the attitude of many English teachers towards personalized learning remains ambiguous at best. Remember from earlier chapters, many English teachers subscribe to a belief in a 'personal growth' model of English learning. For them, there is some unease that personalized learning might be interpreted in a more reductive way as simply setting targets and providing narrow learning pathways that do not allow for unplanned routes or detours.

Perhaps the best place to end the chapter is with Jane and Laura, following the end of their teaching placement. It is now mid-February; however, this time they have not come to see me – usually a good sign! It is our first seminar group meeting in over two months and both Jane and Laura, like the other trainees, are excited and relieved to have come through their ordeal relatively unscathed. The group are reflecting upon their experiences and what they have learnt; this is the first stage in getting them to move on, through reflection, towards their final placement, which begins in less than a month.

Interestingly, when asked to comment on the area of their training in which they have made most individual progress, both choose supporting the needs of individual pupils. Jane has grown and developed, her resilience and sense of humour have obviously served her well. She describes her experience at times as 'feeling like the ringmaster in Billy Smart's Circus' – but at least she was the ringmaster; she could have still been spinning plates, balancing on a high wire or pelted with custard pies! What she says she has particularly realized, though, is that although her pupils might have a wide range of needs, the important thing is that each of them feels that their needs are being particularly catered for on a frequent basis, but not all of the time. It is this sense of making her planning realistic that has been her major revelation over the past six weeks.

As for Laura, her words can speak for themselves:

What I was doing before was labelling the pupils, putting them into boxes, trying to make them fit into certain categories. That was the mistake I was making. As soon as I started to see them as individuals, and how their strengths could change from one activity to another, I could see what I needed to focus on.

Addressing and catering for the individual abilities, aptitudes, interests and needs of pupils is a challenge that faces all teachers. However, the important thing is that you do see them as individuals, each with their own story, each deserving the opportunity to develop to their full potential.

WHAT THE RESEARCH SUGGESTS

Because of their close links with individual pupil attainment, the issues of inclusion, differentiation and now personalization have become frequent areas for study and research. Projects have often focused upon the educational impact of such issues as social class, race, gender and place. Indeed, much of the current developmental work around personalized learning stems from research findings indicating that, in spite of decades of work to counter the educational effects of social disadvantage, there remains a significant over-representation of such groups among the lowest attainers. Within the relatively recently developed personalization field, Professor David H. Hargreaves has been a leading figure, focusing in particular upon learning and working alongside the Specialist Schools and Academies Trust to produce nine pamphlets on the themes of personalizing learning and the reshaping of schools.

Paul Black and Dylan Wiliam have been highly influential writers upon the whole field of assessment, their comments always practical and well considered. '*Inside the black box: raising standards through classroom assessment*' (1998) provides an invaluable introduction to formative assessment. More recent work upon assessment for learning, (for example, *Assessment for Learning: Putting It into Practice*, Black et al., 2003), explores the effectiveness of treating pupils as individuals in target-setting.

Howard Gardner's work on multiple intelligence has been groundbreaking, encouraging schools away from the notion that they should be concentrating their efforts solely on developing intellectual intelligence. His theory was first laid out in *Frames of Mind: The Theory of Multiple Intelligences* (1983), and has been further refined in his numerous works over subsequent years, including *Multiple Intelligences: The Theory in Practice* (1993) and *Intelligence Reframed: Multiple Intelligences for the 21st Century* (1999).

Key points from this chapter

Over the course of this chapter, you have considered a number of key issues concerning inclusion, differentiation and personalized learning. In particular, you have focused upon:

- the importance of seeing your pupils as individuals
- individual abilities, interests, aptitudes and skills
- the ability mix of every class
- the National Curriculum inclusion statements
- the need to plan for differentiation in a variety of ways
- practical ways of achieving differentiation
- creating an atmosphere for learning
- the importance of personalizing learning.

Further reading

Any of the texts mentioned in this chapter will help develop your understanding of the issues involved in teaching pupils with individual abilities, aptitudes, interests and needs. You might find the text below particularly helpful, in terms of further reading.

Clarke, S., Dickinson, P. and Westbrook, J. (2004) *The Complete Guide to Becoming an English Teacher.* London: Sage.
Links educational theory, historical perspectives and current practice in a way that encourages the reader to engage with the issues and critique approaches. Chapter 6 'Inclusion' is particularly relevant as further reading to this chapter.

Fleming, J. and Stevens, D. (2004) *English Teaching in the Secondary School: Linking Theory and Practice.* 2nd edn. London: David Fulton.
Adopts a topic-based approach to English teaching, with chapters on, for example, speaking and listening, reading, writing, teaching poetry, drama, ICT. The final chapter on Inclusion has some particularly helpful ideas.

Pike, M. (2003) *Teaching Secondary English.* London: Paul Chapman Publishing.
Takes a thematic approach, with chapters on assessment in English, literature and literacy at Key Stage 3; popularizing poetry and spiritual and moral development through English. Chapter 9, 'Differentiation and the individual: gender, ethnicity and special needs' offers some interesting points for reflection as you consider the individuals in your classes, and what might best serve their learning needs.

Wright, T. (2005) *How to be a Brilliant English Teacher.* Oxford: Routledge.
A lively and realistic approach, which combines practical strategies for implementing the statutory curriculum and is as entertaining as it is stimulating. Chapter 10 'Differentiation' is particularly relevant as further reading to this chapter.

 Useful websites

Live links to these websites can be found on the companion website www.sagepub.co.uk/secondary.

www.nc.uk.net/nc_resources/html/inclusion.shtml Part of the National Curriculum Online website, this page includes the full statutory inclusion statement. Additional inclusion information on English can be located from here.

www.teachernet.gov.uk/teachinginengland/detail.cfm?id 377 Teachernet is a vast site developed by the Department for Children, Schools and Families as a resource to support the education profession. The inclusion page provides helpful links to further pages dealing with special educational needs, gifted and talented pupils and English as an additional language.

www.demos.co.uk/files/learningaboutpersonalisation.pdf

www.nc.uk.net/inclusion.html

www.publications.teachernet.gov.uk/eOrderingDownload/6856-DfES-Teaching%20and%20 Learning.pdf

www.ssat-inet.net/whatwedo/personalisinglearning.aspx

www.standards.dfes.gov.uk/personalisedlearning/

CATERING FOR AN ASSESSMENT-DRIVEN CURRICULUM

Peter Woolnough

This chapter considers:

- an outline of the nature and structure of assessment models used in KS3, KS4 and KS5
- an exploration of how to prepare to teach each key stage
- evaluation of current attitudes to the tests/examinations and an outline of possible changes
- reflection on how successful teachers approach the challenge of having to prepare pupils for examinations and also plan to meet pupils' holistic needs.

Effective teaching and learning hinges on teachers having a clear understanding of the assessment models adopted at each key stage, and the wherewithal to devise schemes of work that both meet the requirements of these models and at the same time meet the broader educational needs of their pupils. It is a widely documented fact that pupils in England undergo more formal, prescribed assessment than any other pupils in the world, and with this comes the not unreasonable concern that incessant 'teaching to the test' has a damagingly reductive effect on the actual learning experience of our children. Bearing this concern in mind, the chapter not only explores some effective ways of preparing pupils for the tests and examinations, but also critically reflects on the dangers of predicating long-term planning on assessment model imperatives, in isolation. We also consider the proposed changes to the curriculum at each key stage which are likely to come into effect during your first few years of teaching. A close reading of Chapter 5, which deals with the philosophies and practicalities of *assessment*, should be undertaken prior to studying this section, which incorporates examples of standard assessment tasks (SATs), GCSE and AS/A level guidance and assessment information, in addition to transcripts of the reflections of trainees and qualified teachers.

ENGLISH AT KEY STAGE 3

Your teaching at Key Stage 3 will be based largely on coverage of the National Curriculum and the secondary National Strategy. Statutory assessment of pupils at the end of Year 9 began shortly after the initial introduction of the National Curriculum, and although the assessment model has been modified over the years, the basic components remain the same. In the current model, pupils sit three standard assessment tests:

- a *writing* paper (made up of a longer task and a shorter task)
- a *reading* paper
- a *Shakespeare* paper

The tests specifically cover levels 4–7 and are undifferentiated. According to the Qualifications and Curriculum Authority (QCA), who manage the tests, pupils working below level 4 should not be entered for the tests. The performance of such pupils is recorded only in terms of teacher assessment, but the QCA does offer *optional activities* which teachers are invited to use, to help them form an accurate assessment of pupil performance below level 4. It is worth noting, here, that all pupils receive teacher assessment levels, but these levels are not publicized or taken into account when 'league tables' are constructed. In effect, a class teacher's overall assessment of pupil performance is of minimal importance, in terms of external accountability.

The aim of the three SATs papers is to objectively assess pupils' competencies against clear *assessment focuses* (see Chapter 5). Questions in the SATs papers are, in turn, designed to reveal pupils' competencies in relation to specific assessment focuses – and this has important implications for the way you, as the teacher, prepare your pupils for the tests. Look at the assessment focuses for reading, in Figure 7.1, and imagine you have decided to ask the pupils to analyse a tabloid newspaper article.

- What kind of questions could you devise to test pupils' ability in each of the assessment focuses?
- How would you begin to approach teaching the reading skills required?

In order for you to prepare your pupils effectively for these somewhat idiosyncratic tests, it is essential that you look closely at the very detailed mark schemes provided for each SAT paper to gain a working knowledge of what the test-setters are looking for and what the specific weightings are for each section.

The writing paper

The format of the paper is fairly straightforward. Pupils will have to attempt:

- a 'longer' task – worth 30 marks. 45 minutes is allocated, of which 15 minutes should be spent on planning. A planning frame is provided.
- a 'shorter' task – worth 20 marks. 30 minutes is allocated, including planning time.

Each task is linked to a different set of the triplets of writing purposes in the *Framework* (*imagine, explore, entertain/inform, explain, describe/persuade, argue, advise/analyse, review, comment*). Also, some basic information about the nature of each task is included with the question. Given the fact that the tasks can be based on any of the four writing triplets, teachers need to ensure that their pupils have extensively explored the range of writing styles and clearly established the typical features of these styles. This has major implications for planning schemes of work, not least in consideration of the interdependence of reading and writing. Here is the 2007 shorter writing task:

Ready to go

You are a television presenter. You have been sent to your
local town centre, where a charity fun run is about to start. The fun
run is going to be included on the local midday news.

You get this message from the television studio:

> You need to explain what this charity event is all about.
>
> Describe what is happening now, as people wait for the fun run to
> start: crowds, people in costumes, music, and so on.
>
> Are you ready? I am handing over to you now ...

**Describe the scene up to the moment when the fun run starts, for
the television news.**

[20 marks including 4 for spelling]

Complications of the mark schemes

The task you have just looked at seems fairly straightforward. If you have explored and developed the techniques of effective descriptive writing in Years 7–9, your pupils should be well placed to do the task justice. However, preparation for SATs is more complicated than ensuring that pupils know basic writing principles. Perhaps the greatest challenge for teachers lies in the complexity and specificity of the mark schemes for the writing papers. The format of the test seeks to reward pupils for demonstrating specific aspects of writing skills, and to do this the mark schemes detail explicitly what should be produced in relation to each assessment focus. This is a deliberate move away from the best-fit or level-related approach that many teachers have used in the past.

For both writing tasks, assessment focuses are divided into three *strands*. In the *longer writing* these strands are:

- sentence structure and punctuation (SSP) – 8 marks
- text structure and organization (TSO) – 8 marks
- composition and effect (CE) – 14 marks.

In the *shorter writing* the strands are:

- sentence structure, punctuation and text organization (SSPTO) – 6 marks
- composition and effect (CE) – 10 marks
- spelling (SP) – 4 marks.

To add to the complexity, the mark schemes then create up to six 'bands of performance' for each strand. Each of these bands illustrates marks to be allocated and the criteria for the award of marks. The criteria are very specific, and aim to remove subjectivity from the marking process. It is certainly worth accessing a mark scheme pack of SATs tests so that you can begin to get to grips with this. These packs include all the test papers, the mark schemes and exemplified/ annotated pupil responses.

READING	
AF1	Use a range of strategies, including accurate decoding of text, to read for meaning (KS2)
AF2	Understand, describe, select or retrieve information, events or ideas from texts and use quotation and reference to text
AF3	Deduce, infer or interpret information, events or ideas from texts
AF4	Identify and comment on the structure and organization of texts, including grammatical and presentational features at text level
AF5	Explain and comment on writers' use of language, including grammatical and literary features at word and sentence level
AF6	Identify and comment on writers' purposes and viewpoints, and the overall effect of the text on the reader
AF7	Relate texts to their social, cultural and historical contexts and literary traditions (KS4)
WRITING	
AF1	Write imaginative, interesting and thoughtful texts
AF2	Produce texts which are appropriate to task, reader and purpose
AF3	Organize and present whole texts effectively, sequencing and structuring information, ideas and events
AF4	Construct paragraphs and use cohesion within and between paragraphs
AF5	Vary sentences for clarity, purpose and effect
AF6	Write with technical accuracy of syntax and punctuation in phrases, clauses and sentences
AF7	Select appropriate and effective vocabulary
AF8	Use correct spelling

Figure 7.1 Assessment focuses of reading and writing

Points for reflection

To what extent would you, as a class teacher, share the mark schemes with your pupils? Would it be important or helpful for them to know that, for example, spelling is not assessed in the longer writing task? How might your planning and teaching reflect the relatively greater importance of composition and effect, in both tasks? Would it be useful to use the criteria in the bands to show pupils how they can gain more marks, and, if so, how might you approach this?

In order to help you respond to the reflection points, I have included transcripts of interviews with two PGCE trainees, both of whom were asked to discuss how they had prepared Year 9 classes for the writing paper. Note how they make considered choices about how to approach test preparation.

Trainee 1

I was working with an able group who were soon to take the tests. They had a fairly secure knowledge of the triplets and the key features of various writing forms and purposes. It seemed to me, therefore, that my main priority was to maximize their ability to give the examiners what they wanted. So, I prepared a PowerPoint (with hard copies) containing details of strands and bands and actually made pupils learn the mark allocation for each test! We then looked at a mark scheme for the 2006 test and began to identify the key features required for good answers in each of the strands. Next, we conducted a marking exercise based on a pupil's response to the shorter writing task, and, using the mark scheme, had to decide which band would be appropriate for the script. The final activity was for the class to attempt an actual task in test conditions, and peer assess responses. I think all this worked really well, because it made the pupils fully aware of what the examiners are looking for.

Trainee 2

I had a class of lowish ability, and most of the pupils were expected to get level 4. Given this context, I decided to focus on the actual tasks set and make sure that the kids wrote in the appropriate style for each task. To be honest, I didn't get too involved with the mark schemes because I felt it might actually confuse some of the class. Instead, we did lots of writing and reading activities that acquainted the kids with the conventions of the triplets and I tried to get them to recognize the nature of a given task and then apply the conventions. The other priority was technical accuracy. We did plenty of skills work relating to spelling, punctuation and para-graphing. So, although what I planned did take into account the mark schemes, I chose not to share this too much with the class. I think that this approach met their needs and was effective.

The reading paper

This paper consists of a *reading booklet with three texts*, on a linked theme. Pupils spend 15 minutes reading the booklet and making notes on it (without access to the questions) and then they spend one hour tackling approximately 15–17 questions. The paper is worth 32 marks, and individual questions range from 1 to 5 marks. A series of questions for each text is printed, and each question is linked to one assessment focus.

The texts chosen can exemplify virtually any genre that Key Stage 3 pupils should access and study within the National Curriculum. As an example, the 2007 paper, entitled 'A Change for the Better' (QCA, 2007) and based on the theme of extraordinary changes, included:

- the opening to a *story*, in which a man wakes up to discover that he has turned into a gigantic beetle
- an extract from a *factual book* about scientists, revealing how a Dutch scientist dramatically changed people's understanding of insects
- an *article* reporting on research which explains why adolescents behave as they do.

The style of the questions

In common with the writing tasks, the reading paper attempts, in its assessment model, to make the process as objective as possible. The questions set range from simple AF2 activities,

Give two quotations from paragraphs 1 to 3 which show that Gregor is finding it difficult to control his movements. (1 mark)

to challenging AF4 questions worth 5 marks,

The writer shows Gregor beginning to feel desperate as he hears his mother's voice (paragraph 5)
How does the writer build up a sense of Gregor's increasing desperation In paragraphs 5 to 9? Support your ideas with quotations from paragraphs 5 to 9.

Pupils need to be aware that questions can appear in a variety of forms in the answer booklet. Some will simply require prose answers, but others will involve box-ticking and completion of charts. The mark schemes are very detailed and supported by exemplar answers (Ref: QCA/06/2772, KS3 SATs Mark Scheme for 2006).

How best to approach the reading paper?

Given the fact that this is an undifferentiated, compulsory paper that covers levels 4–7, it can be difficult for teachers to decide how to tackle it. Pupils working at level 4 might find some of the texts hard to access, and the more challenging questions are, indeed, challenging. However, the following are strategies that successful teachers have used, which should be of some assistance to you.

Use of the 15 minutes *reading and note-making* time is crucial. Pupils need to be trained to approach this time in a systematic manner. They should first establish the theme linking the passages. Then, they should actually write down the following three questions and use them as a basis for annotating each text, in turn:

- What kind of text is it?
- What is it trying to do?
- How does it try to do it?

The answer to the first two of these questions will be brief, but in answering the questions the pupils will have identified genre and purpose. Having done this, the pupils should (hopefully) bring into play their knowledge of the typical features of these text types and go on to produce heavy annotation based on the third question. Language choices, mood, structure, layout and effectiveness will therefore be identified before the pupils actually view the questions. This kind of activity could be undertaken, as a guided or shared reading task, from Year 7 onwards, and the skills of annotation and prediction can then develop in tandem with the pupils' growing knowledge of different text types. This is not teaching to the test, but developing important reading skills in a structured way.

Pupils can also be coached to *understand and interpret the phrasing of the questions*. Many lower-ability pupils find that the greatest barrier to success is their inability to grasp the demands of the question. There are two fairly obvious ways to help the pupils with this. The first is to teach the pupils the skill of linking each question to an assessment focus. If the pupils can do this, then they will know what kind of information is being required by the question, and they can, through regular practice, adopt a formulaic approach and form the appropriate answers. Another useful strategy is to explore the links between the *phrasing of the questions* and the assessment focuses they are likely to be linked to. So, for example, AF2 (understand, describe, select or retrieve information) questions tend to include:

List ...
Give a reason ...
What?

In contrast, AF5 questions that demand some comment on the writer's use of language, might include:

What is the effect of ... ?
What impression do we get ... ?
What does the phrase suggest ... ?

Another important strategy is to apply the *Assessing Pupils' Progress* (DfES, 2006) model (detailed in Chapter 6) to identify specific areas of weakness in certain pupils, and then target these areas in subsequent task setting. You can access the APP materials via the companion website www.sagepub.co.uk/secondary. On a broader basis, it is important to recognize that the entire key stage should be used to *systematically develop pupils' reading skills*. This does not mean that all reading activities during Years 7–9 should be bite-sized or predicated entirely on pupils practising SATs-style activities. What it does mean is that schemes of work should be designed to include analysis of the entire range of text types; study of the class novel should be designed to develop pupils' abilities to utilize specific reading and writing skills; and knowledge acquired from reading tasks should inform pupils' writing, and vice versa. In my view – and it is an entirely personal one – coaching specifically for the actual SAT reading paper is best left to Year 9. The QCA would argue that schools are better served by taking up the optional tests (see useful websites at the end of this chapter) in Years 7 and 8 (QCA: 2007) because they mirror the format of the SATs and provide solid assessment data. I cannot disagree with the latter points, but believe they should be weighed against the danger of reading becoming a tedious activity solely undertaken for test purposes.

A particularly helpful PowerPoint guide, entitled 'Teaching Reading at KS3', created by Jo Wallace, can be accessed on the website. Also on the website are two other PowerPoint presentations that you might find useful. The first outlines the principles of *Assessing Pupils'* *Progress* and the second, 'Ways of Approaching Fiction at KS3', offers some general pointers without specific reference to SATs.

Points for reflection

How far should the formal assessment model dictate teaching time and approach? Or, put more simply, is there a danger that teachers spend too much time preparing pupils to pass tests – at the expense of a broader based, holistic education? Is the SATs model an effective preparation for GCSE?

The Shakespeare paper

Arguably the most contentious section of the KS3 English SATs, the Shakespeare paper is actually only worth *18 marks*. In terms of teacher time, however, it is probably the most demanding paper. Each year, schools select one of three plays. The plays for 2008 were *The*

Tempest, Much Ado About Nothing and *Richard III.* Pupils are required to study one of the three plays in its entirety. From each play, two sections are set for detailed study. In 2008, the set sections were:

The Tempest	Act 3 Scene 2.
	Act 4 Scene 1. Lines 139-262
Much Ado About Nothing	Act 4 Scene 1. Lines 196-325
	Act 5 Scene 4.
Richard III	Act 1 Scene 2. Lines 33-186
	Act 4 Scene 4. Lines 194-342

The key features

- One question is set for each play.
- Forty-five minutes' duration.
- The paper will test the same AFs as the reading paper, with pupils having to demonstrate understanding of the chosen play.
- The test will contain an extract from each of the sections set for study. Extracts will amount to approximately half of the lines set for study.
- Pupils' answers will need to draw on both extracts.
- Questions will focus on one or more of the following areas targeted for assessment:

  character and motivation
  ideas, themes and issues
  the language of the text
  the text in performance.

- For assessment, the mark scheme provides six bands of performance and a range of exemplified pupil responses.
- Over time, just as on A level syllabuses, texts are removed from the list and replacements introduced.

The questions

In some respects, the questions are formulaic. Given the four areas targeted for assessment, this should be expected. The 2007 question on *The Tempest*, for example, was based on *character and motivation*, and read, 'What do you learn about Prospero from the ways he treats the different characters in these extracts?' The question for *Richard III* related to *the text in performance*, and read, 'Imagine you are going to direct these extracts for a classroom performance ... How should the actors playing Richard and Buckingham show the relationship between the two characters in these extracts? The *Much Ado About Nothing* question demanded analysis of *the language of the text* and *character and motivation*. However, despite the formulaic bent of the questioning and the potential for teachers and publishers to predict likely questions, there is a problem with this model. Giving pupils of a broad ability range (levels 4–7) a compulsory question – with no alternative – seems unnecessarily harsh. Pupils studying literature at GCSE and A level invariably get a choice of questions on texts studied for terminal examination, so it seems strange that the Year 9 pupils do not have a similar option. In recent years there have also been instances where English teachers have complained bitterly about the unhelpful phrasing and sheer difficulty of some of the questions. Tales of tearful pupils who have spent months studying a play and then failed to fully comprehend the set question flood the *Times Educational Supplement* (*TES*) message boards each May. It is clearly an issue that the QCA should address.

How best to prepare for the paper

Much depends on the nature of the class you will be taking, but the first thing to say is that there is a wealth of material to help you. As soon as the set sections for a given year are known, publishers, advisers, departmental colleagues and the QCA will be feverishly at work, producing guides, sample questions, annotated copies of the scenes, schemes of work and multimedia packages. So resources and materials will not normally be much of an issue. When to start studying the play and how to do it certainly will be issues. Before you start, however, bear two things in mind: the study of the play should not be allowed to dominate the entire school year, and it can be fun. One way of organizing a scheme of work, would be to think in terms of three phases:

Phase 1 would include your own preparation: close reading of the chosen play; annotation of the selected sections; collation of resources from texts, the Internet, DVDs, and so on; mapping out activities and timings for medium-term plans and devising a series of sample questions based on the four areas targeted for assessment. I would then map out my first few weeks' individual lessons, giving particular consideration to how the play and the world of Shakespeare can be 'sold' to the pupils.

Phase 2 would be devoted to studying the play and the set sections. Pupils' initial contact with a play need not, and indeed should not, be a tedious crawl through the text. You could, for example, tackle pupils' preconceptions and fears about the archaic language by presenting your class with a page or two of Shakespeare's finest insults (see the Insults Starter on the website). A study of *The Tempest* could begin with the sort of empathetic island-based games suggested in 'The Tempest: teachit KS3 Interactive Pack.' A gripping narration of the dastardly deeds of Richard III, followed by a guided viewing of the Ian McKellen film version is another possibility. When it comes to reading the play or studying the set sections, you might consider introducing the four assessment areas and devising activities based on them as you go. Role-playing events and hot-seating characters can bring the thing to life, while DARTs activites can lead the pupils to active engagement with the text.

Phase 3 would be devoted to helping the pupils to apply the knowledge they have of the play and the set sections. Once they have a good working knowledge and heavily annotated personal copies of the key scenes, you begin the crucial tasks of introducing the areas of assessment, considering possible SAT questions and developing ways of answering those questions. Of course, these processes will be largely dictated by the abilities and aptitudes of your pupils. Some groups will need intensive scaffolding to secure such skills as recognizing the demands of the question, structuring an essay, blending argument with appropriate evidence and making effective use of quotation. It is essential that you anticipate in advance what the specific requirements of your class will be, and make a realistic estimate of the time and resources required. During this phase, I would also make use of sample annotated pupil answers, peer evaluation, timed practice and individual target-setting. To maintain enthusiasm and momentum, seeing a good live production of the play would be beneficial, too. Refer to Chapter 5 for sample lesson plans and assessed pieces of work.

Points for reflection

- What do you think are the major barriers to learning related to the Shakespeare SAT?
- Is it acceptable to avoid a detailed or complete class reading of the chosen play?
- How would you go about structuring a Shakespeare scheme of work for a lower-ability group?

Two useful PowerPoint presentations, created by Lynne Warham, can be found on the website. They are entitled 'Shakespeare Seminar' and 'Shakespeare Lecture', and both explore approaches to Shakespeare at KS3.

SATs: the politics and the fury

The continued existence of the Key Stage 3 SATs, in their current form, is an extremely contentious issue. Successive governments have argued that SATs are the only reliable indicator to parents of children's progress at the mid-point in their mainstream schooling. It has also been argued that the presence of SATs ensures that pupils' entitlement, in terms of the National Curriculum, is met. Supporters of SATs and optional tests additionally assert that the tests have led to a rise in standards and they emphasize the value of the assessment data that the tests produce.

Many within the teaching profession, however, believe that SATs are an unsatisfactory means of assessing pupils. They argue that the English tests are ill-conceived, poorly administered and unreliable. Their principal complaints are the following:

- The tests lack differentiation (unlike science and maths, both of which offer two tiers of paper) and therefore disadvantage level 4 pupils.
- The absence of a choice of questions on each Shakespeare play is inexplicable.
- The tests, despite their prescriptive nature, are inefficiently marked. (The English KS3 SATs have more appeals against results than any other public examination.)
- The results, in recent years, have not been available to schools until mid or late August – too late for schools to use them as part of the Year 10 setting process. Prior to 2007, science and maths results have been available to schools in early July.
- The increased importance of the tests, in terms of league tables, performance management and accountability, has led to overemphasis on the tests in terms of teaching time.

Most teachers now accept the inevitability of some form of national assessment in Year 9, but they want an alternative to the current model. Even the QCA has expressed concerns about the testing regime, and in the spring of 2007 government ministers began to consider proposals to modify the KS3 SATs regime.

Introduction of single-level tests

Partially in response to criticisms of the current testing regime and in an attempt to make more effective use of the APP model, the National Assessment Agency (NAA) conducted trials of single-level tests in 2008. As a result of these trials, the new tests will replace SATs in 2009. The information currently available suggests that the tests will be more flexible than SATs. To view the NAA single level tests information, go to our website.

Single-level tests: key features
The express purpose of the tests is to improve pupils' progress during Key Stages 2 and 3. The NAA feel that the drive towards more personalized learning will best be served by testing as and when individual pupils are able to evidence competence at a particular level. Teachers will be expected to make use of APP strategies to progress the skills of individual pupils and thus make personalized learning an effective reality.

- They are for all pupils in both Key Stage 2 and Key Stage 3.
- They are available at level 3 through to level 8.
- They are short: between 50 and 70 minutes depending on the level of the test.
- They are externally marked.
- In English, there are separate tests for reading and writing.
- They are intended for pupils working securely at the level of test.
- They can be taken during one of three testing windows during the year.
- They are designed to be taken when each individual pupil is ready – this will mean that tests can be taken before Year 9.
- They can be attempted more than once by individual pupils.
- If a pupil fails to attain the lowest mark designated as a pass, their test result is recorded as unclassified.

Implications for teachers

There are some obvious positives to emerge from the move to single-level tests, but there are also imponderables and, as yet, unanswered questions. The positives largely relate to the fact that pupils and teachers should no longer have to spend an inordinate amount of time preparing for a single test, and the new tests do focus on the readiness of the individual pupil – so the tests should be much more appropriate for pupils, given that the tests are aimed at discrete levels.

However, the tests do raise a number of interesting questions. For example, if pupils are allowed to sit the tests earlier than Year 9, how will this affect the government's league tables? If pupils can take the tests at a given level more than once, how will this be funded? Will teachers feel even more pressured by having three assessment windows to plan and prepare for? And what of the actual tests themselves? At the time of writing, the nature, structure and assessment models are not widely known – and English teachers (as so often in the past) have no access to any evidence supporting the view that the trials of the tests have gone well. Certainly, the new tests present an opportunity for productive change, but it is imperative that this change is managed rather better than many initiatives in the past have been.

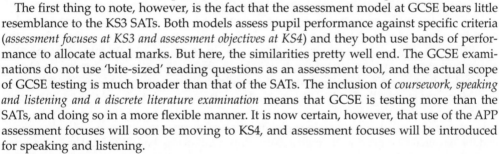

Point for reflection

How will you, as a classroom teacher, balance the twin responsibilities of preparing pupils effectively for tests and providing a varied and stimulating education which fully meets the needs of the pupils?

ENGLISH AT KEY STAGE 4

This phase of English education is dominated by the GCSE examinations, and for most pupils, Years 10 and 11 constitute a two-year examination course. All pupils capable of grade G will be entered for English and the overwhelming majority of pupils will also take the *English literature* examination. The general criteria for these examinations were issued by the QCA in 2001, and the various examination boards created their own specifications, based on the general criteria. It would not be productive or practical, in this chapter, to detail the specifications of Assessment and Qualification Alliance (AQA), Edexcel, Welsh Joint Education Committee (WJEC) and others, but the chapter will outline the basic principles of the GCSE and reflect on practical approaches to course management, planning, assessment and delivery of specific components. You can, of course access the respective examination board details through our website.

The first thing to note, however, is the fact that the assessment model at GCSE bears little resemblance to the KS3 SATs. Both models assess pupil performance against specific criteria (*assessment focuses at KS3 and assessment objectives at KS4*) and they both use bands of performance to allocate actual marks. But here, the similarities pretty well end. The GCSE examinations do not use 'bite-sized' reading questions as an assessment tool, and the actual scope of GCSE testing is much broader than that of the SATs. The inclusion of *coursework, speaking and listening and a discrete literature examination* means that GCSE is testing more than the SATs, and doing so in a more flexible manner. It is now certain, however, that use of the APP assessment focuses will soon be moving to KS4, and assessment focuses will be introduced for speaking and listening.

General criteria for syllabuses

Subject criteria for GCSE *English* require that candidates undertake a range of *reading*, covering the main genres in English: poetry, prose, drama, media and non-fiction texts. In addition, reading must include work from the English literary heritage by at least one major writer, texts from different cultures and traditions, and a play by Shakespeare. In terms of *writing*, candidates must produce work in a variety of forms and genres covering the four writing triplets already discussed in the earlier part of this chapter. *Speaking and listening* is assessed through individual extended contributions, group discussion and interaction, and drama-focused activities. The activities must include the use of speech for a variety of purposes and in a range of contexts.

Subject criteria for *English Literature* demand that candidates study:

- a Shakespeare play
- prose texts written before and after 1914

- poetry texts written before and after 1914
- a drama text written after 1914.

Assessment for both examinations is recorded on a sliding scale

A*   A   B   C   D   E   F   G   U,

in which A* is the top grade, and U translates as 'unclassified'.
Weightings for the respective papers are:

English: 40 per cent coursework, 60 per cent terminal examination
English literature: 30 per cent coursework, 70 per cent terminal examination.

How examination boards interpret the general criteria

The criteria, though specific, do give examination boards the opportunity to create syllabuses with some distinctive features. All the boards offer two *tiers* of paper to candidates: a lower/foundation tier aimed at grades C to G, and a higher tier aimed at A* to D. Another area of commonality relates to *speaking and listening*. Based on QCA directives, speaking and listening in all syllabuses is completed as coursework, internally assessed by class teachers and constitutes 20 per cent of a candidate's total mark for English.

A further feature common to all boards is the use of what are termed *crossover coursework assignments*. In simple terms, this means that certain coursework assignments can be devised to meet the criteria of both the *English* and the *English literature* examinations. This reduces the workload of pupils and encourages teachers to be imaginative and flexible when creating coursework tasks. An obvious example would be the Shakespeare assignment, which is required in both examinations. Elsewhere, we might find an assignment based on a Dickens text being used to meet the English literary heritage criterion for *English* and the pre-1914 prose criterion for *English literature*. The examination boards have also gone to some lengths to make it easy for teachers and candidates to exploit the elements common to coursework submissions and the terminal examinations in each subject. Pupils following the WJEC English courses, for example, are required to produce coursework assignments based on 'open' (imaginative/ descriptive) and 'closed' (factual/persuasive) writing. In the two terminal examination papers for *English*, candidates have to also attempt imaginative and factual writing tasks, thus encouraging teachers to exploit the features common to both coursework and terminal examinations.

As already stated, a detailed, comparative analysis of what each board offers is not feasible here, but it is worth highlighting some of the main differences in emphasis and approach. The largest examination board, the AQA, produces an *anthology* which includes poetry from different cultures and traditions (leading to two questions in the *English* terminal examination) and a selection of poems written before and after 1914 (leading to a question in the *English literature* terminal examination). The WJEC, in contrast, has a syllabus option without an anthology which results in the production of a more traditional 'set book' *English literature* paper and allows teachers the freedom to select poets of their own choice to cover the relevant criteria in the coursework element of their *English* examination. If you do use an anthology, you might want to consider the following questions before you begin studying it:

- Should the pupils read and closely study all the poems?
- How do you approach the comparative process?

- Do answers have to comment in equal detail on each poem?
- Are the named poets supposed to be studied discretely?
- How do teachers plan to deliver the range of materials and skills required? How can time be effectively managed?
- How can teachers help pupils to develop the generic skills required?
- How do teachers ensure that the process is not tedious for the pupils?
- How should pupil files and sample copies of the anthology be organized?
- What use can be made of the question model?

These, plus other issues related to anthologies and approaches to poetry at GCSE, are discussed in greater detail on the website, in a PowerPoint presentation created by Lynne Warham and myself, entitled 'Poetry for GCSE' (10).

You might also find it useful to view Lynne's presentation entitled 'GCSE Crossover Coursework' (11) which examines approaches to crossover elements in the AQA specification. Links to the websites of all GCSE examination boards can also be found on the companion website.

Point for reflection

What, in your view, are the likely benefits and drawbacks of using an anthology at GCSE?

Mapping out the course: where to begin?

Newly qualified teacher (NQT) comment:

> When I inherited a middle-ability Year 10 set at the start of the Year, I had no idea where to start. The Head of Department gave me two huge files, full of exam board details, training materials, past papers and assignments. It was daunting in the extreme. It took ages to sort out the basic course requirements, and even when I'd managed that I was still really unsure about how to actually map out the course. My biggest fear was that I would miss something important out, or worse still, teach the wrong things. It was only when a colleague sat me down and showed me her planning that I calmed down a bit.

This reaction is not unusual. Even when all the materials are made available to you, knowing how to make sense of them can be problematic. What follows is a list of strategies that might make the process less terrifying.

- Ensure that you have access to all necessary documentation, including: syllabuses, past papers, examination board training materials, the school's own policy and guidance documents, samples of other colleagues' planning and exemplar assessed scripts.
- Arrange to meet a mentor or supportive colleague and go through key documents with them. Have a list of questions ready and do not be afraid to admit to your own confusion.

- After this meeting, review the key documents and file them in a way that will make it easy to refer to them in future.
- When you are ready, try to map out the whole course on a chart, dividing the two years into half-term segments. Remember to combine the imperatives of coursework production with terminal examination preparation and set-book/anthology coverage. A sample segment for the first half-term (based on WJEC English and English Literature) might look something like this:

Half-term 1

- Share course details, structure and key information with class
- Open writing task (*English coursework*) and development of open writing skills (*English Paper 1*)
- Read and begin study of *Of Mice and Men*, characterization and themes (*English Literature exam*) ongoing
- Narrative comprehension skills development and task (*English Paper 1*)
- Speaking and listening group task (*English coursework*)
- Unseen poetry analysis and task (*English Literature*)

- Show your basic planning to your mentor and seek advice about timing and logistics.
- When you are ready to devise or select specific assignments and tasks, make sure that you first consult with colleagues and access what has worked well for them. If you want or have to devise your own assignments, make sure that they meet the specific assessment objectives and guidelines set out in the syllabus. Again, share these with colleagues on completion.
- A final point: always share syllabus coverage and key assessment details with your pupils. Make it clear to them what they are studying, how they will study it and how work will be assessed. This secures joint ownership and makes individual target-setting much easier.

How to assess GCSE work

This is probably the trainee or NQT teacher's second major headache, as indicated by the following *trainee transcript*:

> I collected in the first draft of some open writing coursework assignments and was basically scared stiff in case I got them wrong! I looked at the Assessment Objectives for Writing (En3) and the syllabus grid that said these pieces should be marked out of 20 and correlated these marks with GCSE grades. Then I looked at the detailed mark scheme which divided the 20 into marks: 14 for content and organization and 6 for sentence structure, spelling and punctuation. Each of these subdivisions was divided into bands of performance which gave quite detailed guidance. At this point I decided to mark a few in pencil and show them to the class teacher to see if I was on the right lines.

I would say that the trainee in question did most of the right things. He engaged fully with the syllabus instructions and guidelines and attempted a sample, then sought advice. The only other suggestion I would make is that he could have asked to see a range of assessed and moderated scripts from the previous year's examination entry, prior to looking at the work of his own class.

But what about how *you actually mark work?*
What should be written on a candidate's assignments and essays? Well, if the task is class-work or practice for the terminal examination, then you should follow your department's marking policy. If, however, you are marking *coursework* drafts or final submissions, then certain external directives come into play. Too often, teachers 'over-mark' first drafts of assignments and, in effect, allow pupils to submit fair copies in the final draft. This practice, coupled with evidence of widespread cheating in terms of coursework done at home, has led to the likelihood that coursework in most subjects will be abolished within the next few years. It is your responsibility to offer advice and guidance when marking drafts: nothing more. On a related issue, many teachers have been accused of giving pupils too much assis-tance in terms of assignment organization and structure. Again, this practice is unacceptable because it, in some cases, gives a false impression of a candidate's ability and in others it actually stifles individuality. Whether to put provisional grades or marks on coursework drafts is another issue that concerns many teachers. Some would argue that, in the case of low achievers, this practice acts as a disincentive. Most teachers and schools, however, do encourage this approach – allied, of course, to constructive comment and advice – because it can and should be a key element in target-setting. In recent years, it has become common practice to share grade descriptors and assessment practices with the pupils, and for this to happen, pupils must engage with the grades.

Points for reflection

Do you think coursework should be retained, scrapped or modified? What are the benefits to pupils that would be lost in the event of its abolition?

But what about speaking and listening?
Often viewed as the 'Cinderella' of GCSE, speaking and listening is a hugely important com-ponent. It is worth, as we have said, 20 per cent of the entire *English* examination, and con-stitutes half the coursework marks available. More than this, speaking and listening are essential skills that should be systematically taught and assessed. Teachers should not restrict themselves merely to the required formal assessment tasks, but should realize the full potential of oral work to underpin and enliven reading and writing activities. Careful planning, organizing and assessing oral activities for individuals, groups and entire classes can provide a stimulating access point for literature study and writing tasks. Incorporating these activities within schemes of work is important – and being able to assess them effec-tively is a skill that takes time to develop. All the examination boards produce advice on task-setting and they also produce helpful pro formas for teachers to use to keep oral records. There are also standardizing videos available, with examiner commentary to assist class teachers with their assessment of pupils. Many teachers actually use these videos in lessons and ask their pupils to assess the performances, using the syllabus criteria. This not

only gives the pupils an idea of what the examiners are looking for, but it is an effective way of engaging the pupils in an assessable speaking and listening activity. Some very useful speaking and listening resources have been created by Teachit and the Standards Site, and can be found on our website (12).

The future of GCSEs

As has already been indicated, GCSEs, like the SATs, have been under fire. Proposals are currently being considered to remove the coursework option from most subjects, including *English literature*. The other major change pending is the introduction of *functional skills*. Reacting to criticism from employers, the Confederation of British Industry (CBI) and elements of the media that too many young people (even those with grade C or better) are entering the workforce without basic competence in English and mathematics, the government intends to introduce functional skills tests. At the time of writing, the tests are apparently going through a somewhat troublesome pilot stage and few firm details have emerged as to the exact nature of the tests. What is certain is that pupils who fail to reach an acceptable level on these tests will not be able to gain grade C at GCSE. Sources at the DCSF say that the tests will not be a 'bolt on' construct, but that they will have a specific focus on basic accuracy. It is possible that up to 50 per cent of the marks in *English* could be awarded for functional skills, and the skills tests themselves might be multiple choice. Another very likely feature will be that pupils will be allowed to re-take the tests as many times as they choose. The new GCSE in *English* will be introduced in 2010, and it will definitely incorporate functional skills.

ENGLISH AT AS AND A LEVEL

Discussion, in this section of the chapter, of what is taught at advanced level will, of necessity, be limited by the fact that new specifications are in the process of being finalized. In recent years, universities and employers have argued that the current AS and A level examinations have serious flaws. Principally, their concerns have been that:

- the examinations do not discriminate sufficiently at grade A, leading to difficulties in the allocation of university places
- the current model is less demanding than the original A level (which was in effect a two-year course, without coursework, assessed at the end of the period of study by terminal examination)
- coursework has been devalued as an assessment tool because of widespread plagiarism and excessively directed teaching
- subject content and question-setting have been less demanding
- grade inflation has devalued the 'gold standard' of A levels.

Although some of these assertions are open to debate, the government, through the Department for Education and Lifelong Learning and Skills (DELLS) QCA, in 2006, issued new general criteria for AS and A levels with the intention that examination boards devise new specifications for first teaching from September, 2008. At the time of writing, new syllabuses are available in draft form, and although they are unlikely to change substantially, you are advised to access examination board websites and the QCA site, in order to track developments.

Key changes (for first examination in 2009–10)

2007 specification	2009–10 specification
6 units of study per subject (3 AS and 3 A level)	4 units of study per subject (2 AS and 2 A level)
Structured questions	Fewer structured questions, and more open-ended questions. Also, more questions requiring a synoptic view.
Grades: A B C D E at AS and A level	Grades: A B C D E at AS level Grades: A* A B C D E at A level
Internally assessed coursework units offered at AS and A level	Coursework replaced by extended studies

The move to four units of study does not imply a reduction in content or coverage. Rather, terminal examinations will tend to be longer than those currently in place, and actual content is likely to increase. The inclusion of the new A* grade at A level is indicative of greater challenge in the papers designed for the second year of advanced study. The extended studies tasks in both *English literature* and *English language* are designed to elicit greater independence in terms of candidates' engagement – but the draft specifications are less clear about how the new tasks will reduce plagiarism and other forms of cheating. To give at least a flavour of what is to be offered candidates, the basic *English literature* assessment outlines proposed by the WJEC have been reproduced for you:

ENGLISH LITERATURE

AS (2 units)

LT1 30% 2 hours 30 minutes Written Paper (open text). 75 marks

Introduction to Poetry and Drama

Section A: Poetry post 1900

        Two texts: choice of 1 from 2 questions (50 marks)

Section B: Drama post 1900

        One text: choice of 1 from 2 questions (25 marks)

(Continued)

(Continued)

LT2 20% Internal Assesment. 100 marks

Prose Study and Creative Reading

Section A: Prose Study 1800–1945

> Two texts: one piece of extended writing (75 marks)

Section B: Creative Reading

> One text: one piece of creative writing in response to any literary genre (25 marks)

A Level (the above plus a further 2 units)

LT3 20% Internal Assessment. 50 marks

Period and Genre Study

> Three texts: one piece of extended writing on texts from different periods and genres, including poetry and prose (50 marks)

LT4 30% 2 hours 30 minutes Written Paper (closed text). 75 marks

Shakespeare and Poetry in Context

Section A: Shakespeare and related Drama

> Two texts: choice of 1 from 2 questions (50 marks)

Section B: Poetry pre-1800

> One text: choice of 1 from 2 questions (25 marks)

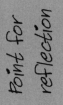

Point for reflection

Compare this summary of assessment with the 2007 version, which can be found on slide 10 of the PowerPoint presentation entitled, 'A Level Literature Teaching', on the website. In what ways does the new model seem more demanding?

 Further details regarding the current AQA specification can be accessed on the website. Look for the PowerPoint entitled, 'Approaches to A Level English Language'. The QCA new specification update information can be also be found on our website.

How to prepare for advanced level teaching

At the outset, you should study the syllabus requirements in detail and make a particular note of the *assessment objectives* of any texts you are going to teach. If you are teaching texts for the terminal examinations, collate any available past or sample examination papers, and create comprehensive lists of assessment objective related questions for your texts. Research and organize your own reference materials, and meet formally with your teaching partners to discuss possible approaches.

Before you meet your teaching group, you should conduct a contextual analysis, utilizing all available information and data. Specifically, you should:

- note the grades your students attained at GCSE
- note any ALIS/ALPS data and the Minimum Target Grades generated for each student. (These are two widely used performance indicator formulas.)

Just as at GCSE, it is important to *share key information with the pupils*. This information can include: syllabus details, study skills advice and strategies, an overview of how the texts will be taught, an indication of the demands that will be made of the students, and a list of any important deadlines. *Lesson planning needs to consider*: the nature of the text(s) being studied, the assessment objectives, time constraints, enhancement and enrichment, and the necessary blend of didacticism with independent study and enjoyment.

Because we are considering, in general terms, two distinctive advanced level subjects, it is not appropriate to detail subject specific teaching strategies in this chapter. However, you might find the following list of *generic teaching strategies*, compiled by PGCE trainees, to be of some assistance when you come to organize your schemes of work:

- asking pupils to pre-read and respond to source material
- creating and disseminating your own explanatory notes/materials
- modelling annotation techniques/note-making
- lecturing on specific elements of the course
- consolidating pupils' analytical knowledge/generic study skills
- asking individual pupils to 'present' certain topics (link to key skills)
- asking individual pupils to interpret and share analysis of published criticism/source material
- producing sample essay plans as part of essay-writing feedback
- copying, sharing and analysing 'good' essays produced by your pupils
- peer marking essays and collectively assessing essays against the marking criteria
- viewing relevant television and film sources and making notes on them
- explaining marking strategies, the assessment objectives and their weighting
- individual target-setting through review points/periodic interviews
- differentiating to meet pupil needs
- varying the format of lessons (teacher-led, group activities, individual activities, problem-solving, role-playing).

This final suggestion is particularly important. Many pupils find the *transition* to advanced level difficult. New demands are being made of them in terms of wider reading and independent study. While it is important to devise effective *induction* processes that enable pupils to adapt to the change in style of lessons, it is also important to build in a sense of continuity from GCSE through continuance of the kinds of varied, interactive teaching strategies that successful teachers use in KS4.

When you are engaged in teaching *extended study units*, you should be aware that such units are designed to develop pupils' independent research and study skills – the kinds of skills that they will need in higher education. The units should also provide an opportunity for pupils to explore topics and genres that interest *them*, rather than the teacher! Good practice that has been applied to the current coursework options will be equally applicable in the extended study tasks. Effective teaching will therefore avoid setting all the pupils a single title and 'teaching to it'. Pupils will be given a range of alternative tasks and texts that fit the assessment objectives – and will be encouraged to come up with their own. Where relevant, the task-setting will be differentiated to challenge the most able and support the less confident. Clear guidance will be given as to *how* to research, manage materials, compile reference lists, structure essays, and integrate received and personal opinion. Supportive teachers will set clear deadlines and identify, in advance, lesson time when they will be available to provide individual support. Most important of all, teachers will be rigorous in their monitoring of the conditions in which the work is produced – and they will not allow copious redrafting.

A final point. The advanced level experience has to be concerned with more than coaching pupils to do well in an examination. It is fundamentally about broadening the intellectual, personal and cultural horizons of the pupils – and preparing them for the future demands of higher education, employment and adulthood. You, as the teacher, must help your pupils to meet the requirements of syllabuses and examinations; but you must also enthuse them, encourage debate, organize trips and residentials, book visiting speakers or performers.

A brilliant history teacher told my A level class, many years ago, that under his guidance we would become historians – and in the process pass A level brilliantly. If you love your subject as much as he loved history, make sure your ambition is as lofty as his.

TEACHING ACROSS KEY STAGES: A BROADER VIEW

Having looked, in some detail, at the assessment models currently operating in each key stage, and having considered strategies for teaching approaches within each key stage, it would be productive at this point to consider the likely differences and similarities in teaching style and emphasis the key stages afford.

Prior to the introduction of the Framework, teachers generally adopted very different approaches to teaching in the discrete key stages. Traditionally, teaching at Key Stage 3 allowed individual departments and teachers much greater flexibility of approach than is now the case, and there was also a distinct change in approach when teachers came to prepare their pupils for GCSE and A level examinations. Although, as we have seen, the current assessment models in Key Stages 3, 4 and 5 seem in some ways to lack obvious progression and continuity, they are still driven by the common imperatives of:

- objective-based lessons
- the recommended lesson structure
- explicit assessment features.

As a result, what actually goes on in most lessons across the key stages is remarkably similar. The principles of Key Stage 3 Framework teaching have, in effect, become the accepted norms in the other key stages too. So, for example, an A level lesson being observed by a senior colleague or inspector would be expected to include the same kind of explicit objectives, lesson structure and interactive teaching strategies that a Key Stage 3 lesson might exemplify. Of course, the A level teacher should employ specific teaching and learning strategies devised to meet the demands of a more advanced context (as discussed earlier in the chapter), but the fundamental approach will largely reflect what has gone on at KS3. The same principles apply at KS4. Teachers of GCSE literature will have to adapt planning and devise strategies to meet the needs of intensive study of a range of literature texts for examination purposes; but the essential thrust of the lessons will reflect Framework principles. The real challenge for the teacher, it seems to me, is to be able to develop the ability to respond to the different contexts of each key stage. Really effective teaching establishes and reflects sound basic principles of continuity and progression, while accommodating the differences in what is actually being studied at each key stage and the increasing maturity of the pupils. Useful source materials, offering guidance on how to plan for progression, can be accessed at the Standards site, via our companion website.

WHAT THE RESEARCH SUGGESTS

Perhaps the most important debate in all three key stages considered in this chapter relates to the issue of standards, and whether they are in fact rising. Sadly, much of the debate tends to be subjective and anecdotal, as exemplified by the QCA-sponsored MORI/CDELL project in 2002. Teachers and pupils continue to be the victims of the debate. When examination pass rates rise, critics argue that the examinations are getting easier. When pass rates fail to meet government targets, then the quality of teaching is blamed. In an attempt to allay fears about grade inflation at A level, Ed Balls, the Secretary of State, has argued (Balls 2007) 'claims that everybody is turning up to university with three A grades at A level are completely wrong. Only 23,000 out of a group of 655,000 reached this level last year'.

This is, in part, a response to the fact that attention has been focused in recent years on steadily rising rates of passes and top grades. At GCSE, the A*–C rate has improved for eight successive years, and the A level pass rate has risen every year for the past 24, nearing 97 per cent in 2006. The proportion of A grades at A level reached 24.1 per cent in 2006 – double what it was in 1990. Naturally, the government seeks to make the case that its reforms, allied to improved teaching, have been the stimulus for what it believes is genuine improvement. Others would contest the assertion that standards are actually rising. At KS3, the percentage of pupils meeting government targets for level 5 in literacy has levelled at around 75 per cent in 2005–07, leading to calls from NATE and the National Literacy Trust for greater emphasis on enjoyment and whole-text study within the English curriculum.

Point for reflection

To what extent do you agree with the assertion that continuously improving examination results at GCSE and A level are indicative of a 'dumbing down' of the examination system?

Point for reflection

Key points from this chapter

In this chapter we have established that:

- the assessment models at each key stage have substantive differences
- teaching and learning across the key stages reflect common principles
- assessment in all three key stages is subject to almost constant revision and change
- effective teaching gives equal weighting to the demands of prescription and the specific context within which the teacher is operating.

Further reading

Brown, J. and Gifford, T. (1989) *Teaching A Level English Literature: A Student Centred Approach.* London: Routledge.
A text that looks beyond the imperatives of specific syllabi. Particularly useful if you have a fairly mixed-ability group.

Keith, G.R. and Shuttleworth, J. (2000) *Living Language: Explaining Advanced Level English Language.* London: Hodder & Stoughton.
Part of the Living Language and Living Literature series. Strong on theory and context, and much more than a mechanistic guide to passing the examination.

Marshall, B. (2000) *English Teachers: The Unofficial Guide. Researching the Philosophies of English Teachers.* London: RoutledgeFalmer.
An intelligent study of what English teaching could and should be about, from one of the more enlightened writers and trainers.

Useful websites

Live links to these websites can be found on the companion website www.sagepub.co.uk/secondary.

Assessing Pupils' Progress web page: www.standards.dfes.gov.uk/secondary/keystage3/respub/englishpubs/ass_eng/
QCA optional tests page: www.qca.org.uk/qca.8659.aspx
Speaking and listening sites: www.teachit.co.uk and www.standards.dfes.gov.uk/speaking and listening/

8

PSHE: DEVELOPING THE WHOLE CHILD THROUGH ENGLISH

Carol Evans

This chapter considers:

- the links between English and many aspects of the non-statutory subject, Personal, Social, Health and Economics Education (PSHEE)
- how teaching English is an ideal means of teaching 'the whole child', and how doing so can address the *Every Child Matters* (DfES, 2004) outcomes
- how PSHEE outcomes can often be naturally addressed in English and media lessons
- how learning to teach English gives you the pedagogic skills necessary to teach PSHE(E) effectively and confidently.

HOW IS PSHE(E) RELEVANT TO ENGLISH?

From September 2008, following the revision of the entire secondary curriculum by the Qualifications and Curriculum Authority (QCA), a new specification for PSHE(E) was implemented, alongside the revised National Curriculum (2007) for English. In this chapter I will focus on the 'Personal Wellbeing' aspects of the QCA website's specification. Although PSHE is taught in many schools as a separately timetabled subject, sometimes with specialist or visiting speakers as key teachers, some schools involve all their teachers in PSHE delivery, and some expect it to be delivered integrally through main curriculum lessons, rather than as a separate subject, and it is this integrated approach which will be addressed in this chapter..

As an English teacher, you'll find frequent opportunities to plan for and teach the knowledge, understanding and skills – known as 'key concepts' and 'key processes' in the specification (QCA, 2007a) – within your English lessons. Above all, this chapter aims to help you to become confident in approaching what, to many teachers, may be a relatively unknown and initially daunting curriculum, requirement. Throughout this chapter, I will use the revised PSHE curriculum, as found on the Qualifications and Curriculum Authority (QCA) website. The PSHE curriculum can be accessed via the companion website www. sagepub.co.uk/secondary. Follow the two links on the website, and you can read the entire PSHE curriculum specification for Key Stage 3 and 4. A print-off would be useful as you read on. It will also be helpful to access to the secondary English National Curriculum as you work through the chapter, again available via the companion website www.sage pub.co.uk/secondary.

WHAT IS PSHE?

'PSHE: Personal wellbeing', as it applies to the secondary age phase, is a non-statutory programme of study at Key Stages 3 and 4, whose curriculum aims are closely linked to all other National Curriculum subject aims, and are underpinned by the *Every Child Matters* (ECM) (DfES, 2004) outcomes. By accessing the QCA website using the link provided, you can see that the QCA states:

> Learning and undertaking activities in personal wellbeing contribute to achievement of the curriculum aims for all young people to become:
>
> - successful learners who enjoy learning, make progress and achieve
> - confident individuals who are able to live safe, healthy and fulfilling lives
> - responsible citizens who make a positive contribution to society (QCA, 2007a: 243).

The programme of study goes on to define more closely what the importance of personal well-being is – and I hope you will forgive me for what is quite a long extract, as I feel it is important for you to consider the QCA's rationale before asking you to consider it within your English teaching:

> Personal wellbeing helps young people embrace change, feel positive about who they are and enjoy healthy, safe, responsible and fulfilled lives. Through active learning opportunities pupils recognise and manage risk, take increasing responsibility for themselves, their choices and behaviours and make positive contributions to their families, schools and communities. As pupils learn to recognise, develop and communicate their qualities, skills and attitudes, they build knowledge, confidence and self-esteem and make the most of their abilities. As they explore similarities and differences between people and discuss social and moral dilemmas, they learn to deal with challenges and accommodate diversity in all its forms. The world is full of complex and sometimes conflicting values. Personal wellbeing helps pupils explore this complexity and reflect on and clarify their own values and attitudes. They identify and articulate feelings and emotions, learn to manage new or difficult situations positively and form and maintain effective relationships with a wide range of people. Personal wellbeing makes a major contribution to the promotion of personal development (QCA, 2007a: 243).

If I had asked you to suggest what you thought the content of a PSHE curriculum might include, offering you this definition of purpose, I suspect that you might have suggested 'drugs', 'sex', 'alcohol', before any mention of the development of 'qualities', 'skills' and 'attitudes'; and you would have been among many of my former trainees, whose memories of PSHE/PSE or similar acronyms from their own school days centre around the more scientific, perhaps embarrassing or sometimes entertaining (to 11–16-year-olds) topics covered. What needs to be made clear from the start, then, is that PSHE as it now exists concerns a broad range of 'key concepts' and 'key processes', in addition to knowledge-based aspects such as sex and drugs education, and it is this broad, 'personal well-being' aspect of the PSHE curriculum on which this chapter focuses.

Another curriculum dimension on which I do not intend to focus here, but which is often confused or conflated with PSHE, is citizenship education. Just to be clear, citizenship education is a statutory element of the secondary curriculum; in David Bell's words as Her Majesty's (former) Chief Inspector of Schools, in his Ofsted lecture to the Hansard Society on 17 January, 2005, he stated:

> the perceived close relationship between citizenship and PSHE is proving problematic. Taking the broad view, *PSHE is about the private, individual dimension of pupils' development, whereas citizenship concerns the public dimension.* They do not sit easily together, particularly when little time is devoted to them. Often, schools claim the content of lessons is citizenship when it is in fact PSHE (Bell, 2005: my emphasis).

Although, therefore, you might see aspects of the PSHE and English curricula which lend themselves to a citizenship slant, I intend to concentrate in this chapter on the more 'private', or personal dimension of pupils' development, even though this will also involve social aspects of their experience and reflections.

PSHE, ENGLISH AND EVERY CHILD MATTERS

Again on the QCA website (2007e), you can find a useful elucidation of how English can contribute to the ECM agenda. I see the underpinning philosophy here as one of *whole-child* development – something that I feel is crucial for English teachers to remember if we are to enhance what might become a fragmentary, skills-based approach to the English curriculum – something which the National Curriculum (2000) (www.qca.org.uk) and other national Frameworks were accused of encouraging (albeit unintentionally, perhaps) by some educationalists, since their inception. As you read on, consider how far you feel you have already observed learning experiences in schools/actually taught lessons in line with the approaches described:

English, personal development and Every Child Matters

Enjoy and achieve

The contribution English makes to pupils' enjoyment stems from the opportunities it gives them to explore their identity and place in the world, engage actively, have their assumptions challenged and challenge the assumptions of others. Pupils appreciate the opportunities it gives them to express themselves, whether by presenting their ideas and opinions to persuade readers and listeners or by creating new worlds, both familiar and unfamiliar, in poetry and narrative. Pupils enjoy being exposed to the richness and breadth of literature. They relish the way that reading can present familiar settings and dilemmas one moment and then ask them to empathise with situations and characters that are beyond their experience the next. Pupils value the ways in which English helps them achieve, in the subject, across the curriculum and in the world beyond, by developing their ability to communicate clearly and effectively.

Be healthy

Central to English is reading for pleasure – encouraging pupils to read as a way to relax and be transported from their day-to-day worries and concerns. Similarly, literature can

(Continued)

(Continued)

help young people work through problems and dilemmas they face by suggesting how they may deal with such problems. Both these aspects of reading have an important role to play in ensuring pupils' mental health and sense of well-being.

Stay safe

English gives pupils the confidence to ask questions, rather than taking things at face value. It provides them with the skills to examine the validity of what they are told or read and challenge it on grounds of logic, evidence or argument. Through reading a variety of texts and discussing issues, English can provide opportunities to explore situations and dilemmas that will help pupils make the right choices to stay safe.

Achieve economic well-being

English plays a central role in contributing to young people's long-term economic well-being by developing the literacy and communication skills essential to any job. It encourages them to be adaptable and find creative solutions to problems, plan and prepare to put their views and ideas across for maximum effect, and work effectively in groups. All these are skills and attributes valued by employers.

Make a positive contribution

English provides many opportunities for pupils to get involved and contribute positively by working collaboratively, most obviously as part of a group discussion or drama performance, but also through the emphasis on pupils evaluating and providing constructive responses to each other's work. Another key aspect of making a positive contribution is being involved in the community, and in English pupils have the opportunity to speak, listen and write for purposes and contexts beyond the classroom (QCA, 2007e).

HOW CONFIDENT (OR COMPETENT) ARE TEACHERS TO TEACH PSHE?

An Office for Standards in Education (Ofsted) report *Personal, Social and Health Education in secondary schools* (2005), drew on evidence from whole-school inspections and surveys by Her Majesty's Inspectors (HMI) from the previous two years. Many improvements in the teaching and learning of PSHE were noted, and the Executive Summary highlighted the finding that: 'Good PSHE lessons provide opportunities for pupils to reflect on their own attitudes and values as well as those of others. They will have opportunities to further develop key skills such as those of communication and be able to know when and how to be assertive' (Ofsted, 2005: 3). A distinction is clearly drawn between such schools and those which:

> perceive achievement in PSHE only in terms of pupils' subject knowledge and understanding; no attempt is made to judge whether there has been any impact on their attitudes, values and personal development ... In too few PSHE lessons were pupils given opportunities to analyse, reflect, speculate, discuss and argue constructively about their understanding of issues (Ofsted, 2005: 3).

The sections on teaching and learning in the report began, again, with a distinction between specialist teachers' relative security when teaching what I will call 'scientific' aspects of the curriculum (drugs/sex), and that of non-specialist teachers in these topics. Less competence, too, was seen in teaching the affective domain elements – feelings or emotions, often referred to as 'emotional intelligence', further defined as 'the ability to perceive emotions, to access and generate emotions so as to assist thought, to understand emotions and emotional knowledge, and to reflectively regulate emotions so as to promote emotional and intellectual growth' (Salovey and Sluyter, 1997: 3–31).

The Office for Standards in Education found that: 'Often PSHE programmes emphasise knowledge and understanding at the expense of other objectives … for example, four out of ten lessons taught by form tutors, as against one in ten lessons taught by teachers with specialist knowledge, fail to explore what pupils think or to challenge existing attitudes' (Ofsted, 2005: 5). 'Form tutors' here are subject specialists, such as yourself, and Ofsted went on to identify the skills which best allowed for pupils' personal development:

> If pupils are to be able to analyse, reflect, speculate, discuss and argue constructively about their understanding of issues, they need to develop appropriate skills. Where provision was good, pupils had opportunities to develop:
>
> - communication skills, such as putting forward a point of view and listening to those of others
> - decision-making so that they can make sensible choices based on relevant information
> - the ability to make moral judgements about what to do in actual situations and put these judgements into practice
> - interpersonal skills so that they can manage relationships confidently and effectively
> - assertiveness
> - the ability to act responsibly as an individual and as a member of various groups (Ofsted, 2005: 5).

Points for reflection

Keep these findings in mind as you read on, and return to them as you reflect on your own developing, transferable skills. You might also like to think back to the sample lessons which you have seen on the companion website (Ian, Monika and Sarah). Consider to what extent their lessons enabled their pupils to develop these skills.

CURRICULUM CONTENT AND LINKS WITH ENGLISH

So how does the PSHE curriculum link to English? A review of what you have just read from Ofsted, from the QCA, about emotional intelligence and about the *Every Child Matters* outcomes should point to obvious connections with English. If you take each of the bullet points above (from 'communication skills' to 'various groups'), it would be difficult not to address one or more of these personal skills in an English lesson. Once you realize this, planning for the development of pupils' personal well-being should be much easier. What follows is an exploration of how you might combine your English and PSHE planning in literature, language and media lessons, and in your pedagogic approaches.

LITERATURE AND PSHE

As an example using literary study, look at Figure 8.1, which shows how PSHE key concepts and key processes might be addressed through an English text often used at Key Stage 4. The text chosen is Willy Russell's musical play, *Blood Brothers*, which tells the fictional life stories of twins separated at birth because of economic and social hardship. The musical drama is emotive, often challenging and invariably (in my experience) engaging for pupils of the 14–16 age group, prompting much reaction, through both laughter and tears.

Figure 8.1 itemizes the subheadings within the first PSHE key concepts section, and it would be helpful if you had in front of you both the PSHE curriculum document for Key Stage 4 and the English specification (each available via the companion website). It is worth checking the explanatory notes offered within these documents by the QCA, to help you to see exactly what might be meant within each 'concept'. Using these documents, notice how the text could be used as a means of enhancing both English skills and understanding, and PSHE or cross-curricular development in your pupils.

Although I would vehemently warn against forgetting that any piece of fictional writing should primarily be read and *enjoyed* rather than being seen merely as a vehicle for the delivery of an aspect of curriculum, this particular play is rich in potential for the development of pupils' English and personal skills and understanding. For example, if you look further into the key concepts section, you will find aspects of 'Healthy lifestyles' (1.2a: 'Recognizing that

PSHE Key Stage 4: key concepts	Topical connection to English text	National Curriculum English link
1.1 Personal identities		
a Understanding that identity is affected by a range of factors, including a positive sense of self	Links with Willy Russell's *Blood Brothers*: themes of self esteem/ unemployment/equality and inequality/economic struggle affecting friendships and family relationships/personal choice	**Key processes: 2.2 Reading** The author's craft. Pupils should be able to understand and comment on: j how texts are crafted to shape meaning and produce particular effects;m how writers present ideas and issues to have an impact on the reader;p how texts relate to the social, historical and cultural context in which they were written
b Recognizing that the way in which personal qualities, attitudes, skills and achievements are evaluated affects confidence and self-esteem		
c Understanding that self-esteem can change with personal circumstances, such as those associated with family and friendships, achievements and employment		**Range and content: 3.2 Reading** The texts chosen should be: b interesting and engaging, allowing pupils to explore their present situation or move beyond it to experience different times, cultures, viewpoints and situations **Curriculum opportunities: 4.2 Reading** c develop reading skills through work that makes cross-curricular links with other subjects

Figure 8.1   Links between PSHE key concepts and English National Curriculum requirements

healthy lifestyles, and the wellbeing of self and others, depend on information and making responsible choices'), 'Risk' (1.3b: 'Appreciating that pressure can be used positively or negatively to influence others in situations involving risk') and 'Diversity' (1.5b: 'Understanding that all forms of prejudice and discrimination must be challenged at every level in our lives'), which are equally applicable to the text and may make fertile ground for rich discussion and debate with reference to the twins and their life chances, self-determination and outside pressures.

Points for reflection

With your two curricular documents (PSHE and English) still in front of you, try the activity in Figure 8.2. A selection of PSHE key concepts and processes are written in, along with some suggested texts which might be useful and relevant. Your task is to try to complete the table as in Figure 8.1, using texts which you know well and consider appropriate for teaching at Key Stage 4, and reviewing the National Curriculum for English specification in order to complete the final column. If you struggle with this exercise, ask your peers or school-based colleagues to add their suggestions.

PSHE Key Stage 4: key concepts/key processes	Which English text would you choose?	National Curriculum English links: key concepts and processes
Key concept 1.1: Understanding that identity is affected by a range of factors, including a positive sense of self		
Key concept 1.2c: Dealing with growth and change as normal parts of growing up		
Key process 2.1e: Develop self-awareness by reflecting critically on their behaviour and its impact on others	for example, *Macbeth*	
Key process 2.3d: Demonstrate respect for and acceptance of the differences between people, and challenge offensive behaviour, prejudice and discrimination assertively and safely	for example, *To Kill a Mockingbird*	

Figure 8.2   Which text would you choose?

SUGGESTED TEXTS

Once you have begun to see these links, and the more you get to know both the PSHE and English curriculum specifications, you will see how integral many aspects of PSHE are to literary study and simply reading for pleasure. You might find the following list of texts, often found in high schools' English stockrooms, useful as a starting point with regard to PSHE connections. I am indebted to Jean Raybould (PSHE Co-ordinator and English teacher) and the rest of the English department at Range High School, Formby, for these suggestions:

Author	Title	Topics
Theresa Breslin	*Divided City*	Sectarianism
Betsy Byars	*Midnight Fox*	Personal growth
Deborah Ellis	*The Breadwinner*	Totalitarianism/gender issues
Mark Hadden	*The Curious Incident of the Dog in the Night-Time*	Diversity/empathy/personal growth
Nigel Hinton	*Buddy*	Relationships
Harper Lee	*To Kill a Mockingbird*	Racism/tolerance/personal growth
Joan Lingard	*Across the Barricades/ 12th Day of July*	Sectarianism/tolerance
Michael Morpurgo	*Why the Whales Came*	Tolerance
Terry Pratchett	*Johnny and the Dead* (play)	War
Willy Russell	*Blood Brothers* (musical play)	Personal growth/social and economic influences/ relationships
Louis Sachar	*Holes*	Delinquency/cruelty/ respect/self-awareness and growth
Barbara Smucker	*Underground to Canada*	Slavery
Robert Swindells	*Stone Cold*	Homelessness
Robert Swindells	*Abomination*	Religious sects

This list gives a flavour of the possibilities at Key Stages 3 and 4. If you consider canonical literature, pre-twentieth-century works and multicultural works you will have no trouble identifying those key concepts and key processes in PSHE and English which could profitably be planned for when you compile your schemes of work. Additionally, some fruitful personal development discussions will occur spontaneously in lessons on literature, though you should not depend on this: plan for PSHE within your English planning, whenever realistic opportunities occur, to do so. For a further, superb list of Key Stage 3 texts which raise many issues relevant to PSHE, look at Jo Westbrook's chapter 5, 'Equal opportunities', in Clarke et al. (2004).

LANGUAGE AND PSHE

As with literary study, so the study of the English language invites easy links to PSHE. An overt example at both key stages lies in PSHE section 2.3, 'Developing relationships and working with others', where working in teams, negotiating within relationships, demonstrating respect and acceptance of difference are targeted. The Key Stage 4 'Explanatory notes' state explicitly here, that 'links should be made … with the functional skill of English (speaking and listening)' (QCA, 2007b: 257). The English curriculum specifies, within the key Process of Speaking and Listening, that

> 2.1 Pupils should be able to:
> e. listen and respond constructively to others, taking different views into account and modifying their own views in the light of what others say
>
> g. make different kinds of relevant contributions in groups, responding appropriately to others, proposing ideas and asking questions. (QCA, 2007c: 64)

The parallels should be clear to you, and both English and PSHE requirements are easily accommodated.

Similarly, at both key stages, issues of diversity and prejudice (via, for example, work on dialect and accent), how people play multiple roles in society (via work on language variation according to audience and purpose) and information retrieval and evaluation (via the use of Internet or other information texts on language topics) forge obvious links between PSHE and English language, whether spoken/heard or written/read.

PSHE AND MEDIA

Points for reflection

No study of the media in English could ignore a focus on its power to influence individuals, groups or whole societies. Before reading on, try the activity in Figure 8.3.

Media and health education: sample lesson

Recent research (Evans and Evans, 2007) has suggested that new teachers are underconfident about teaching issues such as health education, and this supports Ofsted's findings when surveying non-specialist teachers of PSHE (Ofsted, 2005). Problems revolve largely around a perceived lack of subject knowledge, for example with regard to sex, drugs and healthy eating, and you will need to prepare yourself by accessing resources from a wide range of sources, so that you are equipped for pupils' questions and misconceptions.

The QCA recommend several websites linked to their framework, Social and Emotional Aspects of Learning (SEAL), which you will find referred to on the PSHE programme of study page, and can also be accessed via the companion website, at www.sagepub.co.uk/

Fill in the table below, identifying any cross-over with PSHE programmes of study, and one or more media resource which you might choose for each learning point. The first has been done for you:

English curricular requirement	PSHE curricular topic	Media resource(s) (for example, newspaper/magazine/DVD fiction clip/TV news clip/radio clip/web page …)
1.1b Reading and understanding a range of texts, and responding appropriately	2.2b Find information and support from a variety of sources	Selected webpages/informative magazines/TV documentary clip/leaflets …
1.3b Exploring how ideas, experiences and values are portrayed differently in texts from a range of cultures and traditions		
1.4d Analysing and evaluating spoken and written language to appreciate how meaning is shaped		
2.1i Sift, summarize and use the most important points		
2.2i Understand how meaning is created through the combination of words, images and sounds in multimodal texts		
2.2k How writers structure and organize different texts, including non-linear and multimodal		
2.3b Write imaginatively, creatively and thoughtfully, producing texts that interest and engage the reader		

Figure 8.3   Using media in PSHE

secondary: www.standards.dfes.gov.uk. Following its use in primary schools, SEAL was implemented in secondary schools from September 2007. You should use all such sources of information critically, ensuring that potential misconceptions, prejudices and simplistic interpretations are avoided.

In recent years on the Edge Hill University course for PGCE English, one activity-based session has shown trainees how English and media can be used as a vehicle for the exploration of pupils' attitudes to body image. The session questions some of the simplistic interpretations of government messages about obesity, body size and fitness which have prevailed in recent years (for example, HOC, 2004. For in-depth research and analysis of the issues, see, for example, Evans, 2004, 2006; Evans and Davies, 2004; Evans et al., 2003; papers within Evans et al., 2004).

As an example of how children can be encouraged to take critical standpoints and to consider potential influences on their own beliefs and choices, the lesson:

> uses magazine images to encourage pupils to question the construction of 'healthy' and 'unhealthy' in relation to body size, shape, and behaviour, and broader issues relating to the presentation of bodily norms through media texts in relation to age, ethnicity, gender, sexuality, (dis)ability, etc. Rather than focussing on giving trainees specialist 'health' knowledge, these sessions encourage trainees to recognise the potential which the English curriculum has, to contribute to a broader health curriculum through the use of critical, analytical and interactive methods (Evans and Evans, 2007: 44-5).

Points for reflection

The lesson plan is offered here (Figure 8.4) to help you to envisage such an activity within your own planning and teaching. After you review it, try the activities yourself, along with peers if possible, to see how your own perceptions might be reflected or challenged.

PEDAGOGIC APPROACHES IN PSHE AND ENGLISH

So far, this chapter has focused largely on the *content* of the PSHE and English curricula, in an attempt to demonstrate how addressing many English requirements allows simultaneous attention to be paid to aspects of the PSHE programmes of study, particularly with regard to the development of pupils' self-esteem, self-awareness and emotional intelligence. Next, we consider to what extent the *skills* and *pedagogic approaches* which you will develop as a trainee teacher in English will equip you to teach PSHE confidently.

The Office for Standards in Education suggested that: 'Where schools involve tutors in teaching PSHE, senior managers should ensure that tutors receive specialist training to help them improve both their subject knowledge and their use of appropriate teaching approaches' (Ofsted, 2005: 4). The teaching approaches which led to the most effective lessons involved:

- use of a well-structured lesson with clear, realistic learning objectives
- lesson activities that were matched to the lesson aims
- high expectations of the pupils, taking due note of their prior experiences
- good subject knowledge, manifested in the high quality of teacher exposition
- effective use of a range of strategies including group work, role play and whole-class discussion
- creation of a climate that allowed and encouraged pupils to express their views on their feelings
- promotion of respect for the views of others (Ofsted, 2005: 7).

If you consider this list in light of what you have hopefully already learned about good English teaching, from this book and your training to date, you will see how many of the qualities listed by Ofsted correspond with advice given here.

PGCE secondary English lesson plan: all key stages

Class (including ability range): Any KS3/4 English/PSHE
Length of lesson: 2 hours (split over two lessons)
Topic: Media/PSHE

Aim (What is your key purpose in this lesson?): To encourage pupils to recognize how the media can construct norms, to help them to resist pressure to conform to these norms and how it may affect their self esteem.

Learning Objectives: *by the end of the lesson, pupils will:*

English
LOb1:   Explore magazines to extract surface and subconscious effects on readers with regard to body image
LOb2:   Form own opinions and outline own reactions to magazines
LOb3:   Explore with others how they respond to magazines
LOb4:   Analyse the power of images combined with text in magazines

PSHE
LOb5:   Explore possible links between magazines, influences on readers' self-esteem and health implications
LOb6:   Reflect on the potential health risks for themselves and others, attached to media pressure
LOb7:   Identify potential reinforcement of prejudice and discrimination in magazine image choices

Learning Outcomes: *What will pupils produce in this lesson?*

- group collages of images from magazines
- notes on cards reflecting on images
- discussions reflecting on media 'messages'
- posters to show 'norms' in magazine images
- reflective discussion about power of media and potential for individual resistance

Differentiation   (What strategies will you use to cater for the different abilities in your class?):
The tasks are all image based. More academically able students can choose to work with text rather than purely images, and those who feel more comfortable working only with images can do so.

Assessment: You will tell pupils/students that you will be looking for the following specific evidence of their learning, when you assess their oral/written work:
All LOs: assessed via discussion responses and via plenary

Resources needed:
Teenagers' magazines, pens, A3 paper, scissors, glue.

Key NC/Literacy Objective/Examination Syllabus References specifically targeted in this lesson:

English:
R2.2e   Assess the usefulness of texts, sift the relevant from the irrelevant and distinguish between fact and opinion
R2.2f   Recognize and discuss different interpretations of media texts, justifying their own views on what they read and see, and supporting them with evidence
R2.2g   Understand how audiences and readers choose and respond to texts
R2.2i   Understand how meaning is created through the combination of words (and) images in multimodal texts.

Figure 8.4   PSHE and English/Media lesson plan sample

Figure 8.4   (Continued)

PSHE:
1.1c   Understanding that self-esteem can change with personal circumstances …
1.2a   Recognizing that healthy lifestyles, and the well-being of self and others, depend on information and making responsible choices.
1.3b   Appreciating that pressure can be used positively or negatively to influence others in situations involving risk.
1.5b   Understanding that all forms of prejudice and discrimination must be challenged at every level in our lives.

Content, including introduction, teaching and learning methods and activities, timings and review session:

NB. It is important for all of these tasks that it is instant reactions that are gained. For this reason the timings for each task are short. Students should be made aware of the amount of time for each task and that exploration is important, rather than right' or 'wrong' answers.

Hour 1

Introduction (5 mins)
Background to the debate about how media can affect people (especially young people) – make reference to debates about media and eating disorders, and media and aggressive behaviour (film classifications, copycat crimes, desensitisation and so on).

Methods and activities (30 mins)
Pupils are split into small groups (approx. 4 per group). NB. It is important that the pupils choose to be in friendship groups. Preferably single sex groups.

Tasks:
1.   Pupils are given a magazine each. They should work on their own, flicking through the magazines and tearing out any pictures or articles that catch their attention. (3 mins max.)
2.   Students should work in their groups, collating their articles/pictures. They should split the pictures into several (5) categories, 'healthy', 'unhealthy' and 3 *of their own choice* and name these categories. (5 mins.)
3.   As a group, students should write down the title of the category and what the pictures in it represent. (5 mins.) [Optional extra if time: each group presents one category to the rest of the class.]
4.   Looking at these categories and the pictures/articles within them, students should make a poster about what messages are being conveyed. (15 mins.)

Review (15 mins)

Final time should be spent in class discussion comparing what each group has done and pulling out similarities.

Key points to note are (links to English/PSHE curricula in brackets):

* Differences in focus of girls' and boys' magazines. Girls' focus on image and getting a boyfriend – passive, submissive role; boys' are activity based – sport, computer and so on represented in pictures (How choice of form layout and presentation contribute to effect.)
* This means that the messages are different about boys' and girls' roles in society. (How meaning is conveyed in texts.)
* In terms of audience, these magazines target a specific audience, but also tell this audience what they should want. Which came first? (How audiences and readers choose and respond to media.)

(Continued)

Figure 8.4 (Continued)

- The images present a norm. This is done through repetition – a lot of groups' categories will be the same. Are 'alternative' lifestyles represented? (How choice of form layout and presentation contribute to effect.)
- Deconstruct ideas of healthy vs unhealthy. Stress that thin, fit and healthy are not necessarily the same thing. They are just presented in this way in the media. Encourage students to recognize that fat is not bad and thin is not necessarily good! (What influences health, including media).

NB. Keep the groups' images for next lesson

Hour 2

Introduction (5 mins)

Continue from previous lesson to look at how the messages and content of media can affect how happy we are with ourselves (self-esteem).

Methods and activities (40 mins)

Pupils return to the groups they were working in last lesson, and receive the posters they made and the folders with their image categories and selected images in.

Tasks:

1. Working on their own, students should select 3 pictures/articles which make them feel good about themselves and 3 pictures/articles which make them feel bad about themselves. They should write down on a card/poster why they make them feel good/bad about themselves. (10 mins.)
2. In their groups, students should select 2 pictures and answer the following questions about the pictures: (15 mins.)

   - What message does the picture convey?
   - How does it make you feel?
   - Who benefits from the picture?
   - How do they benefit?
   - Who, if anyone, could be hurt by the picture?
   - How could they be hurt?

3. Using these images and the posters made at the end of hour 1, students should consider how the media represents the world: what are the overall messages? Are these realistic? How have different people/ voices/pictures (fat people, ethnic minorities, gay/lesbians and so on) been excluded from the magazines? students should create a poster showing who is the norm according to the media. (15 mins.)

Plenary (10 mins)

Pupils to discuss in pairs, then open to class discussion/drawing conclusions:

How can the media influence people in different ways?
How have your own thoughts and feelings been affected by the sessions?

- Link to last lesson – certain people/lifestyles presented as normal, ideal and linked to healthy
- This can exclude people and hurt people, and make people think they have to change themselves. (Recognize pressures.)
- The people who aim to gain are big companies – advertising, magazine sales and so on. They make us unhappy and then sell us products aimed at changing ourselves. Because we know this is the case, we can resist this pressure and recognize that being different isn't bad. (Use assertiveness skills to resist unhelpful pressure.)

Dr Bethan Evans (Manchester Metropolitan University) and Carol Evans (Edge Hill University)
With acknowledgements to colleagues at Loughborough University, where the idea for this lesson originated.

Points for reflection

Briefly consider the bullet point list above. Note down beneath each one how you could already demonstrate your pedagogic competence in delivering PSHE lessons, based on your practice to date, in English. If any points remain, consider how you might plug the gap by furthering your own practice or personal and professional research.

Typically effective skills demonstrated by good English trainees, and considered equally essential in good PSHE teachers, can be seen in Figure 8.5, based on informal research which I have conducted, in which teachers of PSHE and other subjects responded to a series of written questions. Again, consider these in relation to your own pedagogic approaches in your English lessons. Look, particularly, at how many of the approaches involve basic drama techniques. I have deliberately not included a separate section on PSHE through drama in this chapter, as I believe that effective English teaching in any element of the English curriculum (literature, language, media/speaking and listening, reading and writing) will benefit from a pedagogic approach which makes appropriate use of drama techniques. For further discussion of the historical debates around, and more recent position of drama in the curriculum, read Jonathan Neelands' excellent chapter, 'Drama sets you free – or does it?' in Davison and Moss (2000: 73–98).

ASSESSING PSHE

One of the most criticized aspects of PSHE in Ofsted's report was its assessment. There is no current requirement to assess PSHE formally at Key Stages 3 and 4, though guidance from QCA (QCA, 2005b) is available on the website. Be aware, however, that this was written prior to the curriculum review, and will undoubtedly be updated by September 2008.

One very obvious way in which assessment applies to PSHE objectives targeted within your English teaching is in the form of self and peer assessment, and you can see a prime example of these in practice in Sarah's lesson on the website. Notice how she uses both peer and self assessment in a very structured way at the start of her lesson, as a means of encouraging collaborative working, focusing pupils on learning objectives from previous homework, recapping that work in order to contextualize today's learning and enabling pupils to develop the PSHE key processes in 2.1:

b reflect on personal strengths, achievements and areas for development
c recognise how others see them and give and receive feedback
d identify and use strategies for setting and meeting personal targets in order to increase motivation. (QCA, 2007a: 245)

Although Sarah did not specify these PSHE objectives on her lesson plan, she might well have done so, as she certainly addressed them effectively here.

If you wish to/your school requires you to report on PSHE progress to parents, or even to give feedback in this form to pupils, themselves, Figure 8.6 shows a school report proforma,

Suggested by	Skills and qualities of good subject/PSHE teachers	Your reflection in relation to your own pedagogic practices
Angela Mayer, Assistant Head Lower School, Year 7 PSHE Co-ordinator and Food Technology teacher: Parklands High School, Specialist Language College, Chorley	– Ability to generate discussion – Provision of stimulating teaching material – Having the confidence to develop pupils' creative ideas – Using role play, drama, group tasks and lots of discussion	
Jean Raybould, PSHE Co-ordinator and English teacher: Range High School, Formby	– Ability to lead discussion – Confidence in dealing with questions, and being willing to say, 'I don't know, but I know someone who does!' – Encouraging growth of emotional literacy – Understanding how PSHE underpins learning and the ability to learn, by promoting confidence and self-esteem in pupils – Seeing literature as an appropriate vehicle for consideration of 'issues' in PSHE	
Anthony Rider, PE/PSHE teacher: Holy Cross Catholic High School, Sports and Science College, Chorley	– Being approachable – Being adaptable – Being able to generate interest and inquisitiveness – Being confident with groups – Being knowledgeable – Adapting information to suit the group	

Figure 8.5   What effective PSHE teachers need: practitioners' views

quoted by HMI in Ofsted's report (QCA, 2005b), which should help you, once again, to see what overlap there is between PSHE and English skills, and how transferable your own assessment practices should be in addressing this.

HOW YOU CAN HELP YOURSELF

No amount of training, reading or research can ever equip you to meet every classroom circumstance or every pupil's question with supreme confidence. When trainee teachers – and many experienced teachers – are faced with teaching a lesson which is not in their specialist

In the following example, the school provides a report for parents on PSHE. The report comprises:

Name of pupil: Teaching group:
Name of teacher: Date:
Course description
Grades are given for achievement and effort participation/contribution against the key criteria:

- understanding of the course content
- ability to express personal opinions in writing
- ability to express personal opinions orally
- ability to respond to the opinions of others
- contribution to group work
- ability to work co-operatively with others
- interest shown in social and moral issues.

Figure 8.6   A PSHE report (QCA, 2005b)

subject, they are often nervous. What you can best do to prepare, however, is to make and take every possible opportunity to develop your knowledge and skills in advance of being alone in the classroom.

In recent research, (Evans and Evans, 2007), former PGCE English trainees were asked what they felt would have enhanced their training for PSHE teaching. Top of the list for some was further development of their factual knowledge about topics such as drug and sex education, and, more generally, ideas about what, exactly, to cover. Others would have liked more advice about how to incorporate PSHE into their English teaching. While I hope that this chapter has gone some way to addressing the latter, it is up to you to research the facts and myths of sex and drugs education before venturing into these topics in the classroom. These aspects of the non-statutory PSHE curriculum, however, are also statutory within the science curriculum, so are covered from a scientific angle there; in addition, in many schools, such sensitive topics are delivered by specialist teams or visiting speakers. The advantages and disadvantages of this approach are debatable, though one teacher's caution is worth considering:

Areas such as sex education, or maybe drugs [might be felt problematic by new teachers] ... This is due to the fact that the children may actually know more about drugs and similar issues than the teachers do. (PSHE teacher, 2007, in response to questionnaire)

When you are expected to teach such sensitive topics, while needing to prepare your subject knowledge in advance, you should remember the cross-curricular skills and the range of pedagogic approaches which this chapter has shown that you are developing as part of your expertise as an English teacher, many of which involve your own sensitivity in establishing an open, approachable, professional relationship with your pupils. As one trainee once wrote, 'I think you need to learn from experience and get to know the kids you're showing how to put a condom on a wooden stick!' (former trainee teacher, in response to questionnaire).

A second way in which you can prepare yourself for PSHE teaching is to use your teaching placements in two ways. First, make a point of arranging a discussion with the PSHE co-ordinator. Ask about the way the curriculum is managed and planned: who teaches on PSHE? What is the timetable arrangement for PSHE? What resources are used – and, if possible, can you borrow and/or copy resources for future use?

Thirdly, bite the bullet and ask to be timetabled for at least one PSHE class. Request observation of experienced and successful PSHE teachers first, then ask to be allowed to co-plan and co-teach with one or more of these teachers; and ask to be allowed to deliver PSHE lessons yourself, with the expert teacher observing, and giving you feedback after each lesson. This training scenario is just as useful as it is in your English training, yet it is often forgotten and leaves you at a loss when you start your newly qualified teacher (NQT) post. As Mead (2004) discovered, few trainee primary teachers involved in his research had had more than one or two opportunities on teaching placements to teach PSHE.

Finally, but by no means of least importance, make a decision to include PSHE curricular objectives, as appropriate, whenever you plan your English lessons. In this way, you will become increasingly familiar with the PSHE programmes of study, and it will become second nature for you to capitalize on opportunities to develop personal and social skills relevant to every child.

In summary, I will return to the final statement of Ofsted's (2005) 'Executive Summary'. In order to give you confidence that you really do have the range of skills needed, I would ask you, as you read this, to consider to what extent this statement might be applicable to good *English* teaching and learning, as well as to PSHE:

> The pupils have the last word. When asked what value they placed on their PSHE lessons, a group of Year 10 pupils responded:
>
> 'PSHE is not just about learning facts. We have had the chance to reflect on our own and other people's feelings and friendships and have been helped to understand our physical and emotional development. We enjoy the chance to talk about issues that are important to us now and in the future' (Ofsted, 2005: 2).

WHAT THE RESEARCH SUGGESTS

Other than Ofsted's report (2005) and the more lengthy QCA publication which draws largely on Ofsted's findings (QCA, 2005a), little research relating directly to the delivery of PSHE through English is revealed on an electronic search. The subject association for PSHE, however, (see link in our companion website) planned its first national conference in 2008. Evans and Evans (2007) provide some food for thought with regard to recent trainees' levels of confidence in teaching PSHE in the early years of their careers, and this chapter draws on its findings.

More specific research about healthy eating, body image and the dangers of associated, simplified messages equating 'fit' with 'thin' and 'unfit' with 'fat' make important reading if unsafe dichotomies are to be avoided in the classroom. See any of Evans, 2004, 2006; Evans and Davies, 2004: Evans et al., 2003; papers within Evans et al., 2004.

Mead's (2004) research in primary schools also provides a rather dismal reflection on how little experience of PSHE teaching trainees might get during school-based experience, and should encourage you to press for greater involvement during your own placements.

Key points from this chapter

- Many aspects of PSHE are a genuinely integral part of the English curriculum.
- Remember that you can be confident in your ability to teach PSHE both within and outside your English lessons, knowing that the pedagogic strategies which you use in teaching English effectively will also enable you to teach PSHE effectively.

Further reading

Because this chapter is largely about how to teach PSHE within your English teaching, further reading might include almost any resource which allows you to adopt an interactive, socially constructivist approach to learning. One of the key pedagogic approaches which will assist you in enabling pupils to explore their – and other – worlds is drama, and many books by well-established drama practitioners (such as Dorothy Heathcote and Jonathan Neelands) will help you to gain confidence in using drama technique in exploring values and attitudes. In *Beginning Drama 11–14*, Neelands writes,

> Drama has been, and can still be, an important means of making the hidden influences of a community's culture visible, discussible and changeable. Drama represents how we live, how we have come to live this way, and how we might live differently. It both uses and comments on the webs of rules, conventions, status, traditions, collective identities, taboos and other shared meanings that constitute a community's culture. Making drama involves pupils in discussing and commenting on these cultural concepts. It allows them to 'play' with images of who they are and who they are becoming, to invent alternatives and to physically experience the difference of being 'someone else' (Neelands, 1998: 38).

Stephen Clarke, Paul Dickinson and Jo Westbrook's comprehensive book, *The Complete Guide to Becoming an English Teacher* (2004) is a rich source of ideas, activities and resource suggestions for any aspect of your training. In relation to PSHE in English, I would particularly recommend you to start with chapter 5, 'Equal opportunities' (Jo Westbrook), chapter 6, 'Inclusion' (Stephen Clarke and Sue Dymoke) and chapter 19, 'Teaching practical drama' (Sarah Gooch).

Mark Pike's (2004) chapter, 'Spiritual and moral development through English', in his *Teaching Secondary English* offers some helpful ideas about how you might address pupils' spiritual and moral development, 'in a way that is true to the aims of the "personal growth" model [of English teaching] and is itself morally justified' (Pike, 2004: 169).

Pastoral Care in Education is the international journal for pastoral care and personal-social education published monthly on behalf of the National Association for Pastoral Care in Education. It contains articles of both a scholarly and practical application, and with a research focus.

Useful websites

Live links to these websites can be found on the companion website www.sagepub.co.uk/secondary.
For access to PSHE resources, start with any of the commonly used websites, which are extensive and do need to be reviewed, critically.

www.teachernet.gov.uk/subjects/pshe links directly to the SEAL site (Social and Emotional Aspects of Learning).

www.citized.info is strictly beyond the scope of this chapter, but a valuable site for resources and authoritative articles about citizenship education.

www.pshe-association.org.uk is the subject association for PSHE whose home page states its mission as 'helping teachers and other PSHE professionals to better plan, manage, deliver, evaluate and monitor PSHE provision, raising its status and quality and increasing its impact on, and relevance to, learners in the 21st century' (accessed 20 April 2008).

9 USING ICT IN ENGLISH

Lynne Warham

This chapter considers:

- the advantages and pitfalls of using various forms of ICT in the classroom
- the development in ICT use in recent years and areas for further development within the English teaching profession
- how to use computer basics to engage pupils in active learning
- interactive whiteboards and 'Whizzy' resources
- basic web tools and how they can be successfully used as teaching and learning tools.

WHY USE ICT?

Regardless of your own level of expertise when it comes to information and communication technology (ICT), there can be no doubt that the pupils you teach will have more knowledge of and access to such technologies than ever before. Clear evidence of this comes not just through observations of society around us, but from research such as that conducted for the Literacy Trust in 2005 and 2008 (discussed later in the chapter). It seems that 'on-screen texts' are currently outperforming traditional printed texts in terms of popularity when it comes to children's reading preferences.

This is something that cannot be ignored when it comes to considering the types of texts you will discuss, explore and analyse in your lessons. If you want to appeal to the interests and needs of your pupils, it seems appropriate that you, at least on some level, engage with the technologies which currently fuel their interest in the written word. This does not, of course, mean that you ignore the traditional text in favour of 'virtual' equivalents – but that you make room for them, including a fair balance of text formats within your teaching repertoire.

The new National Curriculum for 2008 also reflects this shift in text status by adopting a more integrated approach to ICT within subjects. Rather than appearing in a separate strand, ICT now appears in various appropriate places throughout the English curriculum. For example, pupils are to consider the 'influences on spoken and written language, including the impact of technology' (3.4d) and study of the author's craft is to include consideration of such things as:

> non-linear and multimodal texts, [which] could include using links and hyperlinks or interactive content on websites or CD-ROMs, or editing and sequencing shots in moving-image texts.

Layout and presentation: This could include the use of: print and web pages: titles, headings and subheadings, illustrations and pictures, font size and style, graphs, tables, diagrams and bullet points. (DfES, 2007: 66)

Given that the Office for Standards in Education's (Ofsted's) 2004 report, *ICT in Schools* (DfES, 2004; discussed later in this chapter), criticized the general lack of integrated approaches to ICT within English, it seems only fitting that the curriculum has been adapted to encourage improved practice in this area both within and across departments.

Points for reflection

- What are the advantages and disadvantages of using ICT to teach English?
- What does ICT have to offer that traditional teaching methods do not?
- How could ICT be used constructively in the classroom?
- What classroom management issues might you encounter?

However, it is also important to remember that, when using ICT within your teaching of English, you give careful consideration as to its appropriateness to learning objectives. If pupils' achievement is not enabled and enhanced by your proposed use of ICT, it becomes redundant. Similarly, if you are too ambitious, opportunities for teaching and learning become lost in a chaos of technological confusion. In other words, make sure your use of ICT is fit for purpose, that its demands lie within both the means of yourself and your pupils, and that it provides a suitable vehicle for achieving teaching and learning objectives. Even the simplest of approaches and task types can result in highly successful outcomes.

Information and communication technology can be used in a variety of ways to enhance the teaching of many aspects of reading and writing particularly. These might include:

- using programs designed to enhance pupils' understanding of texts
- websites which provide information useful for research and information retrieval
- using word processing for effective drafting and redrafting of work
- using software to design media texts such as newspapers and magazines
- using digital and/or recording cameras to create visual representations or 'snapshots' of texts
- using media hardware to create and edit moving images
- using recording equipment to create audio-resources such as tapes, CDs and podcasts
- designing websites
- creating online texts such as email and blogs.

Further examples of the ways in which technology might be applied to English teaching and learning are outlined the British Educational Communications and Technology Agency (Becta's) document, *Entitlement to ICT in Secondary English* a link to which can be found on the companion website.

NOT AN ICT WHIZZ?

You are not alone. One of the biggest ICT-related anxieties for many teachers, new and established, is that pupils' knowledge of technology will exceed their own. This can result in some teachers avoiding ICT use almost completely, with perhaps only tokenistic inclusion of it (such as GCSE pupils typing up coursework into a word-processed document). However, you would be surprised at how effective simple technology can be in engaging pupils and enhancing their achievement. Consequently, the real purpose of this chapter is to outline some of the simple and practical ICT tools you might put to effective use within the English classroom.

The British Educational Communications and Technology Agency, the organization which leads a national drive in improving technology- based learning, recently published a *Checklist for Practitioners* (available on companion website), outlining a few simple steps that you, as a practising teacher, can take to enhance your ICT skills:

1. Learn from your colleagues. Find out who is already using technology effectively, what works well for them and how you can use it.
2. Find out more about the technology your school, college or learning provider has — can interactive whiteboards, laptops, the internet or video conferencing help you do your job better and engage your learners more?
3. Find out more about how you can better use technology to make learning fun for you and your students.
4. Can technology help you keep in touch with learners, parents or local businesses? Can you put updates on your website or send group texts or emails?
5. Get the skills you need to take full advantage of the technology at your fingertips. Find out what training is available to you. (www.nextgenerationlearning.org.uk, accessed 18 January 2008).

Perhaps the most useful and readily available to you is the first of these. As a trainee teacher, you will become well practised in focused observation and will have many opportunities to observe others teach. If using ICT is something that daunts you, there is no reason why you should not ask your mentors in school to provide access to some of the technology available and to opportunities to see it being put to effective use. In this way, you can begin to take on board approaches and tasks you are capable of managing comfortably. Also remember that your fellow trainees will be exposed to a range of different practices and ideas – so, establishing a network for sharing these can be extremely beneficial when it comes to developing your repertoire of lesson ideas and practical resources.

In addition to this, there are a number of websites which offer guidelines as to how various aspects of ICT might be usefully implemented. The following would be worth consulting if you feel the need for an introduction to some of the basics (live links are provided on the companion website www.sagepub.co.uk/secondary):

- Initial Teacher Education
- Becta website
- DfES website
- ICT in Education
- Teachernet

Teachers' TV offers a further source of ideas and inspiration when it comes to using and managing technology in the classroom. The website contains programmes (available to watch and download) which demonstrate the use of specific technologies in English teaching. For instance, using digital and/or recording cameras to create visual representations or 'snapshots' of texts, is demonstrated in the programme *Shakespeare Shorts: Pupils Plotting* (on the companion website). The programme effectively demonstrates how a range of both simple and more complex technology can be used to enhance pupils' engagement with and understanding of Shakespeare's plays. The results of simple approaches like the creation of narratives through the sequencing of digital photographs or the filming of puppet-style miniatures are clear to see. Alongside programmes such as these, Teachers' TV also provides extremely useful *Resource Review* programmes such as *ICT Special: Secondary English* (on the companion website), which consider the benefits and issues related to the use of various software and technologies such as Picture Power 3, an application that creates multimedia slideshows.

Points for reflection

- List what you consider to be your personal strengths in terms of ICT use.
- Against each of these strengths, jot down some basic ideas about aspects of your teaching you might use them in.
- List what you consider to be your weaknesses in terms of ICT use.
- Against each of these weaknesses, identify strategies you will try to improve your knowledge and its practical application to your teaching.
- Make a list of colleagues in your current school, fellow trainee teachers and university-based staff who you could approach for support in improving your use of ICT in relation to your identified needs.

COMPUTER BASICS: THE HUMBLE WORD PROCESSOR

Humble it may be when compared to some of the fancier software on the market, but the word processor is far from past its sell-by date when it comes to usefulness in the classroom. For instance, Table 9.1, which appears on the Initial Teacher Education website, highlights how simple word-processing functions can be used to generate effective ways of supporting pupils' writing.

Similarly, ICT can be used to enhance the teaching of reading in a number of ways. For example:

- cloze procedures can be used to focus on language in both fiction and non-fiction texts
- word processors can be used to map the features of a text
- tables can be used to compare two texts.

Millum and Warren's book, *Twenty Things to Do with a Word Processor* (2001), provides a series of highly effective tasks which support such reading and writing in the classroom. Indeed, as part of the PGCE and undergraduate English teacher training courses at Edge Hill University, trainees sample some of their suggested activities and have reported very positively on their potential uses and outcomes. The exemplar tasks which follow can be accessed in full via the website which accompanies this book.

Table 9.1   Word Processor Activities

Word-processing function	Relevant activities
Cut and paste	for example Sequence jumbled text
	Poetry writing – children collect relevant phrases and then move them around to create a poem
	Select key information from non-fiction text to include in table
Insert text	for example Children add connectives to simplified text and consider the impact on meaning
	Insert missing punctuation, for example speech marks
	Cloze procedure
Delete text	Note-making – children delete irrelevant parts of text
	Deletion of adjectives focuses attention on their role in the meaning of text
Changing presentation of text	Exploring the impact of font in the presentation of poetry
	Insertion of images
Providing a flexible frame to support children's writing	A non-fiction writing frame for instruction writing created in shared writing is used and adapted by individuals in creating their own recipes for a class recipe book

Source: www.ite.org.uk (accessed 18 January 2008).

- *Relay writing*: an activity which explores how ICT can be used in relation to creative writing. Working from a basic outline, small groups write in relay to complete a short story. The idea is that one pupil begins to write, and then passes the story to the next person at a certain point. This could be after a certain amount of time, or after a certain number of words. You should encourage pupils to write instinctively, and to write their thoughts and ideas without stopping to correct mistakes or edit their text. When the story is complete, the group should then read the end result, and collectively edit and redraft. If you do not have a suite of computers to work with, this activity can be completed by small groups of pupils working at one computer.
- *Cloze activities*: using software such as Hot Potatoes (downloadable free from http://hotpot.uvic.ca/) enables both you and your pupils to create effective interactive resources using simple computer technology. Using aspects of the software such as JCloze, pupils can explore various text types, concentrating their attention upon the use of various aspects of language by carefully constructing cloze exercises. Tasks can be made more challenging, with opportunities for pupils to analyse texts, using various types of on-screen text marking, and rewriting texts for different audiences.
- *ICT and DARTS:* you can encourage your pupils to engage creatively with texts by using the editing tools available on a word processor. Pupils work on an electronic passage of prose and the aim is to create a piece of writing that looks and reads like poetry. The activity has four main stages:

1. Reading and highlighting the passage
2. Trimming and deciding on the line breaks
3. Editing the final piece so that it reads like a poem
4. Formatting the final poem.

So, you could take a text such as *The Tell-Tale Heart* by Edgar Allan Poe (as used in the full version of this task on the website), asking pupils to select an extract that they find particularly powerful. They would then copy and paste this passage into a new Word document. Thinking about the language, content and form of the passage, including imagery and use of metaphor, they embolden all the words or phrases they felt worked well, appeared vivid or held their interest. The text would then be trimmed to include only the emboldened aspects, and line breaks inserted, restructuring the text into poem format and focusing their attention on structure.

Points for reflection

- Go to the website accompanying this book and download one of the tasks outlined above. Work through the task, being mindful of how your pupils might respond to and engage with it if you were to use it with them.
- Note any positive reflections and possible concerns or questions which the task raises.
- Now, using a different text or text-type, plan a lesson which follows the same or similar principles to the one you have just rehearsed, bearing in mind the ability levels of pupils within the class and how you might differentiate accordingly.

INTERACTIVE WHITEBOARDS

Use what you have

I wonder how many of you have seen interactive whiteboards (IWBs) used solely for those 'comfy-slipper tasks' such as showing a PowerPoint or the film version of a Shakespearean play? Yes, it seems there are many in the English teaching profession who have yet to discover all the joys the IWB has to offer.

The British Educational Communications and Technology Agency online guide to interactive whiteboards (link on the companion website) provides a useful starting point for our consideration of the place of this technology within the English classroom:

Interactive whiteboards are by their very nature interactive, and this interactivity extends and develops the teaching styles that teachers have traditionally used, as well as offering opportunities to use resources in new and different ways.

In an English classroom, for example, the advantages of using the whiteboard to display video clips include not only the size of the image but also the facility for pupils to control the playback and to make notes on the same screen. (www.schools.becta.org.uk, accessed 25 January 2008)

A crucial point is made here – that IWBs *extend* and *develop* traditional teaching methods and enable us to explore and utilize resources in new and exciting ways. The key to making the IWB work *for* you is to take tried and tested teaching strategies and resources as your starting point, then wave that whiteboard wand over them to transform them into dynamic and interactive resources.

Just as Becta's example above refers to the potential of on-screen note-making as an enhanced use of video and DVD, so there are other ways of making your existing resources work for you. For example, printed worksheets you have created can be displayed on the IWB and then 'acted upon' by both yourself and pupils. If you were looking at lexical cohesion with a highly able GCSE group, you might display texts and then get pupils to use the highlighter function to colour-code various groups of words which are semantically linked. Pupils could also annotate to record their thoughts about the impact of various words and phrases on the reader. Thus a humble piece of text becomes a working and interactive resource which pupils can collaboratively invest in and save to return to at another point – in turn encouraging them to revisit their initial responses and reflect critically on their initial ideas.

Many English teachers have already invested time and energy into pooling their resources for precisely such uses – and many of them are downloadable for free from websites such as Teachit, the *Times Educational Supplement* and Teachernet. However, it is important that you reflect critically on the resources you use from these sites, giving careful consideration as to their appropriateness and suitability to your lessons.

Chris Warren, one of Teachit's trainers (with a key role in ICT development on the site), is keen to point out that this is a crucial issue which they are actively trying to address. Given that the website is currently seeing download rates in the region of 13 million resources per year, Chris and his colleagues have become increasingly aware of what he describes as their 'responsibility' to the English teaching profession. Their aim is to encourage individual teachers to adapt and to personalize the resources available on the website so that they better suit planned learning objectives and outcomes. For this reason, they have recently introduced 'Teachit trails' and 'Tweakits' sections, designed to encourage English professionals to consider the different ways in which resources might be utilized and adapted to suit different audiences and purposes. In this way it is hoped that English teachers will continue to benefit from sharing resources, while avoiding the constraints of making lesson activities 'fit' a downloaded resource created by a fellow teacher. Teachit's resources offer a potentially dynamic and, therefore, endless source of starting points for effective teaching and learning. Further discussion of the various interactive tools on offer will be discussed in the 'Whizzy things' section later in this chapter.

PowerPoint

Although talk still rages about 'death by PowerPoint', it surely has an important role to play if, like all other resources, it is used selectively and is appropriate to learning objectives? It can be used successfully for things such as:

- presenting key information about a topic
- presenting series of images to provoke discussion and/or writing
- summarizing key points from previous learning
- pupils' presentation of ideas/issues related to a key aspect of study
- plenary activities such as quizzes and *Who Wants to be a Millionaire*-style games related to learning.

For example, in preparation for study of Afrika's poem 'Nothing's Changed', studied by many pupils for GCSE assessment (as outlined in Chapter 7), you might use PowerPoint to present a series of photographs which provide key information about the issues explored in the poem. This allows pupils free range to speculate about the poem's content and the poet's attitude. Such discussion also provides a useful starting point for you to assess pupils' prior knowledge about South African history and the issue of apartheid. This could then be followed up with pupils linking lines and phrases from the poem to the various images on the slides, thus exposing them to the poem's content indirectly and giving them time to absorb and process it. Such an approach to poems from other cultures and traditions would complement others suggested in Chapter 4 of this book.

A further example of an effective use of PowerPoint is demonstrated through approaches such as the *Who Wants to be a Millionaire*-style quiz. When studying Shakespeare, for instance, pupils could spend a lesson engaging in online research into Elizabethan theatre, background necessary for their study of Shakespeare, the use of the *Millionaire*-style quiz during the plenary would enable you to both consolidate pupils' learning and to assess their knowledge of the topic prior to the follow-up lesson. Alternatively, pupils themselves could be involved in creating such a resource as a means of presenting and consolidating their research findings.

Points for reflection

- Refer to a recent university session or to your own schemes of work.
- Identify one point at which using PowerPoint might be appropriate to present information visually and/or to stimulate discussion.
- Using an Internet search engine and PowerPoint software, create a series of slides that you could use with pupils to enhance their knowledge and understanding of the relevant text and/or issues.

Whizzy things

Teachit's 'Whizzy things' now have a dedicated section of the website of their own, such is their popularity and expanding bank of ready-to-use resources. The applications and activities provided mean that English teachers can 'embed ICT into every lesson with ease', making 'the most of your computers and interactive whiteboards' (www.teachit.co.uk, accessed 25 January 2008).

Their current repertoire boasts an impressive range of handy IWB-based templates and resources which will enable you to incorporate ICT activities into many aspects of the English curriculum:

- *Interactive*: text can be arranged and rearranged, can be puzzled over, matched and associated, can be ranked and prioritized.
- *Scramble*: based on the classic game *Countdown*. Simply try to make the longest word in the time limit.
- *Anagram*: the computer selects a word from one of three lists and displays its component letters randomized. Players simply try to find the word in the time limit, rearranging the tiles as appropriate. If the word is correct the program will present another word.

- *Word Whiz*: new suite of random generators for exploring sentence structure. Students have control over the *structure* of the randomly generated texts, and they can copy and paste especially felicitous results into Word for later editing/polishing.
- *Choptalk*: gives the brain a thorough word-workout. To begin with it is all word-level work – hard decoding, spelling, punctuation, wrestling with fragments, searching for connections. Next, as the pieces come together and meaning begins to emerge from the fragments, we engage sentence level. And last, we have to think at text level, working on textual coherence and general sense until we know we have got it right.
- *Syntex*: takes punctuation marks and sentences and gives each component, or word, a tile of its own. On a special interactive screen, you can move the tiles around within the sentence. You can join one tile to another so that a number of words form a unit (ideal to show phrases and clauses) and you can move the whole unit around, say from the beginning of the sentence to its end. You can split units up. You can remove sections of the sentence to a temporary scratchpad while you work on the rest. You can add or subtract your own words at will. You can illustrate speech punctuation and parenthetical commas. The list is endless.
- *Magnet*: a digital word tool. Drag them and drop them. Assemble strange phrases or masterpieces of poetry. Be creative or analytical. Write your own verse or reconstruct a de-sequenced text.
- *Cruncher*: crunch, collapse or analyse texts. Computers can manipulate short texts – or very long texts – with lightning speed and enormous accuracy. Cruncher does just that. It offers students, teachers and researchers a range of powerful tools. Patterns of usage that you have not recognized before emerge like revelations (www.teachit.co.uk, accessed 25 January 2008).

The website does include some freely available ready-made resources which enable would-be users of the site to try out some of the 'whizzier' resources on offer. Those who subscribe to the website have access to a wider range of these resources and, more importantly perhaps, to templates which can be used to generate tailor-made resources for personal use. As with all such resources, the key to their success lies in selective and appropriate usage, lest the cause of PowerPoint's supposed demise leads to a similar fate.

Where used effectively, however, such tools can be invaluable – not only in terms of improving the efficient management of your planning and preparation time, but in actively involving pupils in the teaching and learning process and engaging them in creative and collaborative learning (as discussed in Chapter 4).

For instance, 'Magnet' enables the construction of fridge magnet-type words or lines of a text which can be dragged and dropped into different positions on the page. Such a tool can be used for such things as enhancing pupils' reading skills by focusing on the structure of a text. A poetry text, such as a Shakespearean sonnet, broken down into separate lines and reordered, can be used to engage pupils in using such things as rhyme scheme as an investigative tool with which to recreate the original text.

This IWB tool provides an 'on-screen' version of the much loved 'cut and paste' activity and an extremely time efficient whole-class approach to such a task which might, for example, serve well as a plenary activity after exploring aspects of poetic structure during a lesson. This tool also enables you/pupils to colour-code various aspects of the text, thus providing opportunities not only for exploring structure generally, but for highlighting patterns in structure and diction. It also enables the teacher to target specific pupils in order to assess their understanding of newly acquired knowledge by getting them up out of their seats and interacting with the text on the IWB.

In the spirit of the previously mentioned aim of Teachit's staff, to promote creative and personalized use of their resources, such tools have designated 'Help' sections which suggest various creative ways of using these tools and adapting them to best suit your objectives and the needs of your pupils. The *Teachit Works* newsletter is also available to subscribers and contains activities you can try out in order to maximize the potential and the creative scope of the resources and templates available – a sample activity sheet, 'Whizzing Word Classes', taken from the Autumn 2007 newsletter is available on the companion website.

And finally, a word of caution – remember that the 'interactive' aspect of such IWB activities is not always going to be successful in actively engaging *every* pupil in your classroom. Where the IWB is concerned, there will inevitably be opportunities for a limited number of pupils to physically interact with the text on screen (unless you have access to a class set of computers/laptops). So, you will need to think of ways of maximizing inclusive involvement over a period of time, and avoid thinking of such IWB tools as outright replacements for more conventional approaches to tasks, such as cut and paste, which will enable the active involvement of all pupils at any given point.

WEB TOOLS

Some of the things discussed in this section will be well known to you already, perhaps more so from a consumer standpoint than that of a teacher. Many of you will undoubtedly have blogs of your own, an account with Facebook, will use email as a major communicative tool. Being familiar with these does not automatically translate into using them as teaching and learning tools, however. Given that research (outlined later in the chapter) tells us that websites, emails and blogs/networking sites are more popular with young readers than ever, it seems not only fitting, but wise, to incorporate such things into your repertoire of resources and activities. Interviews conducted by Teachers TV for the programme *Professional Knowledge – English* (link 13 on companion website), further supports this. Discussions with teenagers about their experiences of blogging, My Space, YouTube, and podcasting, along with comments from experts in the field emphasize the important role of digital technology and media in today's society and, therefore, in the English classroom.

Email

Electronic mail has become one of the most powerful communicative formats of the twenty-first century, surpassing traditional 'snail mail' in popularity due the increasing availability of the Internet and the instantaneous delivery of mail from sender to recipient.

It may be stating the obvious to identify the ways in which email may be used as a potential resource and basis for pupil activity in your English lessons, but some are worthy of mention:

- exploring the conventions of email, how they differ from traditional letter writing
- pupils write emails 'in character' to demonstrate knowledge and understanding of a character(s) from a novel, play or poem
- pupils respond to a character's email as another character from the same text
- pupils write an email of complaint to an official of an organization, for example, a local council.

In each of these cases, such activities could be published on school websites as well as forming the basis for assessment of pupils' reading and/or writing skills.

Blogs

The web log, as it is formally named, has spawned a new generation of online communicative text. Lovingly labelled the 'blog', this online phenomenon has swept the globe at lightning pace in recent years. At 25 April 2007, Technorati Data suggested that there were around 15.5 million active blogs in existence worldwide, proving the genre's increasing popularity (www.businessweek.com, accessed 18 January 2008 – link 14 on companion website). In keeping with this, research discussed later in this chapter also highlights the popularity of blogs when it comes to children's preferred reading materials outside the classroom.

Many of your pupils will, therefore, be accustomed to 'blogging', thus making it ripe for exploitation in the English classroom. Blogs can be used for a number of curriculum-related purposes, enabling you to support pupil progress with various English skills. These might include the following:

- writing for different audiences and purposes, thereby exploring appropriate conventions of written text types, for example, informative, persuasive, descriptive and so on
- reading skills, such as demonstrating understanding/insight into character(s) in a studied text, for example, pupils might write a blog as the character from a novel, short story or poem using appropriate language and textual details
- information retrieval and selection, for example, researching and gathering information to be used in a blog to support or to illustrate ideas
- drafting and redrafting of written work – given that the blog is a public medium, it has the potential to reach a larger audience, thus enabling a wider range of input and critical comment which will enable the writer to revise and redraft effectively
- group work and speaking and listening skills – blogs provide an excellent forum for collaborative work (discussed in more detail in Chapter 5), with groups of pupils being able to work together on preparing and compiling articles for a blog site. In addition, given that blog pages offer the scope for multiple contributors, pupils can publish their materials side by side, offer commentary on each others' work and enter into a dialogue about published materials.

This is not intended to be an exhaustive list of the blog's potential uses in the English classroom, but rather to provide some starting points to highlight how easily this popular medium can be put to good use in your teaching. To gain further insight into how blogging can form an effective part of an English scheme of work and indeed can prove a useful assessment tool, it would be well worth watching the Teachers' TV programme *KS3/4 English and Media – Building Blogs* (link 15 on companion website). This programme demonstrates how blogging can form an effective basis to support a combination of reading, writing and speaking and listening skills. A group of Year 9 pupils engage in a project which culminates in a 'Newszine' blog aimed at their peers. The scheme of work involves them in collaborative work in a number of ways: researching topical issues; discussion and selection of appropriate information, content and style; production of journalistic written texts; peer evaluation; and editing and redrafting of work.

A number of successful outcomes clearly emerge from such a project. The collaborative aspect assists in building pupils' confidence, encourages positive risk-taking and enables pupils to take ownership of the learning process (as discussed in Chapter 4). The teacher of the class quite rightly draws attention to the fact that she, in this case, becomes more of a monitor and adviser, with pupils taking on the role of teacher; simultaneously taking ownership of their learning. An additional benefit of such a role reversal is that you, the teacher, can learn from your pupils, thus increasing your own technological knowledge.

The final product, the blog site itself, enables a range of pupils, teachers and parents to comment on the various articles published therein. This provides opportunities for pupils to receive feedback on their work in a much less intimidating way than the usual 'red-pen' mechanism that teachers use – an extremely useful way of implementing formative assessment.

Setting up a blog is relatively easy to do and does not require any specialist technological know-how. Blog packages and templates are freely downloadable from a number of websites such as Blogger, My Space, Word Press and SOS Blog (links on companion website). Such sites will guide you through the process of getting all the basics in place and getting your blog site ready for use. All you need then is the assistance of your school's network technician to help you to download it onto the school system, ensuring you and your pupils have access to it. It really is as simple as that.

Podcasts

To put it simply, 'Podcasting is basically the creation and distribution of amateur radio' (Richardson, 2006: 112). Given that many of your pupils will already have access to MP3 players and iPods, the podcast can be an incredibly powerful tool in developing and enhancing learning in English.

As well as providing a platform for pupils to create their own broadcasts, the World Wide Web now houses a huge number of ready-made podcasts, many of which can be used effectively in an educational setting or, indeed, have been purpose built to support pupils' educational needs. For instance gcsepodcast. com (on companion site) has been specifically designed to support GCSE students with various aspects of the Key Stage 4 curriculum and with revision of key examination topics. A plethora of search engines also exist, with websites such as podcast.com, podcastalley.com and the iTunes store providing a quick and easy way to search for podcasts about specific topics and issues.

In terms of supporting pupils' learning podcasts can be used very successfully in two key ways:

1. Pupils listen to and engage with ready-made podcasts. This approach can be put to good use in the following ways:

   - developing and refining listening skills
   - as memory aids for the learning of key material
   - for revision of key topics for examination
   - for revision of lesson material in an out-of-school setting
   - pupil engagement in peer assessment
   - for supporting independent learning, with pupils accessing teacher-generated podcasts for homework tasks

- for supporting pupils with specific learning needs
- supporting pupils who have missed lessons because of absence.

2. Pupils actively engage in the creation of their own podcasts. This approach can result in the following successful outcomes:

    - developing and refining speaking for specific purposes and audiences
    - pupils' creation of succinct audible summaries of learning which not only consolidate recently acquired knowledge and skills, but also prove highly effective revision tools
    - opportunities for pupils to engage in peer teaching
    - opportunities for a range of assessment – teacher, self and peer based;

When it comes to the mechanics, podcasting is a simple process which is possible provided you have some sort of digital recording equipment available, such as a computer and microphone, an MP3 player or iPod, or a mobile telephone capable of recording sound. As with blogging, a number of websites exist to support users in creating and publishing podcasts online. One such site is voices.com (on companion site) which offers free online tutorials and guidance about the process from start to finish. For those wishing to create a more polished finish to their MP3 audio broadcasts, audacity.sourceforge.net provides a free cross-platform sound editor which enables you and/or your pupils to improve the quality of recordings as well as editing, cutting and reorganizing sound clips.

Websites and the Internet as a research tool

It goes without saying that the Internet provides a wealth of information which can support and extend pupils' knowledge and skills within English lessons. In fact, it is likely that this particular aspect of ICT is the most commonly used in the secondary classroom, albeit sometimes as a tokenistic activity in teachers' attempts to meet National Curriculum requirements.

However, as with everything else discussed in this chapter, when used selectively, appropriately and in a carefully managed way, the Internet can prove an invaluable source of ideas and information for both you and the pupils you teach. It seems futile to attempt any sort of generic guide to the Internet at this point, given that English teaching has such huge scope in terms of potential subject matter and focal issues. However, it is appropriate to bring your attention to an extremely useful resource which appears on  Becta's website: *Becta ICT Advice: Using Web-based Resources in Secondary English* (downloadable on the companion website). It aims to:

> describe a number of lessons in which ICT is used effectively to support the teaching and learning of English at Key Stages 3 and 4. The examples show just one of the many ways in which these web-based resources can be used by students and teachers in both whole-class and individual work. (Becta, 2004: 1)

The publication also provides a range of useful websites and URLs to sites which will provide material to support a range of English study, such as:

- Film education
- Key Stage 4 prose fiction study, including texts such as *Lord of the Flies, Of Mice and Men* and *To Kill a Mockingbird*
- Shakespeare
- drama texts
- media and advertising
- poetry writing and analysis
- grammar.

Ultimately, the key to using the Internet effectively (in the classroom in particular and with larger numbers of pupils) is careful planning. If you're intending to engage pupils in a task which involves them accessing the Internet for research purposes, do some online searching yourself first. You can then compile lists of websites you wish pupils to use, thus ensuring that they access relevant sources of information immediately, rather than wasting valuable time ploughing through endless search engine results. For example, the companion website contains examples of prompt sheets used to support pupils in researching. While reading Zephaniah's *Refugee Boy*, Year 8 pupils conducted research into the causes and manifestations of refugeeism in different parts of the world. The teacher (myself in this case) investigated a range of websites prior to the research lesson and produced a list of websites for pupils to consult – websites which I knew contained the information they would need in relation to the area they had been allocated. Such preparation ensures that you maintain control over the task and pupils' interaction with it, while also facilitating independent learning and achievable learning outcomes – the perfect balance one might say. To see an example of the presentations prepared by students, visit the companion website www.sagepub.co.uk/secondary.

The Internet also provides an extensive range of printed and media texts for use within the classroom. Most newspapers are now available in an online format, this giving you access to a wide range of articles for developing reading and writing skills. Comparing newspaper articles and styles can be made all the easier when they are displayed side by side on a split screen. In this way pupils can text-mark and make notes on texts using basic word-processor tools. Similarly, websites such as You Tube and the Internet Movie Database (IMDb) provide a wealth of moving image texts which can be used in the teaching of media – advertisements, film trailers and film clips are easily downloadable and manipulated for classroom use. Using IWBs moving image clips can be paused at significant points to enable pupils to engage in discussion about imagery and the effects of devices such as camera angles, shot types and sound effects.

Points for reflection

- Look back at the web tools outlined above. Under key headings, make a list of the ways in which you might use each of them in your current schemes of work for each of your teaching groups.
- Liaise with relevant staff at your current school to find out what technology is available to support the use of web tools by both you and your pupils.

- Select one scheme of work/class you could realistically use web tool(s) with this term, and review/amend your scheme of work accordingly.
- When it comes to actually using these web tools in the classroom, critically reflect on their use for both teaching and learning and include in your written lesson evaluation(s).

WHAT THE RESEARCH SAYS

When considering the reasons why using ICT in English teaching is so important, it is worth noting research such as that conducted by Foster and Clark for the Literacy Trust in 2005. Their national study of children's reading habits revealed that 'on-screen texts' are out-performing the traditional printed texts we associate with the classroom of old. When asked about preferred reading materials outside of school, respondents rated websites (63.6 per cent) and text messages (61.0 per cent) very highly, being exceeded only by magazines in popularity (Clark and Foster, 2005: 22). More recently, Clark et al.'s study into *Young People's Self-perceptions as Readers* (2008) has further reinforced the popularity of online texts, with websites (63.2 per cent), emails (58.7 per cent) and blogs/networking sites (53.1 per cent) occupying three of the top four spots. The message to us is clear. Young people are including these texts types among their preferred reading material, thus making them likely sources of pleasure and engagement if used appropriately in the classroom. In your quest to inspire and involve your pupils in their own learning process, the resources and strategies that ICT offers can positively influence the teaching and learning cycle.

In terms of ICT use in schools in recent years, Ofsted's 2004 report, *ICT in Schools* (DfES, 2004), suggests that overall it has improved in English, although the disparity between best practice and that found in the majority of schools at the time was marked. It is clear that, where used effectively, ICT has a positive impact upon both teaching and learning in the English classroom. One area of apparent strength in the use of ICT among many teachers is its effective use for planning, creating resources and generating recording systems. However, there are greater inconsistencies in its successful application to learning within the classroom.

This can be partially accounted for by limited access to various technologies within some schools – although it should be noted that ongoing investment has resulted in significant improvements in equipping schools. More often than not, these inconsistencies arise from the fact that ICT is not always well integrated across departments, with 'pockets of exper-tise' which are not fully exploited. This is exacerbated by the fact that, within English departments, the effective use of ICT is witnessed 'within isolated units of work' (DfES, 2004: 4) rather than comprehensively across all schemes of work, and there is little evidence to suggest that departments have yet addressed the notion of progression when it comes to developing the sophistication of pupils' ICT use: 'Few English departments have addressed the issue of progression in ICT skills as pupils move through the school. As a result, too many pupils repeat activities from year to year, often without any noticeable increase in challenge or sophistication, either in developing literacy or ICT' (DfES, 2004: 4).

Thus, in schools where the use of ICT as a teaching tool was deemed unsatisfactory, many pupils were not successfully engaging with the technological aspects of the work presented to them: either because their ICT knowledge outstripped that demanded by tasks created by teachers, thus presenting no challenge; or, as was the case with pupils with poor reading skills, tasks were too difficult and, therefore, inaccessible. Such evidence clearly highlights the need for English teachers to assess pupils' ICT capabilities more effectively and to cater for a range of ability levels in their planning for ICT use. The Office for Standards in Education's findings also emphasize the fact that teachers must carefully consider whether ICT facilities will enable them to meet curriculum objectives and result in pupils successfully achieving specific learning objectives.

Despite the shortcomings identified by Ofsted in their report, they do provide clear examples of what might be considered 'best practice', thus demonstrating the sorts of things English teachers could and should do in order to exploit ICT as a consistently effective teaching and learning tool. For example, in effective practice: 'ICT is the vehicle through which learning English is to be achieved. Tasks given to pupils motivate them by using ICT appropriately, for instance to focus on purpose and audience for writing or on text manipulation and experimentation in layout and presentation' (DfES, 2004: 6). Carefully selected and screened Internet-based resources also proved highly successful in assisting pupils with skills such as research and information retrieval.

The overwhelming message, regardless of the form in which ICT appears in English lessons, is the need for teachers to weigh up the benefits of using technology against the potential pitfalls and distractions that may result from its use. For instance, the Internet can present pupils with a wealth of information and ideas which might otherwise be inaccessible: however, if not managed carefully by the teacher, its use could result in pupils embarking on useless and unproductive searches which undermine learning objectives completely. Likewise, such 'misuse' of technology can result in problems with pupil motivation and behaviour – a reminder to us all that ICT use is not the magical key to good behaviour.

Key points from this chapter

In this chapter we have established that:

- outside of school pupils are increasingly engaging with virtual texts, and this must be taken into consideration in the modern English classroom
- ICT is only truly effective when it is used in a considered way which is appropriate to teaching and learning objectives
- the use of even the simplest of technologies can result in improvements in the quality of teaching and learning, and in encouraging pupils to engage and enjoy
- interactive whiteboards are increasingly available for use within the modern classroom and can be used to promote pupils' active engagement with a range of traditional and media texts
- web tools offer innovative and creative ways of consolidating and reinforcing pupils' learning in ways which appeal to their interests and sense of enjoyment
- the Internet provides an endless source of information which can prove valuable to teaching and learning, but its use must be monitored and controlled carefully
- there remains a need for greater coherence in approaches to using ICT in English, with ICT-based activities being integrated into lessons on a regular basis rather than in tokenistic ways.

Further reading

British Educational Communications and Technology Agency (Becta) (2004), *Becta ICT Advice: Using web-based resources in Secondary English* (available to download from link 3 on the companion website).
A highly useful resource which provides links to various online resources for use with different aspects of the English curriculum at Key Stages 3, 4 and 5.

Harris, S. and Kington, A. (2002) *Innovative Classroom Practices Using ICT in England: The Second Information Technology in Education Study* (available to download from link 27 on the companion website).

Millum, T. and Warren, C. (2001) *Twenty Things to do with a Word Processor: ICT Activities for the Secondary English Classroom*. Derby: Resource Education.
Does exactly what it suggests, leading you through easy and highly usable word-processor activities to engage pupils more actively in learning.

Useful websites

Live links to the these website can be found on the companion website www. sagepup.co.uk/secondary.

www.animationfactory.com	www.nate.org.uk
www.blogger.com	www.nfer.ac.uk
www.blogsearch.google.com	www.ofsted.gov.uk
www.createblog.com	www.podcast.com
www.english-online.org.uk	www.podcastalley.com
www.englishandmedia.co.uk	www.qca.org.uk/curriculum
www.futurelab.org.uk	www.schools.becta.org.uk
www.gcsepodcast.com	www.sosblog.com
www.hotpot.uvic.ca	www.teachernet.gov.uk
www.imdb.com	www.teachit.co.uk
www.ite.org.uk	www.tes.co.uk
www.learning2goblog.org	www.wordpress.org
www.myspace.com	www.youtube.com

10 BEYOND ITT: What Next?

Carol Evans and Peter Woolnough

This chapter considers:

- career entry procedures and how they work
- how to construct and maintain your CEDP
- the newly qualified teacher (NQT) year: your rights, responsibilities and opportunities
- Masters level study and being research active.

BEYOND INITIAL TEACHER TRAINING: THE CAREER ENTRY AND DEVELOPMENT PROFILE

Towards the end of your initial teacher training (ITT) course (known as 'transition point 1'), you will prepare a career entry and development profile (CEDP). You can find full informa-tion about the CEDP and your induction year, from our website link (1), where you'll read the Teacher Development Agency's (TDA's) introduction to the CEDP: 'The career entry and development profile (CEDP) is primarily an online resource and is aimed at trainee and newly qualified teachers (NQTs). It will encourage you to focus on achievements and goals early on, and discuss your professional development needs.' The site goes on to outline the basic structure of the CEDP:

> It is in three transition points. Transition point 1 is towards the end of initial teacher train-ing (ITT), point 2 is at the beginning of the induction, and point 3 is towards the end of induction.
>
> At each transition point there are guidance notes, a set of prompt questions and sample formats that can be selected or adapted for making notes. In addition, there are resources to help you set objectives and write induction action plans.

The document is a reflective tool – reflection continues throughout your career! – and it gives you the opportunity to consider the strongest aspects of your teaching, to identify areas that you feel need further development and experience, and to consider the nature of support that you would like in your induction year. Perhaps for the first time in your training, it also gives you a chance to consider your longer-term career goals.

The CEDP is an important document: your training provider is required to support you in completing it and tell you about statutory induction arrangements; your NQT school also has a statutory responsibility to support you. In terms of your own responsibility, completing your CEDP is a key way in which you address standard Q7b: 'Identify priorities for [your] early professional development in the context of induction'.

The completion of the document should be relatively straightforward, especially if you have reviewed your professional development in a systematic and effective manner during your training course. What we offer you here is guidance on what you might include, and how you might express your needs.

The information which you write in the profile is in response to four key questions relating to your course and professional development to date: what has been interesting and rewarding? What have been your main strengths and achievements? What future, further experience and support do you need? What are your longer-term career aspirations and goals?

Guidance on the four questions is generally clear. Particularly in respect of questions 2 and 3, we would encourage you to consider including statements under each area of the Professional Standards. Remember that you are seeking to set a development agenda that forms a training requirement for you in the next stage of your career.

As far as style is concerned, the use of bullet points is appropriate, as is continuous prose. Avoid writing too much: your NQT tutor will not want to read your life story! As the document is available online, word processing is appropriate and generally leads to a professionally presented document, which you will be happy to present as a printout to your NQT tutor. You might want to cross-reference your statements to the Standards. For example, you might write, 'I have been successful in providing an effective learning environment though good classroom management. I achieved this through careful planning and appropriately pitched lessons, using a range of resources and activities in sessions (Q25, Q30, Q31', but this is entirely optional.

One word of warning: be very careful about the wording of your response to the third question, 'What future, further experience and support do you need?' By the time you finalize your CEDP, you will be at the end of your initial training course and you will have produced evidence that you have achieved *all* the Professional Standards – otherwise, your training provider would not be able to recommend you for QTS. Consider, therefore, the message given by the following: 'I haven't taught any pupils with special educational needs … ' Does this mean you haven't really achieved Q19: know how to make effective personalized provision for those they teach, including those for whom English is an additional language or who have special educational needs or disabilities … ? It would be better to write: 'I understand the theory and some of the practical and pedagogic strategies to help those with SEN to make progress, and I would now appreciate the opportunity to shadow an experienced member of staff before teaching pupils with SEN, alone.'

Similarly, be careful not to give your NQT tutor or head of department carte blanche to load you with work: avoid 'I need more practice in assessing GCSE examinations'; better 'I would like further, guided, confidence-building experience of assessment at GCSE, and would like to co-mark with an experienced teacher, to begin with.'

The key thing to remember, as already stated, is that this document is important in setting your agenda as a beginning teacher. A cursory completion of the document will not help you in 'putting down markers' as to what you feel will help you as you proceed, while not making excessive and unrealistic demands on your school. A full and carefully completed CEDP allows you to demonstrate not only that you are already operating as a reflective practitioner, but that you are also very clear about the next stage of your professional development and advancement.

Point for reflection

How might you word an entry in your CEDP which suggests that you need further help with 'stretching' more able pupils in Year 11?

During your induction year, the CEDP should be reviewed in the first four weeks of your new post. It acts as a discussion point to enable the induction tutor to establish further targets against the next phase of standards – the induction standards. This early observation is to ensure that you continuously receive feedback and further focus. All 'targets' should be mutually agreed, and reviewed again at the next observation.

Towards the end of your induction year, you and your induction tutor should meet to review your continued professional development (transition point 3). This process may well feed in to the school's performance review/appraisal system, and should lead to the identification of further development support/opportunities that are appropriate to you at this time. In this way, the continuous nature of professional development is established from the very start of your career, and should enable you to build up a portfolio of evidence of your training and achievements.

STARTING YOUR NQT YEAR

Taking up your first teaching position can be an extremely stressful experience. Once the initial euphoria of having secured a job has worn off, it is often replaced by a period of uncertainty. Concerns regarding teaching groups, planning, and access to materials and support rear their heads, and the tension mounts as your starting date draws near. This section of the chapter gives you practical advice on how to reduce the neurosis and take control of your induction and subsequent professional development. All schools have formal induction processes, but they will vary in terms of detail and efficacy – so it is essential that you are both organized and proactive prior to beginning the job and throughout your first year. Make sure you also maximize the help that will be available to you, as outlined in this chapter.

Prior to starting

When you accept the offer of employment, the induction process begins. Your school will almost certainly invite you and other new colleagues to attend one or more formal *induction days*. These induction sessions usually occur late in the summer term and they will provide you with details of whole school policies, curriculum and pastoral structures, routines and key dates. A member of the senior management team (SMT) will have specific responsibility for induction and NQTs, and this colleague will be an important figure in your first year of teaching. In most schools, induction days usually include time for you to meet your head of department or subject mentor (very often, one and the same person). If this is the case, you should be provided with detailed information regarding the department, its policies, schemes of work, resources and your personal timetable. It is always advisable to prepare for such meetings in advance. Make a list of the things you feel you need to know – and make sure that you raise these items if they are not covered by the formal presentations.

So, what happens next? In the worst case scenario, several weeks of the summer holiday pass by and you hear nothing more from the school. You begin to worry because you do not know your timetable yet, you do not have key syllabus documents and you fear that you will be under-prepared at the start of term. To avoid this scenario, we strongly suggest that you consider the following actions, recommended by former trainees:

- After the formal induction, ask if you can come in to school for a day or two before the summer holidays to have further discussions and look at resources. Bring lists of questions when you do visit.
- Exchange contact details with your head of department or mentor and ask if it would be possible to arrange to meet them towards the end of the holiday – or at least stay in touch to discuss your classes and any planning you have already undertaken.
- Make sure that you have been given all the essential documents: set lists, departmental handbook, examination syllabuses, schemes of work, rooming details. Read them, and contact your mentor if there is anything you do not really understand.
- Go into school in the holiday and spend time looking at resources, sorting out your room (if you have your own!) and copying materials you will use with classes in the first few weeks.
- Read all the school documentation carefully. Anything you do not fully comprehend should be noted and brought to the attention of your head of department (HOD) for clarification. Initially, the biggest problem will be getting your head round all the initials, acronyms and codes that school handbooks tend to contain.
- Introduce yourself to the office staff. They will be able to offer advice on administration and procedures relating to reprographics.
- Respond positively to all offers of help. Departmental colleagues (beyond your head of department) often have much to offer.
- Once you know your timetable and have access to resources, begin to organize your folders, your long- and medium-terms plans – then *show them to someone* to make sure you are on the right lines!
- Ask to look at mark schemes, GCSE and other work to get an idea of standards and how the department approaches assessment.
- Offer to share any of your own materials/resources that the department might find useful. A bit of ingratiation always helps!
- Make sure that your HOD or mentor has access to your CEDP and reads it.

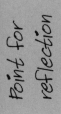

Point for reflection

What preparatory actions and activities will you undertake to ensure you embark on your first day in post feeling confident?

The first few weeks

Unsurprisingly, the start of the school year is extremely busy. As a new teacher, you are subjected to a multitude of pressures and demands, and each of these will seem to be imperative. During this time, *careful planning of your lessons and management of your time will be your biggest priorities*. At the outset, make sure that you have access to all the baseline data available on your teaching groups and tutor group, and ensure that these details inform your plans. As an NQT, you will be on a reduced timetable, but the actual contact time will still far exceed anything you have experienced as a trainee. Examine your timetable closely, and try to map the likely pressure points. Equally important, scrutinize *the whole-school calendar*. When will your groups be undertaking examinations and assessment? When will you be expected to attend meetings? When are the holidays?

The early weeks of your teaching career are also hugely important in terms of *relationships* and becoming part of a team. Not only will you be establishing yourself as an important figure in the lives of the pupils you tutor and teach, but you will also be developing relationships with your departmental and other colleagues. The vast majority of NQTs find themselves welcomed into supportive, well-organized departments, with colleagues keen to assist you and get to know you. We will consider what to do when this is *not* the case, later in the chapter, but whatever the dynamics of the department you join, you are strongly advised to make connections with colleagues on both a formal and informal basis. Spend break and lunchtime with people in your team, make the most of offers of help, engage particularly with the thoughts of other NQTs and recently qualified colleagues – and never apologize when asking for advice. Your colleagues will want you to do well, and they will expect you to need support. Additional, external support will be available through the local authority (LA). Most authorities organize a programme of NQT meetings, and in many cases the LA literacy adviser or school link adviser will arrange a series of meetings with you personally to help you develop and progress during the NQT year.

Formal structures and monitoring

Elsewhere in the chapter, you will have read of the importance of the CEDP and the procedures that accompany it. When developing the CEDP file, remember that it is a document that will form an evidence base not just for your first year in teaching, but for your subsequent development and advancement aspirations. View it as the start of a *portfolio of evidence* that can be used to illustrate your successes, achievements and ambitions. This will be crucial if you decide, at the relevant time, to apply for Teacher of Excellence or Fast Track Status. Extremely helpful information regarding these areas and others, including developing your CV, early professional development and induction standards, can be found on *teachernet*, which can be accessed through our website.

Point for reflection

Where do you see yourself in five years' time? How can you plan ahead to ensure that your professional profile will be adequate to meet your career development aspirations?

In order for you to meet the requirements of the key *induction points* in your NQT year, you will have to develop and maintain your CEDP, as outlined earlier in this chapter. In addition, you will have to undergo three lesson observations, one per school term. At least one of these will be undertaken by your line manager (head of department or mentor), and the SMT colleague in charge of NQTs will usually undertake the other two. The focus for these observations should be clarified and discussed in advance of the events actually taking place.

Another hugely important aspect of the NQT year is the formal *NQT training programme*, arranged and often delivered by the relevant SMT member or professional mentor. These sessions should constitute a comprehensive induction to the specific school coupled with training designed to meet the broader curriculum and pastoral needs of NQTs. A programme might, for example, include sessions exploring:

- behaviour management
- special educational needs (SEN) and inclusion issues
- working with other professionals in school (teaching assistants, learning mentors)
- the *Every Child Matters* (DfES, 2004) agenda
- assessment for learning
- use of ICT facilities/systems
- use and management of performance indicators and other key data
- the school's own priorities and its development plan
- reporting procedures and protocols.

This list is neither comprehensive nor exhaustive, but it does, hopefully, provide an idea of the likely content of the sessions. In many schools, the NQT co-ordinators arrange joint sessions with ITT students, and it is common practice for 'guest' speakers with particular specialist knowledge to deliver some of the programme. In a limited number of instances you will find that the entire programme is organized and delivered by the LA advisory team.

Ensuring that you are fully involved

We have looked at the formal structures in place that are designed to support and develop you during the NQT year, but the question remains: what can *you* do to maximize the experience?

The simple answer is to be proactive. Within your *department*, you should definitely take every opportunity to share and develop good practice. Discussing your schemes of work with colleagues is a useful starting point, but you might also engage in peer observations, volunteer to be a member of a working party, actively participate in departmental meetings, offer to take on specific curriculum developments, run or participate in trips and theatre visits and ask if you can represent the department at examination board or LA meetings. If there is a particular area of your practice or knowledge that you feel you need to develop, why not research the details of relevant courses and submit a formal request to attend a course? The school's professional mentor will have details of what is available to you. Activities such as these send out the message that you have aspirations and that you want to make a substantial contribution to the work of the department.

Another way of maximizing your role would be to consider running a club or project. Many English departments organize reading clubs, drama groups, media productions and newspapers. Could you contribute to or initiate activities like these? If so, the school hierarchy will be pleased and the children who benefit will be delighted. One word of caution, though. Remember that the NQT year will be a challenging one, and although you want to be perceived as enthusiastic and ambitious, you need to avoid being overloaded.

What if there are problems?

We naturally hope that you will have a completely rewarding, trouble-free NQT year. But who do you turn to, if this is not the case? For most issues, the simple answer is your immediate colleagues. Every teacher has experienced 'problem' classes, disconcerting incidents, difficulties with planning and the like. Most of your colleagues will, as we have already stated, be happy to help you to resolve problems – and you should not let the fact that some of those colleagues will be responsible for monitoring your performance put you off. Sensitive management acknowledges difficulties colleagues might have and applauds individuals who strive to overcome their problems.

But what if the management structures and support are, themselves, poor? This is surely a more acute problem. When a school fails to deliver an appropriate induction programme, when a mentor is too busy to offer advice or when the school's behaviour sanctions are ineffectual, where do you turn for assistance? There is obviously no single answer to these disparate scenarios, but a general guide would be to use the hierarchy of support, in the first instance. So, if there is no appropriate induction programme being run by the SMT, refer it in the first instance to your head of department who could, *in extremis*, consult with the mentors of other NQTs and raise the issue with the head teacher. If your subject mentor is failing to support you, discreetly make your SMT line manager aware of this. If the school's discipline system is not helping you, try enlisting the support and involvement of an individual colleague who is able to have some influence on the pupils' behaviour.

The message is, therefore, that most problems have solutions. In the unlikely event of you feeling that no one in the school can or will help you, a sensible course of action would be to contact your LA subject adviser who, in turn, could act as a mediator or even put you in touch with colleagues in other schools.

Do remember, though, the likelihood is that you will not encounter major problems during your NQT year. These suggestions are merely a safety blanket!

Point for reflection

What do you hope to have achieved by the end of your NQT year, and how will you try to meet these objectives?

Point for reflection

MASTER'S-LEVEL STUDY: BECOMING RESEARCH ACTIVE

In recent years, there has been encouragement for trainee teachers and those in and beyond the NQT year to become qualified at Master's level. Many higher education institutions enable you to complete your initial teacher training year wholly or partially at this level; this has tied in with Ed Balls's (Minister for Education) recently announced initiative, recorded on the Teacher Developement Agency (TDA) news website as follows:

Government extends teaching diploma
TdaNews Direct
Published: 14 March, 2008

The government has announced the launch of a new Master's qualification to boost teaching. Ed Balls, children, schools and families minister, told the ASCL conference that the Master's in Teaching and Learning would help the country 'compete' internationally. 'Our aim is that every teacher over time should have the new Master's in Teaching and Learning,' he explained. This ought to ensure that the status of teachers is raised and they 'get the recognition that they deserve', he added. (See our website (3) for further details.)

In order to achieve Master's level, either on or after the ITT year:

your assignments will need to demonstrate:

- an ability to reflect on your own and others' professional practice and/or learning in order to improve;
- an ability to engage with, and critically evaluate, recent research and literature in your subject specialism or other educational issues;
- an ability to combine complex information and/or sustain a complex level of argument and reflection;
- an ability to adapt skills and design or develop new procedures/knowledge for professional situations (Edge Hill University, 2008: 35).

Many universities offer modular courses, which can be completed over several years, and which often refresh your enthusiasm as a reflective teacher. You might find opportunities exist in school to request partial funding for further study, and you will find practitioner research or action research a focused and personally rewarding means of linking such further study with your day-to-day teaching, as well as being a possible means to promotion within your career. Many trainees and teachers throughout their careers begin by being apprehensive about taking on further academic study, and only you can decide when or whether it is right for you. It can, however, be far more manageable than you may at first think: several trainee teachers (from the Edge Hill University cohort 2007–08) said how much they had gained from undertaking a small-scale, practitioner research project, as part of their Postgraduate Certificate of Education (PGCE) work, finding that preconceptions about teaching and learning were often challenged by their findings, and their practice had developed and matured as a result. Perhaps most importantly, your own professional development should lead to better opportunities for pupils to 'enjoy and achieve' one of the key outcomes of *Every Child Matters* (DfES, 2004).

While we understand and endorse, to a degree (no pun intended), the government's ambition to create a teaching workforce that is highly qualified academically and engaged in continued reflection and research, we do recognize the potential pitfalls for ambitious NQTs who feel obliged to embark on Master's courses very early in their careers. There is something to be said for the view that your main priority as an NQT or 'novice' teacher is to establish yourself as a confident, competent classroom practitioner. As we have already stated in this chapter, the start of your career is likely to be a challenging experience, and you should therefore consider carefully your capacity to take on additional research and study activities during this time. One possible approach would be to fully engage with your school responsibilities in the first year and use this time to discover where your true passions and interests lie. Then, once you are certain that you can manage your time and workload effectively, you can consider accredited

Master's-level options that will enhance your knowledge and career profile – and be of benefit to the school you are currently working in. The risks of burnout and absence resulting from work-related pressures are particularly high in NQTs, and you need to think about the much discussed 'work–life balance'.

Finally, we would remind you that teaching – and particularly the teaching of English – can and should be a wonderfully rewarding experience. You are entering the profession at an exciting time, where creativity, engagement and flexibility are being placed on the same pedestal as functionality, and where there seems to be a genuine acknowledgement that prescription is not necessarily the best way forward. Enjoy your teaching, aspire to inspire, and you will make a real difference to the lives of countless individuals.

Key points from this chapter

In this chapter we have established that:

- career entry procedures exist to support and develop you as a teacher
- the CEDP is an essential document which needs to be effectively written and maintained
- the NQT year must be planned, supported and executed in a professional manner
- opportunities for Master's-level study and other research activity should be carefully considered.

Further reading

Bubb, S. (2004) *The Insider's Guide to Early Professional Development: Succeed in Your First Year as a Teacher.* London: RoutledgeFalmer.
Some practical advice on a wide range of topics and situations.

Liebling, H. (2007) *Newly Qualified Teachers.* Stafford: Network Continuum Education.
A contemporary guide, with contextualized advice and guidance.

Rogers, B. (2006) *I Get By With a Little Help.* London: Paul Chapman Publishing.
Drawing on his experience as a teacher, researcher and educational consultant, the author shows how the support of colleagues in schools makes a difference.

Useful websites

Live links to these websites can be found on the companion website www.sagepub.co.uk/secondary.

TDA Induction www.tda.gov.uk/teachers/induction/cedp.aspx
Teachernet www.teachernet.gov.uk

REFERENCES

CHAPTER 1

Beard, R. (1998) *National Literacy Strategy: Review of Research and other Related Evidence*. London: Department for Education and Employment.

Bolinger, D. (1980) *Language, the Loaded Weapon: The Use and Abuse of Language Today*. London: Longman.

Cameron, D. (1995) *Verbal Hygiene*. Oxford: Routledge.

Cater, R. (1997) *Investigating English Discourse: Language, Literacy, Literature*. London: Routledge.

Clarke, S., Dickinson, P. and Westbrook, J. (2004) *The Complete Guide to Becoming an English Teacher*. London: Sage.

Cox, B. (1991) *Cox on Cox: An English Curriculum for the 90s*. London: Hodder & Stoughton.

Davison, J. and Dowson, J. (2003) *Learning to Teach English in the Secondary School: A Companion to School Experience*. 2nd edn. Oxford: Routledge.

Davison, J. and Moss, J. (2000) *Issues in English Teaching*. London: Routledge Falmer.

Department for Education (DfE) (1995) *English in the National Curriculum*. London: HMSO.

Department for Education and Employment (DfEE) (1998) *The National Literacy Strategy Framework for Teaching*. Sudbury: DfEE Publications.

Department for Education and Employment (DfEE) (1999) *The National Curriculum for England: English Key Stages 1–4*. London: DfEE and QCA.

Department for Education and Employment (DfEE) (2001) *Key Stage 3 National Strategy: Framework for Teaching English: Years 7, 8 and 9*. London: DfEE.

Department for Education and Skills (DfES) (2004) *Every Child Matters: Changes for Children*. London: DfES.

Department of Education and Science (DES) (1975) *A Language for Life. Report of the Committee of Inquiry Appointed by the Secretary of State for Education and Science*. (The Bullock Report). London: HMSO.

Department of Education and Science (DES) (1988) *Report of the Committee of Enquiry into the Teaching of English Language*. (The Kingman Report). London: HMSO.

Department of Education and Science (DES) (1989) *English for Ages 5–16*. (The Cox Report). London: DES.

Department of Education and Science (DES) (1990) *English in the National Curriculum* (No. 2). London: HMSO.

Eagleton, T. (1983) *Literary Theory: An Introduction*. London: Blackwell.

Fleming, J. and Stevens, D. (2004) *English Teaching in the Secondary School: Linking Theory and Practice*. 2nd edn. London: David Fulton.

Harrison, C. (2002) *Key Stage 3 English, Roots & Research*. London: DfES.

Marenbon, J. (1987) *English Our English: The New Orthodoxy Examined*. London: Centre for Policy Studies.

Marshall, B. (2000) *English Teachers: The Unofficial Guide: Researching the Philosophies of English Teachers*. Oxford: Routledge.

Meek, M. (1992) *On Being Literate*. London: Heinemann.

Phillips, M. (1997) *All Must Have Prizes*. London: Little, Brown.

Pike, M. (2004) *Teaching Secondary English*. London: Paul Chapman Publishing.

Qualifications and Curriculum Authority (QCA) (2005) *Taking English Forward*. London: QCA.

Qualifications and Curriculum Authority (QCA) (2007) *The National Curriculum for English*. London: QCA.

Sampson, G. (1921) *English for the English*. Cambridge: Cambridge University Press.

Williamson, J. (2001) *Meeting the Standards in Secondary English: A Guide to the ITT NC*. London: Taylor & Francis.

Wright, T. (2005) *How to be a Brilliant English Teacher*. Oxford: Routledge.

CHAPTER 2

Atherton, J.S. (2005) *Learning and Teaching: Bloom's Taxonomy*. www.learningandteaching.info/learning/bloomtax.htm (accessed 23 July 2007).

Bloom, B.S. (ed.) (1956) *Taxonomy of Educational Objectives, the Classification of Educational Goals – Handbook I: Cognitive Domain*. New York: Longman.

Bowkett, S. (2007) *100+ Ideas for Teaching Creativity*. 2nd edn. London: Continuum.

Clarke, S., Dickinson, P. and Westbrook, J. (2004) *The Complete Guide to Becoming an English Teacher*. London: Sage.

Davison, J. and Dowson, J. (2003) *Learning to Teach English in the Secondary School: A Companion to School Experience*. 2nd edn. London: Routledge.

Department for Education and Employment (DfEE) (2000) *English: The National Curriculum for England: Key Stages 3 & 4*. London: HMSO.

Department for Education and Employment (DfEE) (2001) *Framework for Teaching English: Years 7, 8 and 9*. London: DfEE.

Department of Education and Science (DES) and Welsh Office (1990) *The Statutory Order: English in the National Curriculum*. London: HMSO

Department for Education and Skills (DfES) (2004) *Every Child Matters*: Change for Children. London: DfES.

Fleming, M. and Stevens, D. (2004) *English Teaching in the Secondary School*. 2nd edn. London: David Fulton.

Harrison, C. (2002) *Key Stage 3: National Strategy. Key Stage 3 English. Roots and Research*. London: DfES.

McBer, H. (2000) *Report on Research into Teacher Effectiveness*. London: DfEE.

Myhill, D. and Fisher, R. (2005) *Informing Practice in English. A Review of Recent Research into Literacy and the Teaching of English*. HMI 2565. London: Ofsted.

National Strategy (2004) *Pedagogy and Practice: Teaching and Learning in Secondary Schools. Unit 3: Lesson Design for Lower Attainers*. London: DfES.

Office for Standards in Education (Ofsted) (2005) *English 2000–05. A Review of Inspection Evidence*. HMI 2351. London: (Ofsted).

Pike, M. (2004) *Teaching Secondary English*. London: Paul Chapman Publishing.

Vygotsky, L. (1986) *Thought and Language*. Cambridge, MA and London: MIT Press.

Wright, T. (2005) *How to be a Brilliant English Teacher*. Oxford: Routledge.

www.standards.dfes.gov.uk/secondary/

www.teachernet.gov.uk/teachingandlearning/subjects/english/

www.teachit.co.uk

www.qca.org

CHAPTER 3

Bleiman, B. (2001) *The Poetry Book*. London: English and Media Centre.

Brownjohn, S. (1994) *To Rhyme or Not to Rhyme? Teaching Children to Write*. London: Hodder & Stoughton.

Corbett, P. (2002) *How to Teach Poetry Writing at Key Stage 3*. London: Fulton.

Corbett, P. (2004) *Jumpstart: Literacy Games*. London: Fulton.

Davison, J. and Dowson, J. (eds) (2004) *Learning to Teach English in the Secondary School*. 2nd edn. London: RoutledgeFalmer.

Department for Children, Schools and Families (DCSF) (2008) www.standards.dfes.gov.uk/ secondary/framework/english

Department for Education and Employment (DfEE) (2001) *Framework for Teaching English: Years 7, 8, and 9*. London: DfEE.

Department for Education and Skills (DfES) (2004) *Pedagogy and Practice: Teaching and Learning in Secondary Schools. Unit 13: Developing Reading*. DfES 0436 2004 G. London: DfES.

Department for Education and Skills (DfES) (2006) *English Subject Leader Development Materials/Spring*. 2094-2005 DOC-EN London. DfES.

Eagleton, T. (2006) *How to Read a Poem*. London: Blackwell.

Hodges, G.C. (2004) 'Possibilities with poetry' in J. Davison and J. Dowson (eds), *Learning to Teach English in the Secondary School*. 2nd edn. London: RoutledgeFalmer.

NLT (2006) *Reading for Pleasure: A Research Overview*.

Qualifications and Curriculum Authority (QCA) (2007) *The National Curriculum for English*. London: QCA.

Westbrook, J. (2004) 'The National Literacy Strategy', in J. Davison and J. Dowson (eds), *Learning to Teach English in the Secondary School*. 2nd edn. London: RoutledgeFalmer.

Yates, C. (1999) *Jumpstart Poetry in the Secondary School*. London: Poetry Society.

CHAPTER 4

Cowley, S. (2006) *Getting the Buggers to Behave*. London: Continuum.

Department for Education and Employment (DFEE) (2000) *Raising Standards, English at Key Stage 3, Training 2000: Speaking and Listening*. London: DfEE.

Department for Education and Employment (DfEE) (2001a) *Key Stage 3 National Strategy: Framework for Teaching English: Years 7, 8 and 9*. London: DfEE.

Department for Education and Employment (DFEE) (2001b) *English Department training (2001), Grammar for Writing*. London: DfEE.

Department for Education and Skills (DfES) (2004) *Every Child Matters: Change for Children*. London: DfES.

Department for Education and Skills (DFES) (2006) *Grouping Pupils for Success*. 03945-2006DWO-EN. London: DfES.

Department for Education and Skills (DFES) (2007) *Guidelines for Teaching Shakespeare in Key Stage 3*. 00037-2007DWO-EN. London: DfES.

Gibson, R. (1998) *Teaching Shakespeare*. Cambridge: Cambridge University Press.

Kerry, T. and Wilding, M. (2004) *Effective Classroom Teacher: Developing the Skills You Need in Today's Classroom*. London: Pearson Education.

Kounin, J. (1970) *Discipline and Groups Management in the Classroom*. New York: Holt, Rinhart & Winstone.

Kyriacou, C. (1998) *Essential Teaching Skills*. 2nd edn. Cheltenham: Nelson Thornes.

Lunzer, E. and Gardner, K. (1979) *The Effective Use of Reading*. London: Heinemann Educational Books for the Schools Council.

Moy, R. and Raleigh, M. (1980) 'Comprehension: bringing it back alive', *The English Magazine*, ILEA Centre, Autumn.

Muijs, D., Harris, A., Chapman, C., Stoll, L. and Russ, J. (2004) 'Improving schools in socio-economically disadvantaged areas: an overview of research', *School Effectiveness and School Improvement*, 15 (2): 149–76.

Pollard, A. et al. (2005) *Reflective Teaching: Evidence Informed Professional Practice*. 2nd edn. London: Continuum.

QCA (2008) *National Curriculum*

National Curriculum, English Key Stage 4 – available online at http://curriculum.qca.org.uk

Vygotsky, L.S. (1978). *Mind and Society: The Development of Higher Psychological Processes*. Cambridge, MA: Harvard University Press.

Wragg, E.C. (2001) *Class Management in the Secondary School*. London and New York: RoutledgeFalmer.

CHAPTER 5

Black, P. and Wiliam, D. (1998) 'Assessment and classroom learning', *Assessment for Learning*, 5(1): 7–68.

Black, P., Harrison, C., Lee, C., Marshall, B. and Wiliam, D. (2002) *Working Inside the Black Box: Assessment for Learning in the Classroom*. London.

Black, P., Harrison, C., Marshall, B. and Wiliam, D. (2003) *Assessment for Learning: Putting It into Practice*. Buckingham: Open University Press.

Clark, L. (2005) 'The teacher who wants to ban failure in the classroom', *Daily Mail*, 20 July: 25.

Clarke, S. (2005) *Formative Assessment in the Secondary Classroom*. London: Hodder Murray.

Department for Children, Schools and Families (DCSF) (2008) www.standards.dfes.gov.uk/secondary/framework/english

Department for Education and Skills (DfES) (2001) *Key Stage 2/3 Transition Units*. London: DfES.

Department for Education and Skills (DfES) (2004) *Every Child Matters: Change for Children*. London: DfES. www.dcsf.gov.uk/publications/childrenactreport

Department for Education and Skills (DfES) (2005a) *Assessment for Learning: Whole School Training Materials*. 2nd edn. 1115–2005 G. London: DfES.

Department for Education and Skills (DfES) (2005b) *Handbook for Assessing Pupils' Progress in English*. 1789–2005 CDO – EN. London: DfES.

Henry, J. (2002) *Forget the Marking, Start Talking*. www.tesco.uk (accessed 20 February 2008).

Petty, G. (2000) *Teaching Today*. 2nd edn. Cheltenham: Stanley Thornes.

Qualifications and Curriculum Authority (QCA) (2000) *Secondary English National Curriculum*. www.qca.org.uk

Qualifications and Curriculum Authority (QCA) (2005) *Assessment for Learning*. London: QCA.

Tanner, H. and Jones, S. (2003) *Marking and Assessment*. London: Classmates.

Wiliam, D. (2001) *Level Best? Levels of Attainment in National Curriculum: Assessment*. Association of Teachers and Lecturers.

Wragg, E.C. (2004) *Assessment and Learning in the Classroom*. London: Routledge.

CHAPTER 6

Black, P. and Wiliam, D. (1998) 'Inside the black box: raising standards through classroom assessment', *Phi Delta Kappan*, October: 139–48.

Black, P., Harrison, C., Marshall, B. and Wiliam, D. (2003) *Assessment for Learning: Putting It into Practice*. Buckingham: Open University Press.

Clarke, S., Dickinson, P. and Westbrook, J. (2004) *The Complete Guide to Becoming an English Teacher*. London: Sage.

Daw, P. (1995) 'Differentiation and its meanings', *English and Media Magazine*, 32: 11–15.

Department for Children, Schools and Families (DCSF) (2007) *The Children's Plan*. London: TSO.

Department for Education and Skills (DfES) (2006) *2020 Vision: The Report of the Teaching and Learning in 2020 Review Group*. London: DfES.

Fleming, J. and Stevens, D. (2004) *English Teaching in the Secondary School: Linking Theory and Practice*. 2nd edn. London: David Fulton.

Gardner, H. (1983) *Frames of Mind. The Theory of Multiple Intelligences*. New York: Basic Books.

Gardner, H. (1993) *Multiple Intelligences: The Theory in Practice*. New York: Basic Books.

Gardner, H. (1999) *Intelligence Reframed: Multiple Intelligences for the 21st Century*. New York: Basic Books.

Pike, M. (2003) *Teaching Secondary English*. London: Paul Chapman Publishing.
Stradling, R. and Saunders, L. (1993) Differentiation in Practice: Responding to the Needs of all Pupils, in *Educational Research*, vol 35(2): 13.
Thomas, P. (2006) 'G & T English: a progress report', *The Secondary English Magazine*, 9(5): 8–9.
Wright, T. (2005) *How to be a Brilliant English Teacher*. Oxford: Routledge.

CHAPTER 7

Balls, E. (2007) 'Let's celebrate exam success and then make sure it continues', TES, August, 2007.
Brown, J. and Gifford, T. (1989) *Teaching A Level English Literature: A Student Centred Approach*. London: Routledge.
Department for Education and Skills (DfES) (2006) *Assessing Pupils' Progress in English*. DfES 03957–2006 CDO-EN. London: DfES.
Keith, G.R. and Shuttleworth, J. (2000) *Living Language: Explaining Advanced Level English Language*. London: Hodder & Stoughton.
Marshall, B. (2000) *English Teachers: The Unofficial Guide: Researching the Philosophies of English Teachers*. London: RoutledgeFalmer.
MORI/CDELL (2002) Public Examinations: Views on maintaining standards over time: Accessed 8 September 2007. www.qca.org.uk/qca_7673.aspx.
Qualifications and Curriculum Authority (QCA) (2007) *A Change for the Better: KS3 English Mark Schemes*. London: QCA.

CHAPTER 8

Bell, D. (2005) 'Citizenship'. Hansard Society/Ofsted Lecture www.ofsted.gov.uk/assets/3821.doc (accessed 20 June 2007).
Clarke, S., Dickinson, P. and Westbrook, J. (2004) *The Complete Guide to Becoming and English Teacher*. London: Sage.
Davison, J. and Moss, J. (eds) (2000) *Issues in English Teaching*. Oxford: Routledge.
Department for Education and Skills (DfES) (2004) *Every Child Matters: Change for Children*. London: DfES.
Evans, B. (2004) '"Be fit not fat": broadening the childhood obesity debate beyond dualisms', *Children's Geographies*, 2(2): 288–91.
Evans, B. (2006) '"Gluttony or sloth?": critical geographies of bodies and morality in (anti)obesity policy' *Area* 38(3): 259–67.
Evans, C. and Evans, B. (2007) 'More than just worksheets? A study of the confidence of newly qualified teachers of English in teaching Personal Social and Health Education in secondary schools', *Pastoral Care in Education*, 25(4): 42–50.
Evans, J. and Davies, B. (2004) 'Sociology, the body and health in a risk society', in J. Evans, B. Davies and J. Wright (eds), *Body Knowledge and Control: Studies in the Sociology of Physical Education and Health*. London: Routledge.
Evans, J., Davies, D. and Wright, J. (eds) (2004) *Body Knowledge and Control: Studies in the Sociology of Physical Education and Health*. London: Routledge.
Evans, J., Evans, B. and Rich, E. (2003) '"The only problem is, children will like their chips": education and the discursive production of ill-health', *Pedagogy, Culture and Society*, 11: 215–40.
House of Commons (HOC) (2004) *Health Select Committee Report: Obesity*. London: The Stationery Office.
Mead, N. (2004) 'The provision of personal, social, health education (PSHE) and citizenship in school-based elements of primary initial teacher education', *Pastoral Care*, June: 19–26.
Neelands, J. (1998) *Beginning Drama 11–14*. London: David Fulton.

Office for Standards in Education (Ofsted) (2005) *Personal, Social and Health Education in Secondary Schools*. HMI, doc ref 2311. London: Ofsted.

Pike, M. (2004) *Teaching Secondary English*. London: Paul Chapman Publishing.

Qualifications and Curriculum Authority (QCA) (2005a) *Personal, social and health education: 2004/5 annual report on curriculum and assessment*. London: QCA.

Qualifications and Curriculum Authority (QCA) (2005b) *PSHE at Key Stages 1–4: Guidance on Assessment, Recording and Reporting*. Doc ref QCA/05/2183. London: QCA.

Qualifications and Curriculum Authority (QCA) (2007a) www.qca.org.uk/libraryAssetsmedia/ PSHE_Personal_Wellbeing_KS3_PoS.pdf, pp. 243–51 (accessed 4 August, 2007).

Qualifications and Curriculum Authority (QCA) (2007b) www.qca.org.uk/libraryAssets/media/ PSHE_Personal_Wellbeing_KS4_PoS.pdf, pp. 253–61 (accessed 4 August, 2007).

Qualifications and Curriculum Authority (QCA) (2007c) www.qca.org.uk/libraryAssets/media/ English_KS3_PoS.pdf (accessed 4 August, 2007).

Qualifications and Curriculum Authority (QCA) (2007d) www.qca.org.uk/libraryAssets/media/ English_KS4_PoS.pdf (accessed 4 August, 2007).

Qualifications and Curriculum Authority (QCA) (2007e) www.qca.org.uk/secondarycurriculum/review/ subject/ks3/english/links/personal-development/index.htm (accessed 2nd July, 2007).

Russell, W. (1986) Blood Brothers *Studio Scripts* (ed. D. Self). London: Nelson Thornes.

Salovey, P. and Sluyter, D.J. (1997) *Emotional Development and Emotional Intelligence: Educational Implications*. New York: Basic Books.

www.standards.dfes.gov.uk (accessed 26 July 2007).

www.teachernet.gov.uk/pshe (accessed 12 July 2007).

CHAPTER 9

British Educational Communications and Technology Agency (Becta) (2004), *Becta ICT Advice: Using web-based resources in Secondary English* (downloadable from www.schools.becta.org.uk).

Clark, C. and Foster, A. (2005) *Children's and Young People's Reading Habits and Preferences: The Who, What, Why, Where and When*. London: National Literacy Trust.

Clark, C., Osbome, S. and Akerman, R. (2008) *Young People's Self-perceptions as Readers: An Investigation Including Family, Peer and School Influences*. London: National Literacy Trust.

Department for Education and Skills (DfES) (2004) *ICT in Schools – the Impact of Government Initiatives: Secondary English*. Ref: HMI 2186. London: DfES.

Department for Education and Skills (DfES) (2007) *English: Programme of study for key stage 3 and attainment targets*. London: DfES.

Harris, S. and Kington, A. (2002) *Innovative Classroom Practices Using ICT in England: The Second Information Technology in Education Study* (downloadable from link 27 on the companion website).

Millum, T. and Warren, C. (2001) *Twenty Things to do with a Word Processor: ICT Activities for the English Classroom*. Denby: Resource Education.

Richardson, W. (2006) *Blogs, Wikis, Podcasts, and Other Powerful Web Tools for Classrooms*. Thousand Oaks, CA: Corwin Press.

Qualifications and Curriculum Authority (QCA) (2008) *National Curriculum*.

CHAPTER 10

DfES (2004) *Every Child Matters: Change for Children*. London: DfES.

Edge Hill University (2008) *PGCE Secondary English Handbook*.

INDEX